LIVING WITH JAPANESE

Terence Kelly

KELLAN PRESS

©Terence Kelly 1997
First published in Great Britain 1997

ISBN 0 9530193 0 6

Kellan Press
127, Sandgate Road
Folkestone
Kent CT20 2BL

This book is copyright. No part of it may be reproduced in any form without permission in writing from the publishers except by a reviewer who wishes to quote brief passages in connection with a review for inclusion in a newspaper, magazine, radio or television broadcast.

Printed and bound by Biddles of Guildford

Contents

Page

Preface

1	Last Days of Freedom	1
2	Boei Glodok Prison	7
3	A Voyage Beyond Belief	26
4	Island of Temples - Innoshima	45
5	The H.K.V.D.C. move in	56
6	Hitachi Dockyard	73
7	The Staple - Food	92
8	The Genki Boys	107
9	Living with the Japanese	121
10	The Second Blessing	155
11	Our incomprehensible Hosts	170
12	Innoshima attacked	199
13	Freedom regained	214

List of Illustrations

Cartoons by Sid Scales	3
Plan of Boei Glodok Prison, Djkarta, Java	11
H.M.S. Indomitable	14
Pilots of 258 Squadron	15
Typical Javanese scene	17
Author and Lambert on readiness in Java	28
Map of author's voyages from Java to Japan	35
Orika Gokei Jin Ja shrine on Innoshima island	46
Warrant Officers F.Cox & H.A Prichard	48
Sketch of typical billet on Innoshima	50
Captain Akiro Nimoto, Camp Commandant	51
Photograph of the camp on Innoshima island	58
Dai Nichi Maru survivors	59
A group of the H.K.V.D.C	60
Another H.K.V.D.C. group	61
Allocated bedspaces	67
The Administration Block	68
The Inland Sea	70
The Seaward Passage	71
Hitachi Dockyard layout	73
Raffs in working uniforms	79
Hachi Dock	83
The Chain of Command - Cartoon	85
Winston Churchill	91
"Make way for a Klim Tin Pie"	99
'Chick' Henderson	110
Ken Forrow's last work card	123
'Look Alikes' - Cartoon	124
Sketch of camp by G.S.Coxhead	127
Letter Card - Address side	128
Letter Card - Contents side	129
Catholic Chapel of St Francis Xavier	132
'Doctor' John Furnell	135
Edward Tandy	136
"Roll on That Boat" - Music and Lyrics	136
Concert Programme frontispiece	139
Part of Concert Programme	140
Humphrey Knight	151

LIVING WITH JAPANESE

TERENCE KELLY

To the vast majority the Japanese remain as much an obscure Oriental race as they were in pre-war days when they were rarely met with in the flesh, almost their only exports were gimcrack copies and the term "Made in Japan" was almost a synonym for rubbish. Yet in today's world they are everywhere present, swamp us with essential high-quality goods and their influence on our lives is enormous, inescapeable and on-going. It is surely important we make an effort to discover how they tick and how under future pressures they are likely to react. How do we best set about doing this? Presumably by getting to know as much as we can of what has been spoken and written about them by those who have had through commercial or other reasons intimate personal contact with them.

Terence Kelly is such a person. A Japanese prisoner of war, after incarceration in a noisome gaol and a voyage of unspeakable horror he found himself in a unique small camp close to Hiroshima where for close on three years learning much of their language he worked side by side with ordinary Japanese, old men who had never known war, young men who had returned after completing two years of military service, seamen off passing ships who spoke English and had been to America and Britain. He shared with them the early days when Japan was cock-a-hoop with victory and the later days when defeat was imminent, when Hitachi dockyard where he worked, pulverized by bombing had almost ceased to function and nothing lay ahead but starvation or shaming defeat.

Moreover his camp was unique in another and most important way. Not only was it far better than most camps (and quite possibly the best camp in which the Japanese housed any of their prisoners) but about half its inmates were ex-Colonials from Hong Kong - men who had been bankers, judges, lawyers, shipowners, taipans - men who knew the Orient and those who lived in it, whose education, background and clout put them poles apart from the largely raw, unfledged servicemen beside whom for the best part of the next three years they were going to have to work as dockyard coolies. It was an extraordinary mixture. A man with the ambition to arrange the social experiment of forcing two groups of men utterly disparate in age, class and experience to live and work together could hardly have chosen a better setting.

Living With Japanese is no hackneyed war story of the enemy's brutality and inhumanity but as well as giving an insight into the ethos of an enigmatic and puzzling race is an exciting examination of the effects of hardship and deprivation in a place where the rules and conventions of normal life no longer apply.

Also by Terence Kelly

Novels

Properjohn
The Carib Sands
The Developers
The Genki Boys
The Blades of Cordoba
Play in a Hot Summer
Revolution on St Barbara
Fepow
Voyage Beyond Belief
The Spy is Dead
Long Live the Spy

Non-fiction

Hurricane Over the Jungle
Battle for Palembang
Hurricane in Sumatra
Hurricane and Spitfire Pilots at War

Books in large print

Properjohn
The Carib Sands
The Genki Boys
Voyage Beyond Belief
The Spy is Dead
Long Live the Spy
Hurricane Over the Jungle
Battle for Palembang

Plays

A Share in the Sun (with Campbell Singer)
Divorce in Chancery
Four Sided Triangle
The Genki Boys
Just Before Dawn (from Elleston-Trevor's
  A Place for the Wicked)
Honest Tom
Carnival in Trinidad
Stella
The Masterminds
Revolution on St Barbara
Crackdown

Professor Ashton-Hill	156
John Stirling Lee	157
The Guinea Pigs - Musker and Hailstone	162
Author and Con 'Buster' Harris	165
Corporal Dai Mogford	168
Two of the newsvendors: Fallon and Reid	194
Freddie Clemo	196
Allied reconnaissance photograph of dockyard	202
A further reconnaissance photograph	208
Ship damaged after bombing	209
General dockyard damage after bombing	210
A 5 yen banknote liberally autographed	222
Leaflet confirming end of hostilities	223
H.K.V.D.C. survivors homeward bound	225

Preface

More than fifty years have passed since the atom bombs dropped on Hiroshima and Nagasaki brought the Far Eastern War to its end and saved the lives of the scores of thousands of Japanese prisoners of war who would quite certainly have been liquidated had the alternative of invading Japan been followed. Through those years many books have been written by survivors with the great majority understandably based on the hardships they endured and the brutality they suffered and any ex-prisoner who writes about his captivity in any other vein is likely to considered disloyal and accused of attempting to vindicate a nation unworthy of such rehabilitation.

Such is not my purpose. As a Japanese prisoner myself, I experienced their callousness at first hand and even after fifty years find it impossible either to forgive them for the quite unnecessary suffering they caused or, as some have done, to accept the simplistic excuse that their behaviour stemmed from an evil system now thankfully put behind them.

But when I look back on my own captivity, I cannot just dismiss those three and a half years as an ugly experience best forgotten for in them I learnt a great deal about myself, a great deal about the behaviour of human nature under stress and I believe rather more about the Japanese than was learnt by the vast majority of my compatriots slaving on railways, working in copper mines or building airfields on remote tropical islands. This came about because after seven months spent in a noisome Javanese gaol followed by a voyage to Japan in conditions of such horror as to beggar description, I found myself in a camp close to Hiroshima which I believe to have been quite unique in the annals of prisoner of war experience.

Not only was this camp far better than most (and quite possibly the best camp in which the Japanese housed any of their prisoners) but about half of its inmates were ex-Colonials from Hong Kong: men who had been bankers, teachers, judges, lawyers, shipowners, taipans - men who knew the Orient and those who lived in it, whose education, background, ambition and clout put them poles apart from the largely young, raw, unfledged servicemen beside whom for the best part of the next three years they were going to have to work as dockyard coolies. It was an extraordinary mixture. A man with an ambition to arrange the social experiment of forcing two groups of men utterly disparate in age, class and experience to live and work together could hardly have chosen a better setting.

And then again, unlike the majority of prisoners who only saw their fellow prisoners and guards, we worked side by side with ordinary Japanese, old men who had never known war, young men who had returned after completing two years of military service, seamen off passing ships who spoke English and had been to America and Britain. We shared with them the early days when Japan was cock-a-hoop with victory and the later days when defeat was imminent and our dockyard, pulverized by bombing, had almost ceased to function. We learnt quite a bit of their language, ate the same food, did the same work, suffered the same injuries and endured the same bombing. And we knew the same privations as towards the end of the war Japan became a country for which, with all the major cities flattened, its shops empty of goods and food in desperately short supply, nothing lay ahead but starvation or shaming defeat. In a word we had the opportunity of getting to know its people in a way that was at the time granted to very few and is certainly not granted to those who do business with them nowadays.

Before the war to most Europeans the Japanese were an obscure Far Eastern race who eked out some sort of living by selling gimcrack copies of largely trivial articles invented by their betters. But now we live in a world in which the Japanese influence on our lives is enormous, inescapeable and on-going. The Japanese decisively affect our economy, swamp us with goods essential to our lives and are everywhere personally in evidence. We cannot disregard them - and we consider them casually at our peril. Yet what kind of people are they? How should we categorize them? How do we relate the quietly-dressed, exceptionally well-behaved and courteous passenger who takes the seat beside us in an aircraft to the brutes of whom ex-prisoners write so damningly? He must surely be of quite a different breed. Or is it that the fifty post-war years of concentration on securing prosperity by commercial rather than militaristic means have utterly changed the ethos of a race of more than one hundred million souls?

Both premises are surely unacceptable. Whereas from time to time the conduct of nations may change, their character is more obdurate. The Common Market has not removed the difference in make-up of say the Germans and the French; deep-seated beliefs and principles handed down from generation to generation are not so easily dismantled. And if this is true of nations living cheek by jowl and pressurized by immediately neighbouring ideologies, how much truer must it be of an island race which for century after century kept itself aloof from outside influences.

Towards the end of the eighth century Japan became an autonomous country with a feudal society, Buddhist in religion, largely cut off from the outside world, and certainly from the Western world, and even the discovery of Japan by the Portugese and Spanish some eight hundred years later, had little impact. From 1638 until 1853 this detachment from outside influences was, if anything, intensified by an edict of the rulers that only a single port, Nagasaki, should remain open to foreign trade with only Chinese and Dutch ships permitted to enter it. A dynasty of governors which had unified the country and established a rigidly enforced regimen had no wish to see it undermined by Western and Christian influences. It took the advent of an American, Commander Perry, to enforce the country's opening-up.

But this created problems never envisaged previously. The influx of foreign goods which were entirely new created a financial crisis and necessitated an industrialization which, seriously hampered as it was by a dearth of the raw materials essential to maintain it, inevitably led to militarism. Surrounding Japan were vast territories ripe for looting once subdued. Over the next eighty years or so Japan took Formosa from China, Kwantung and the southern half of Sakhalin from Russia and annexed Korea entirely. Manchuria and large areas of China itself were occupied and seizing as it saw its opportunity when Europe was plunged into the Second World War, founding what it euphemistically dubbed *The Greater East Asia Co-Prosperity Sphere*, it rapidly occupied Hong Kong, Indo-China, Malaysia, Indonesia and the Philippines.

To accomplish these staggering conquests required the total subservience of its population but with its unbroken history of feudalism this was not difficult to achieve. On the one hand there was an all-powerful military clique working hand in hand with a limited number of great families - the Mitsuis, the Mitsubishis and the like - which controlled the country's industry; on the other a proletariat accustomed by the habit of many centuries to accept orders without demur. And to oil the friction of a hard and little rewarded way of life and quell occasional doubts, there hovered over everything the vague but revered image of the Emperor, in appearance nondescript, in essence divine. Such was the background of those about whom the prisoner of war justifiably complains and such is the background of the hordes of latter-day Japanese nowadays seen everywhere.

There is a question to be posed. Has half a century of commercial triumph changed the ethos of the Japanese people or underlying the apparent Westernization of their culture, does a deep-rooted, perhaps even ineradicable, basically unchanged character remain? And it is perhaps an important question for Japan's current commercial success is, because of its lack of oil and raw materials, always perilously poised and should it falter there will be the temptation to have recourse to the old, familiar ways.

Nowadays two stock notions of the Japanese are generally held and have come to be habitual ways of thinking. The first that held almost universally by their ex-prisoners which fifty years have hardly dented and the second by others that far from being the gimcrack counterfeiters of pre-war days, they have developed into a race of commercial wizards who have put the bad old ways of thinking and behaving far behind them.

But stock notions and habitual ways of thinking are, as Matthew Arnold was at great pains to point out, very limiting and should always be subjected to fresh streams of thought and experience.

And in this lies my second reason for writing this account. In it I offer the reader an opportunity of seeing the Japanese in a broader light than they are normally depicted in books written by those who were their prisoners or is perhaps seen by later generations who do business with them or only meet them in the cosmetic atmosphere of golf course, hotel lounge or restaurant.

Terence Kelly, Marlow, 1997.

This book is dedicated to all Far East Prisoners of the Japanese and especially to those who shared my experiences in Singapore, Sumatra and Java, who were incarcerated in noisome gaols such as Boei Glodok, Djkarta and who were transported on hell ships such as the Dai Nichi Maru to Japan and elsewhere, with my thanks to all who have refreshed my memory with their own accounts of those long and weary years and supplied me with photographs and other memorabilia much of which is reproduced in the pages which follow.

CHAPTER ONE

LAST DAYS OF FREEDOM

On the morning of March 1st, 1942 I was having my own private little war as a lone pilot attacking with a Hurricane the Japanese force invading Java which had arrived a few hours earlier and as I was the sole object on which they could carry out target practice, I was getting the full attention of the escorting warships and to improve my chances doing my strafing from little more than treetop height. It was on one of my sorties that I saw my first Japanese close to. He was wearing a green shirt and yellow shorts and crouching in the surf - and as it has to be far easier for a man with twelve machine guns firing simultaneously to kill another lying on an unprotected beach than for a few warships, however enthusiastically they blaze away, to hit a small aircraft flying low at about three hundred miles an hour, it was reasonable for this fellow to be even more frightened than I was and frightened he certainly was. More than fifty years have passed since that dramatic and exciting morning but the picture of that fellow looking up at me over his shoulder with terror written on his face remains. sharp and clear.

    Another twenty days were to pass before I was to see another Japanese close to and this one was a nondescript bespectacled fellow who had his back against a wall, his rifle firmly gripped and whose eyes flickered in every direction as if he feared at any moment someone might shoot him. The place was a market town in Java called Garoet and I had driven there by private car with Squadron Leader Wigram, a heavily tattoed World War 1 veteran, to organise accommodation for about a thousand men who were currently, and most

Last Days of Freedom

comfortably, encamped at a tea plantation fifty or so miles to the south.

The situation was a curious one. Having, for one hundred and twenty-six years, ruled this beautiful and mountainous island some six hundred miles long which supported sixty million souls, the Dutch high command yielded it with hardly even token resistance to a negligible and poorly equipped Japanese invasion force. The act of capitulation took place on March 8th by which time few of the fourteen thousand Allied servicemen, to say nothing of the Dutch, had fired a shot in anger or indeed been anywhere near the enemy and for the next two weeks or so the roads of Java, winding their way through breathtakingly lovely hills and valleys were clogged with convoys of soldiers and air force groundstaff vaguely wandering around the country wondering where to head for next. Rumour was rife and the only certain knowledge was that so far as they were concerned hostilities were over and escape by sea impossible because all ships that hadn't left in time had been sunk. But as to where the Japanese were exactly was a mystery.

A few more enterprising men made for the beaches in the folorn hope of finding, or even constructing craft in which to attempt the two thousand mile voyage across open sea to Australia or set about equipping themselves as best they could to try to wage guerilla warfare from the jungle, but the majority gradually coalesced into large groups which descended on towns or tea plantations where some sort of order was established and a Shangri-La existence came into being. Food was plentiful and cheap, discipline was light, there was much that was new to discover and experience, the weather was kind, football matches were arranged against teams drawn from the local populace and a remarkable but very strongly held belief took hold that so long as everyone behaved themselves and caused no trouble, the Japanese with far more important things to think about would not be bothered with them and would leave them in peace. And at Palempoek plantation we pilots, the handful who had survived gruelling days of flying and fighting in Singapore, Sumatra and in Java before the capitulation, sharing a native hut wallpapered with pages from newspapers and magazines, bought and cooked chickens, played bridge and conjectured whether our captors would permit us to obtain the necessary materials, to study and complete taking our professional examinations as we knew imprisoned air crew in Germany were doing.

"They look much better when they've lost face!"

These and innumerable similar cartoons were drawn by Sid Scales who was of course also a Japanese prisoner of war

The point was that it was quite beyond us to visualise the Japanese. In pre-war days to the extent that the vast majority of Europeans thought about them at all, they were inclined to be thought of as slit-eyed dwarfs with yellow skins who lived on rice and scratched some sort of living by slavishly copying, and copying poorly, small things their betters made. Pre-war, the term *'made in Japan'* was synonymous with gimcrack. Oddly enough the fact that they had by then chased the British out of Malaya and all but chased the Americans out of the Phillipines failed to change the attitude of mind of the men

Last Days of Freedom

about to be taken prisoner either then or through the ensuing three and a half years before the fortuitous dropping of the atomic bombs on Nagasaki and Hiroshima restored their freedom.

And so, as Wigram and I drove into Garoet, we were not remarkably surprised to find it swarming with our own troops and only speckled with Japanese. The streets were thronged with local people going about their normal business and with British soldiers and R.A.F. groundstaff who had taken over its administration and were controlling the traffic, commandeering accommodation, organising food supplies or simply wandering around shopping and sightseeing. Wigram and I had not been searched for weapons nor could the huge majority of the servicemen about the town have been; to have taken it over from our captors would have been the simplest thing. I do not recall hearing anyone making the suggestion we should do so and I sense this was because the huge majority had not in fact yet absorbed the fact they really were prisoners anyway or could even credit that this handful of scruffy, and often bespectacled gnomes, were henceforth going to control their destiny.

And far from reality being established, as the days passed this curious situation became even more bizarre as more and more prisoners poured into Garoet magnifying the disproportion of prisoners to captors. Presumably the Japanese must have been very puzzled not merely by our apparently spineless capitulation but by the high-handed attitude we, their prisoners, displayed towards them; when we were not utterly ignoring them, we were being overbearing, impatient and rude, almost treating the situation as if we were the victors. As an example, to pass the time and maintain some sort of discipline, daily route marches out of the town far into the countryside were organised and the extraordinary spectacle of long columns of well-booted troops, unaccompanied by guards, winding their way between the paddy fields, singing their smutty marching songs, became a commonplace. Had they chosen to take to the hills and jungles there was nothing stop them; instead they dutifully returned for tea.

Last Days of Freedom

However, after several days during which this remarkable situation continued, the Japanese began to split their captives into groups and send them off to various camps, the group in which I found myself being required to march at night to the nearest railway station there to be entrained to the capital, Djkarta, or, as it was then known, Batavia. It was a remarkable, quite unforgettable march. The air was warm and soft, the fireflies flickered and frogs croaked by the million; the sky was powdered with stars and the night drenched in heavy, tropical scent. We sang as we marched, smartly in step and on either side of the road along which we made our way British soldiers were bivouacked and the lights from their shelters and amongst the many chatting groups who called to us seemed to add a touch of romance. We were young, we were fit, well-fed, optimistic - the Japanese we had discovered to be reasonable people and they were sending us to a major town where there would be better facilities than those we had found in the flea ridden huts of Palempoek.

The train journey was equally encouraging. We were not overcrowded, the seating was comfortable, the Japanese issued to each of us two packets of cigarettes. As we passed through countryside of quite surpassing beauty our thoughts turned again to the way we would pass the months before Java was retaken: we would learn Malay, polish up our bridge and study for our examinations. I suppose there were guards but I do not remember them; they certainly didn't bother us. On the outskirts of Batavia young girls, advised of our coming, were lining the tracks waving to us, again as if we were conquerors, not captives. It was altogether reassuring.

As the train pulled into Batavia Station, Wigram, determined to show the flag, seated himself on the step to our coach which had no doors and thus sailed in to the platform with legs dangling. There were many Japanese awaiting our arrival, amongst them a smartly turned out officer who failed to appreciate Wigram's show of insouciance and proceeded to beat him across the knees with his swagger stick. Shocked, unprepared for this barbarism from an enemy which up to now had behaved in such a civilized fashion, I called out angrily to him to stop but fortunately was dragged back by my shoulders into the carriage and thus avoided similar treatment. But far worse than a mere beating about the knees was soon to follow. We were hustled out of our carriages in short order and directed by cries beyond our comprehension to make our way like a myriad bulls of Pamplona through the streets of Batavia. No semblance of order was allowed - the complacent column out of Garoet, marching in step and belting out its dirty wartime songs, was of a sudden a disorderly, straggling mob, six, seven, eight, nine men wide with drovers yelling incomprehensible Japanese from either side and striking with rifle butts any who incurred displeasure. And so we progressed, affronted and bemused, under the eyes of Dutch, Chinese and Indonesian bystanders along streets at first metalled but soon deteriorating into uneven, dusty, unpaved roads between on the one hand low, shabby, irregularly spaced concrete buildings and on the other a continuous structure of high, limewhited walls out of which projected curious high-roofed corner turrets from which armed Japanese soldiers gazed down on us.

At Palembang in Sumatra when I had for the first time been on the receiving end of strafing by Japanese aircraft, I had been shocked at the sight of the blood red ball of their insignia painted underneath their wingtips as they pulled out not fifty feet above my head - now I was equally shocked by the sight of the same insignia on a white flag fluttering mockingly and by the cry from someone amongst our rabble: *"God, it's a bloody prison!"*

We had arrived; our three and a half years as Japanese prisoners of war had begun.

CHAPTER TWO

BOEI GLODOK PRISON

1

Boei Glodok, as the prison was called, no longer exists; it was demolished some fifteen or so years ago and in its place is a bustling shopping centre still known as Glodok. It was Batavia's gaol and as their Dutch masters regarded the native Javanese as of small account, the facilities now made available for the soldiers, sailors and airmen hastily dispatched in a vain effort to stem the Japanese advance, were sorely limited.

The entrance was unprepossessing: a crude, unpainted concrete portico shaded a set of iron doors with barred openings above. On our arrival the centre pair of doors was open and inside two Japanese soldiers awaited us: the one to count off batches of six, the other to act as tallyman; every sixth man got a booting in and at each booting the tallyman made a mark. Once within we were roughly dispatched through a forward area towards a 'U' of large cells into which we were counted by more or less the same process and when each cell was considered sufficiently filled, its iron door was clanged shut.

In my cell were about one hundred and fifty. It had a concrete floor and concrete walls and high above a timber roof. It was slightly more oblong than square with the two opposite walls unrelieved by openings while of the other two, one was pierced at high level by a more or less continuous shallow barred opening through which could be seen a line of western sky while the fourth, which overlooked the courtyard around which the 'U' of cells was built, had the door in the northern corner and barred openings whose cills were about chest high. In the centre of the cell was the lavatory which consisted of a hole in the floor and two short lines of glazed tiles on which one was supposed to squat. And that, apart from a large number of trestle tables and rather more straw mats of about table top size, was the whole of it.

For a while utter chaos reigned. Each of the one hundred and fifty occupants had kit which varied from the mere shoulder knapsack of the unfortunate or imprudent to tight as drum kitbags of the canny and farseeing. As, thus laden, we were bundled in we were forced along the passages between the trestle tables by the press of those still pouring in through the door. Tables were sent flying adding to the din and confusion of a mob of shouting, cursing, disbelieving men thrust from the blazing sunlight into the gloom of this unimaginable place. Discipline could not exist, rank was of no account; we were simply a rabble of one hundred and fifty men of differing reactions and emotions endeavouring to adjust to an impossible situation whilst aware that one had only those early moments in which to select the patch of floor, or the trestle table henceforth to be one's home. Some, the more alert, the less emotional, like Klondike miners staked out their claims while others wandered aimlessly watching the bedspaces being snapped up one by one with a sinking awareness they must decide whilst there was still something to decide about or simply sank down on the patch of concrete where they happened to have found themselves marooned.

But it had been a long and tiring day and with the march to Garoet Station having been at night most had had little sleep for the past forty-eight hours or so and weariness mitigated the vileness of the situation. Gradually the cursing and complaining died down as we lay to rest either on the trestle tables, or on straw mats on the concrete, with all around an incredible assortment of suitcases, knapsacks, boxes, kitbags, sacks, billy cans, kettles, caps, loose clothing, spare boots, groundsheets and so on in vast variation, scattered like contributions to an earthquake disaster yet to be sorted out and organised.

Some even slept but not for long for as darkness fell the bugs attacked. They dropped from the timbers of the roof, issued from the trestle tables, and poured from the cracks in the walls and floor in numbers inconceivable. They were small, perhaps four would have covered a fingernail, dark red in colour and when squashed smelt of marzipan and squirted blood. There seemed to be one at least to every square inch of floor and they moved at quite astonishing speed. It is a strange feeling when you are exhausted mentally and physically with your body so insisting on sleep that your mind cannot function properly, to be vaguely aware of an army of bugs approaching you on all sides and to be hopefully turning up the edges of the mat on which you are lying in the absurd hope that this will keep them out. But what cannot be cured must be endured, and there are in any case four edges to a mat. Sleep won eventually and one hundred and fifty men, punch drunk with weariness and dismay, snored and spluttered and ground their teeth escaping from one nightmare into others and the bugs feasted.

At some hour with a harsh and sudden clang the iron door was opened and dimly in our battered consciousness we were aware of a new, strange and continually repeated sound as stacks of metal dishes were banged down on the concrete floor and shovelled in. The only light was a crepuscular gloom filtering in from the courtyard and equivalent to that of an English winter dawn - but it was sufficient to advise that the meal was of two courses if insufficient to inform as to contents. There was a vague morass like a scoop of bog and some substance caked hard into the flat dished aluminium bowls on which rested an object I took to be a spoon. Continually brushing off the crawling bugs, unwilling to risk the ooze, I attacked the second course with this utensil. But the stuff was too hard and the spoon too soft and when it yielded and bent double, I wearily thrust it all from me untouched. Daylight explained: the ooze was a glutinous mess of coconut and some sort of green stuff, the caked substance was a gritty coarse red-grained unpolished rice, the spoon a small morsel of dried and rotting fish.

Man's capacity for rising above his circumstances is impressive. In my seventy-plus years I have had my share of nights of pain, fear, hunger, disappointment and dismay but none that compare with the awfulness of that first night in Boei Glodok. And so I think it was with most of the one hundred and fifty in K.8 (as the cell was named) and in all the other cells which accommodated in total two thousand men. The wetness of bug

Boei Glodok Prison

blood and smell of marzipan, the stink of unwashed bodies, the explosions of excretion, the curses, snoring, teeth-grinding, farting; the sense of disbelief, of helplessness, of anger; the sheer impossibility of such a situation all came together to make that night a hell such as could never again, for all that lay ahead, be surpassed in horror.

In the morning there was a brief visit by the Japanese commandant who accompanied by an interpreter informed us that henceforth he was to be our father and mother, after which we were left alone through a day during which two identical meals were as unceremoniously clattered in in ten high stacks and the time was used in making some semblance of order out of chaos.

On the following day, we were allowed out of our cells and from then on conditions improved. The main problems to be dealt with were the destruction of the bugs which made the days unpleasant and the nights a torment and the organisation of latrine facilities.

The former was dealt with by taking everything, clothing, kit, mats and woodwork out into the courtyard and exposing them to the blazing equatorial sun. The effect was astounding. Bugs by the million poured wildly out of the trestle tables and the new residences they had occupied, scurried around like lunatics in padded cells and died. It was also surprising how the numbers whose homes were in the walls and roof gradually yielded to the unsuitable conditions cleanliness in the cells created for them. We never lost our bugs completely - if you fixed some sort of cupboard against a wall and a few days later took it down, you would expose a seething mass of them - but we did so reduce their numbers as to make nights reasonably tolerable.

As to the problem of human waste, most fortunately there happened to be an open drain which ran through the courtyard. This was obviously a stream from some spring outside the prison which had been canalized into a concrete run off about eighteen inches wide the flow of which never varied. (see sketch of layout below)

Boei Glodok Prison

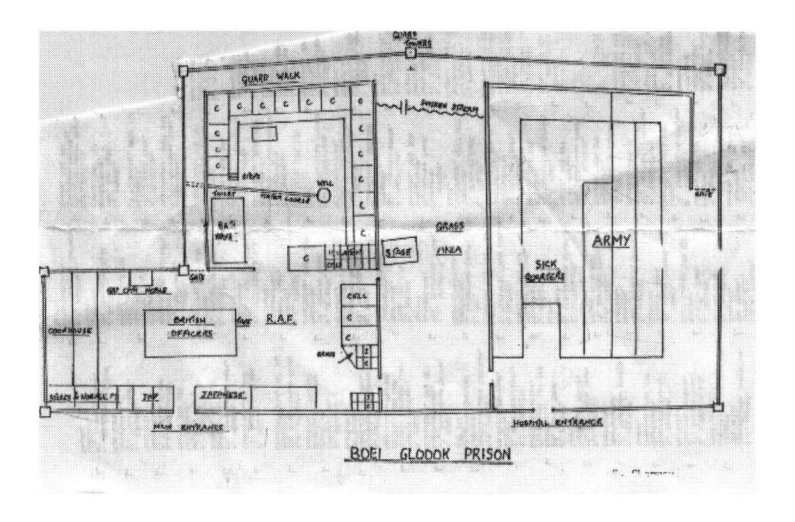

It was decided to allocate the stream in sections: the first, the upstream section to be used for washing dishes; the second for washing clothes; the third for sewage. In due course a fence was built around this section within which one squatted over the drain staring at the backside of the occupant ahead and observing as it passed between your legs of what the one behind had rid himself. Meanwhile the hole in the floor of the cell was cemented in.

For some little time we were scarcely troubled by the Japanese and became, as it were, a service unit operating within the permitted franchise of a higher command. The main structure of rank was re-established and whereas all other ranks were similarly housed the officers enjoyed a way of life as relatively more comfortable as is life in an Officers' Mess when compared with that of the lowest ranks on service stations generally. Daily Routine Orders were issued and posted up in every major cell together with a list of rules and regulations and the punishments which would follow from disobeying them. The R.A.F. were divided into squadrons lettered A to G, with officers and N.C.Os allotted to each. The pilots of my own squadron were in B Squadron but owing to a shortage I was allotted to A - a happening which although of no apparent significance at the time was to result in my being split up from them when the bulk of A Squadron was later shifted to Japan.

Boei Glodok we discovered to be a sprawling place which was divided into two sections with a large grassed and walled in area between. The western section (occupied by the R.A.F) consisted of the large cells built around the courtyard 'U' and other cells which were more open and airy in the forward area by the entrance where the cookhouse, R.A.F. officers and the Japanese administration sections were to be located The eastern section (occupied by Army prisoners) consisted of smaller units which imaginably had been occupied by better class civilian prisoners. Circumnavigating the entire camp was a high double wall with a walkway in between, which was bridged at every turn by a watch tower in which there were always armed Japanese

In the courtyard there was a long ablution shed with a tin roof over a trough of water which had to be scooped out in wooden bowls; there was a line of punishment cells; and there was a section midway between those occupied by Army and R.A.F. which came to be used as sick bay and hospital. The cells were all raised up two or three feet above courtyard level to prevent them being flooded by the frequent tropical rainstorms. What at first sight had appeared an impossible place of habitation soon became acceptable and if the outside world was banished by the circumnavigating walls, at least we had the boon of an open courtyard in which we could stroll and chat largely untroubled by the Japanese.

Within the cells it soon became apparent who were the men of foresight: they were those who had filled kitbags and had chosen places against a wall. There were three good reasons for being against a wall: the first because being able to see a Japanese entering, you were less likely to be caught out and punished for breaking rules or being shown to be in possession of prohibited objects; the second because you could construct cupboards in which to store those things you needed frequently; the third because not only were you not walked upon but you were saved the sense of disorientation living your life out as an island inevitably produced.

For my part having lost almost everything except what I was

Boei Glodok Prison

wearing or had in my pockets when flying out of Singapore and later out of Sumatra, my possessions were few enough to be accommodated in a wicker attaché case I had picked up somewhere and I soon abandoned sleeping in the cell at all and instead occupied a space on the edge of the raised concrete platform off which the cells were built and slept directly on the concrete with a rolled up macintosh as a pillow. When it rained I went inside but otherwise apart from the soreness of my hips I found it pleasant enough lying out in the tropical night, looking up at the Southern Cross and dreaming my dreams of eventual release.

Out here I was not once bothered by the patrolling guards who made their way between me and my cell. Occasionally they would stop and exchange a word as best they could or offer a cigarette - but at that time, and in fact throughout my entire prisoner of war existence, I had a curious pride which militated against being seen to be engaging in conversation or accepting gifts from my captors and mostly I feigned sleep whenever they approached.

Not that many of the prisoners in Glodok had much to do with them; on the whole there was mutual uninterest. With the Japanese very sensibly allowing the management of the camp to pass into the hands of the Army and R.A.F. and secure in the knowledge that escape from within those walls or from an island surrounded by seas they controlled was hardly possible, a handful of strolling guards and a dozen or so at a time in the watchtowers was all they needed; while as for the soldiers themselves, largely drawn as they had been from the muddy unpaved streets and the hovels of the poorer quarters of Japan, the brilliance and luxury of Batavia with its brothels, cinemas and teeming streets was of far more interest than were these curious Europeans who had capitulated to them wihout a fight.

2

A week or two after we had arrived, the Japanese decided it was time we did something to earn our keep and sent us out to Kemajoran Airport to help repair the damage to the runways which the Dutch had mined.

Boei Glodok Prison

To the imprisoned Hurricane pilots there was a curious irony in this. We had arrived in Java by flying our Hurricanes off the aircraft carrier *Indomitable* from some point in the Indian Ocean close to Christmas Island, forty-eight young men cock-a-hoop with confidence they would soon sweep the Japanese with their wooden biplanes out of the skies of Malaya and Singapore.

H.M.S.Indomitable

I happened to be in the first batch of sixteen to land and we arrived to welcoming drinks and lunch in the glittering airport terminal building which overlooked the runways from which we would fly up to Singapore on the following day. There had been twenty-two in my squadron who had set out from England but there were only five in Glodok. Of the other seventeen five had been killed and five injured in aerial combat in the few hectic weeks of fighting over the skies of Singapore, Sumatra and Java. The balance (including the injured) who had been fortunate enough to draw high cards when it was decided that the five who drew the low ones should stay to fly the last few

Boei Glodok Prison

Hurricanes remaining to us in Java, were by now in what was then Ceylon. Of the five who stayed one, Dobbyn, was killed and one, Campbell, was shot own but survived although not to fly again. A sixth pilot, a New Zealander named Vibert, idiotically volunteered to stay on. All five survivors were in Glodok, Lambert and Healey, being with me in K.8, and we worked beside each other filling in the craters in the mined runways

Surviving pilots of 258 Squadron when cards were drawn to decide which ones should stay behind to fly the few remaining Hurricanes. The unlucky ones were: Back Row, leftmost, Dobbyn; fifth from left, author; eighth from left, Lambert. Front row, leftmost, Campbell; second from left, Healey; seventh from left, the volunteer, Vibert.

To get to the airport we had to march for three miles through contrasting sections of what had been to us a very beautiful and fascinating town and in which for a short time (with our Commanding Officer, a man named Thomson, providing us with unlimited funds out of an imprest fund for a ground staff which, following by ship, had most sensibly been diverted away from Java when it was obvious it would fall) we had lived like Lords.

Boei Glodok Prison

The Batavia of those days was a splendid place for those with funds. Here was none of the make do and mend of many pre-war British possessions whose purpose was to provide a profitable way of life enabling its administrators eventually to retire to some English market town or hamlet, but a country in which its Dutch managers expected to live and die. They had, in consequence, built in a totally different idiom. The streets were wide between fine buildings, the hotels flower-embowered, the homes of quality. Batavia breathed permanency. It throbbed with life and colour. Its streets, choked with traffic, car, bicycle, rickshaw, pedestrian, were loud with honks and hoots and shouts and cries and the tinkling of bells and the scrape of iron-bound cartwheels. Flowers, creepers, trees, succulents and vegetables did not struggle to survive but fought each other for the room to luxuriate in a rich red soil which, always moist from cloudburst, allowed a crop of rice to be sown and reaped within a hundred days. The markets were pinnacles of fruits and vegetables in unimaginable variety, the air heavy with a hundred intermingling scents.

This was the town through whose streets we were now, as prisoners, obliged to march to fill in craters in the runways of Kemajoran: a motley lot with each man wearing what he chose out of a meagre selection which included unmilitary items yet still retained something of the coherence of a service - for these were the early days when habit was only fraying at the edges.

We didn't, because this was not our route, pass by old haunts: the splendid Rijswik with its central canal against whose walls we used to idle listening to the koptek's croak while we discussed the evening plans; the Capitool, that fantastic restaurant where we used to try to match the Dutch as trenchermen; the Hotel der Nederlanden where on that fateful morning we drew cards to decide which out of the remnants of a battered squadron should stay behind to fly the last few planes; the Black Cat night club where we used to pile our revolvers on a separate table and drink the new fad, highballs. We didn't pass these places - but we talked of them and because these were the early days when hope of swift release was high were encouraged by the thought that one day we would revisit them and enjoy them all the more.

Boei Glodok Prison

Typical Javanese scene

Our route to Kemajoran was mainly through the shabbier streets of the working quarters, hot and dusty but blazing with bougeanvillea or softened by the hanging stars of white thumbergia. But part of the way was through quarters where wealthy Chinese merchants, apparently untroubled by the Japanese, lay on their verandahs dressed in silk pyjamas, sipping tea and regarding us as we passed with a benign but transient interest. Then, the city left behind, we came to open country, flat and red and very green, with water buffalo and wizened old women working in the rice fields under pointed coolie hats and Malays in tunics and sarongs with pill box caps.

And so to the airfield which, was it a bare three months ago?, we had beat up in formation before breaking into pairs and taxying to that glittering terminal for our welcome feast. That glittering terminal! - what was it now? A nondescript mess of broken glass and twisted metal.

If the Dutch, with the honourable exception of their Navy,

had done as good as nothing to hinder the Japanese air force and army, they had certainly done a splendidly efficient job of mining and the runways had been rendered unusable by huge, neatly-round and very deep craters with the resulting debris surrounding them. Our job was the simple one of pitching the debris back in again. Meanwhile the airfield was in operation for there was plenty of room for aircraft to take off and land on its grassed areas and it was with savage chagrin and desperate jealousy that Lambert, Healey and I watched this activity. But soon it occurred to us that herein lay the only possible method of escape from Java. If, we reasoned, we could steal an aircraft of sufficient range with a bit of luck we could make Australia. Scattered around the field were the burnt out remnants of allied aircraft but amongst them the almost intact fuselage of a Lockheed Hudson. One of us could, we decided, slip into it when the guards were occupied and stay behind and spend a night casing the precautions taken and satisfy ourselves which aircraft were fully fuelled. We saw little difficulty in this initial exercise or in organising things so that one should not be missed through the rough and ready roll call of many hundred men returning to camp - and indeed as future experience was to demonstrate covering up one missing man would have presented little problem. It was a risky idea but it might very well have worked. We had no chance of finding out for another group of pilots, again three in number, upstaged us, attempted almost exactly what we had in mind, were caught and summarily beheaded. Moreover the Japanese made it clear and had it put around that in future if any escapes, or attempted escapes took place, they would presume that those who slept on either side of the offenders were of necessity in the know and would suffer a similar penalty.

To be forced to labour as a coolie was undignified and unpleasant but not without its compensations. It provided escape from a native gaol into the throbbing life outside its walls and on the airfield itself there were consolations to offset the endless days toiling in blistering heat and the agony of the rim of flesh between hand and buttoned down shirt sleeve which the relentless sun burnt into a raw and blistering mess. Bitterly envious though we were of the Japanese pilots, yet with flying having become almost the be-all and end-all of our

Boei Glodok Prison

lives, the activity around us was a reminder of better and exciting days. And then again on the periphery of the airfield imaginative Javanese had set up their stalls for a brand new set of customers and, providing you had the money, not merely were you freely allowed to buy from them but often the guards, always scrupulously honest with your change, would willingly do your shopping for you. Even, occasionally, a guard would use his own money to buy things for a prisoner or a few, a lamentably few, Dutch women would be seen braving the risk of angering their conquerors and standing behind the enclosing wire giving food and money. Being back on Kemajoran had its compensations.

Once the craters had been filled in work at Kemajoran ceased and henceforth working parties ceased to be compulsory and were varied and smaller. If you wanted to go on one you volunteered and were paid a little money; if you didn't want to go, you stayed in Glodok passing the day as you chose scarcely troubled by the Japanese. I suppose I went on a working party about every other day. It made a change, the work was rarely arduous and one never knew where one might go. As often as not you were transported to the place of work in open trucks and waving to the girls one passed and feeling the rush of the humid scented air brought a taste of freedom. Life inside the camp was a still, quiet, unchanging business but outside its walls there was noise, bustle and beauty: a poui in blossom is perhaps even more beautiful to a prisoner.

The money received was of real value. Java at the time functioned on a cheap labour economy and a fertile soil and ample rainfall supplied everything in abundance: eggs, fruit, chickens, vegetables, tobacco, sugar, coffee, tea - all was absurdly cheap. The few cents received for a day's work was very useful and a few guilders bought a sackful. Alas we three, Lambert, Healey and myself, had lived in those halcyon, exciting days before Java fell not wisely but too well - a single day's frugality would have yielded a month of plenty and a little forethought seen us in comfort through our entire stay in Glodok.

Not all had been so improvident. Next to poor men surviving on the ration, sat rich men selecting which cream cake to follow a meal of tinned meat and vegetables; the curious

Boei Glodok Prison

odour from cinnamon cigarettes which were wrapped in vivid saffron-coloured rice paper printed with hieroglyphics and made of a hard and brittle substance which exploded tiny, sparkling crystals as they were smoked, mingled with the tempting scent of mild cigars. But even for the poorest the solace of tobacco of a sort was usually available and the camp food soon improved. It was limited: there were apples, apples in the most astounding quantity, as if an entire shipload of the two gallon tins in which they were supplied had been delivered the day before capitulation; there was bread - for the camp owned its own mobile bakery, a beautiful vehicle, sky-blue in colour, shaped rather like a huge petrol tanker and at least as large; we might in our flying days in the Dutch East Indies have been short of radio receiving sets or spare parts for our Hurricanes, but the commissariat at home hadn't been unmindful of the fact that an army marches on its belly even into a prison camp and had shipped the monster out in the nick of time; there were, after a few months had passed, tomatoes, two per week for each of two thousand men harvested from seeds from a bag of rotting fruit discarded by a Japanese and sown in Java's amazing soil; and there was, on Saturday nights, a hot pot culled from tinned meat and dried potatoes!

Those Saturday nights were never to be forgotten. In them for a precious few hours one could forget one was a prisoner and recover not merely hope but pride as well. Let me set the scene.

The heavy pall of afternoon cloud which has thickened the atmosphere to a dank and gloomy sogginess has given way to great towering sculptures of cumulus gleaming white against brilliant softening blue. Two thousand men are rising from their mats, breaking away from their squatting fours of bridge or solo, putting aside their dogeared much borrowed books or the solitary letter somehow kept and read and re-read a hundred times. With the break up of the cloud sheet, for a while the light is brightening and here and there are tiny patches of sunlight which only at this time of day can penetrate the hard, barred concrete cells. In K.8. as elsewhere are one hundred and fifty living spaces, some neat, some a shambles, no two alike, their owners equally as distinct: bearded, shaven; booted, plimsolled, barefoot; in shirts or singlets; in shorts or

Boei Glodok Prison

underpants. They rise and pour out from the doorways like ants, clutching scraps of soap, ragged bits of towel or torn and worn out shirts pressed as such into service and form queues for the washing places. There is movement everywhere, the splash of water and talk sharpened by anticipation. Back in the cells clothes are coming off and going on, hair is being combed, heads are cocked sparrowlike to reflect in broken bits of orange-backed mirrors such areas of face as their size allows.

In the cookhouse the wise men who had the forethought to volunteer as cooks and are already recognisable by their fleshier frames, are beaming at the waiting orderlies in the knowledge that, even if for the rest of the week they will be envied and mistrusted, calumnied, accused, tonight at least they will be popular The cry rings out and the hot pots are collected - the hot pots and the apple tarts of Saturday nights. Each hot pot, cooked in its separate tin container, has been prepared in the true Lancashire style with layers of thin potatoes parting the succulent meat; the apple tarts are enormous things which have yet to be subdivided with the most precise exactitude. In total bulk together the two courses may not amount to much, but never mind - they are a reminder of the past and of the shape of things to come. Next week (if the rumour that the Americans have landed at Sourabaya, the Australians on Bali and the British on the Celebes is correct) we will be free - by Christmas anyway.

Now the heat is ebbing and the billowing cumulus is rosy pink and gold and heading away to the unknown place to which night always takes it. Men are issuing from the cells in knots of two or three, friends together, or individuals setting off ahead to book places for the Saturday concert. Across the courtyard they go all in the direction of the narrowish opening to The Green. The cells are emptying fast but are never entirely empty for there are always those too ill to leave their bedspace, too morose to be enthused, or taking their turn as guardian to watch over the clutch of limited but infinitely precious possessions the concert audience has left behind.

On The Green the stage is set, promising but empty. The first few rows are hard wooden chairs reserved for the Japanese with their as yet untranslated stars and bars of rank and for the Allied officers in the camp. Behind it is free for all. On the

Boei Glodok Prison

whole it is a well-dressed, undemanding, cheerful audience enduring the early twinges of some vitamin-lack complaint or the first threatening stomach gripes.

High walls hide the prison camp and above them can be seen the tops of creaking palm trees like black tarantulas against a soft sky suddenly, mysteriously, swept naked of cloud and shaded lilac, pink, lemon and steel blue each colour merging, changing imperceptibly one into the other so that nowhere can you say where one begins or another ends. The waiting holds a hum of conversation which dies abruptly so that now can be heard the croak of kopteks and the rasping of cicadas as the floodlights blaze and the night is of a sudden come and the first bright stars are pricking out the sky. And over The Green drifts the rich, warm aroma of tobacco smoke.

The set is never changed - it is of a West End night club with waiters, diners, a dance band and a cabaret. The show is unashamedly sentimental; here are no hard-eyed critics sitting at the end of rows jotting down brilliant epigrams and apothogems alert to rise and leave before the National Anthem, but an audience of young men who average age will be twenty or so which adores the sentimental songs of wartime; the vast majority in it will never have watched television and never have been to a West End or perhaps any night club. They are ready to be transported out of a dreary prison camp into a soft, romantic, luxuriant way of life which has been largely beyond their means and even beyond their ambitions.

The diners on the stage are in evening dress - the men in dinner jackets, the women - the men dressed as women - in long clinging gowns. They are very beautiful these women. Their breasts are firm, their limbs are long, their flesh is powdered, their nails are scarlet, their lips desirable and their hair flows over naked shoulders which invite caresses. The diet has yet to kill the lust from young mens' bodies or prison life to kill the romance in their hearts.

The cabaret turns begin. There are the Eastern Brothers with an act based on the pre-war Western Brothers, who mock the watching, uncomprehending Japanese; there are jugglers, singers, comics. All are enjoyed. But what really matter are the intervals between these turns when with the band playing a favourite dance tune of the time, the self-assured and superbly turned-out men lead their lovely partners out on to the floor and dance close with them under a tropical sky. Then there are unashamed tears in a thousand pairs of eyes and an ineffable yearning for what has been lost.

3

The Drain flowing through the courtyard by now served an additional purpose - as an anodyne for *Happy Feet*..

Happy Feet, or *Electric Feet* as it came to be known in the prison camp of Shamshuipo in Hong Kong, is a curious complaint. The medical term for it is peripheral neuritis and it is an inflammation of the nerves at body extremities. It is caused, or at least was caused in the prison camps, by vitamin deficiency. The first sympton is a slight and not particularly unpleasant tingling of the feet but this rapidly increases to continual and unremitting shooting pains similar to a series of electric shocks and the suffering is abominable. It was discovered by those who were badly affected that the only way to get relief, and thus the only way to get to sleep, was to numb their feet in the surprisingly cold water of the drain passing through the camp. So there they sat, the members of *The Drain Club* as they came to be called, day by day, twenty-four hours on end, (with breaks only to wash and make visits farther downstream), watching the water flowing over their feet, their faces haggard, their suffering unimaginable.

Another malady was known as *Strawberry Balls*. Presumably there is a medical term for this as well but if there is I have never heard it. It was obviously another complaint springing from vitamin deficiency and there were few who did not suffer from it in smaller or greater degree. It attacked the testicles from which one daily lost a skin and the area soon itched, grew sore and became a surprising colour. Occasionally septicaemia set in and I believe in other camps, though not, I think, in Glodok, some deaths resulted. There were of course doctors who'd been taken prisoner but neither they, nor their Japanese counterparts, had the slightest notion how to deal with it and many things were tried the most bizarre of these being exposure of the affected parts to the presumed benificent rays of a tropical sun. On an appointed day all sufferers were

Boei Glodok Prison

instructed to attend a course of treatment on The Green. The length of exposure was to be timed and limited and at a given word of command all were to be instructed to expose their testicles. At the preliminary briefing it was pointed out that the penis was likely to cast a shadow and all patients must make appropriate arrangements to see this didn't happen. Much ingenuity was displayed: there were slings with tapes which tied around the neck; there were tripods; there were posts and strings. One was put in mind of that ever popular prurient classic *Eskimo Nell*.

> 'For eighty tits is a gladsome sight
> For a man with a hell of a stand
> It may be rare in Berkeley Square
> But it's not on the Rio Grande.'

One wonders what flights of fancy the author might have flown if he had witnessed the spectacle of that one thousand men that morning on The Green of Boei Glodok!

Other diseases which spread like wildfire included impetigo which is known to be carried by lice and was presumably, judging by the purple pointillism of many bodies, also carried by our bugs. There was scabies for which as there was no medicine many things were tried including scrubbing the sores with wire brushes and anointing the open wounds thus caused with diluted hydrochloric acid - a process which caused the patient foreseeable agony but so far as I could discover was totally inefficaceous. There was dysentry which killed about seventy men while I was in Glodok and there was dengue fever which can kill but on the whole seldom did. Only about five per cent of the camp escaped an attack of dengue fever which was accompanied by a headache which has to be experienced to be believed and a general feeling of such weakness, helplessness and misery that you could watch the bugs (which for some strange reason were never eliminated from the sick bay) crawling in waves all over you and yet not have the capacity to do more than wave a despairing hand. Recovery commences about a week after the attack, but it is slow and effects linger for a considerable time.

Boei Glodok Prison

And there was that sickness which is the most difficult of all to cure - that of the man who who lies down on his truckle bed, his mattress or his patch of concrete to die. These were the men who could not adjust and there were many of them. One was named Taber. Some of us were deputed to act as wards to these unfortunates and Taber was the man I tried to take under my wing. He was about twenty years of age, had red hair and a freckled face and lived in one of the smaller cells in the forward part of the camp. There was nothing particularly the matter with him except that, like a caged bird which cannot endure its confinement, he had lost the will to live. I used to go across to see him every day, sometimes to encourage, sometimes to bully, sometimes to coax. It was in vain. He appreciated the effort I was making and talked very sensibly about it from the mattress he'd got from somewhere. But nothing would stir him from his apathy, not even the bribe of extra food. When he died his body was wrapped in a shroud of cheese cloth. I went to pay my last respects before they took him away. There was a small moist stain where the cloth touched his nostrils and there were flies on it; it seemed the most disgusting thing. Forty years later I revisited Java and laid flowers on the grave in the military cemetery of Leading Aircraftsman R.E.Taber who had died on the twenty-seventh of July, nineteen hundred and forty-two - only four months after entering Boei Glodok and exactly two weeks after my own twenty-second birthday.

CHAPTER THREE

A VOYAGE BEYOND BELIEF

1

It would be as false to paint an over-rosy picture of those first few months of captivity as it would be to paint them over-black. They were not good days. We had lost our freedom and what should have been the best days of our lives, the days of youth, were dragging by with a painful slowness which was highlighted by following immediately on the most hectic and rewarding weeks we had ever known. They were not good days because in them we had to obey the orders of men we regarded as being of a lesser race. And they were not good days because of the melancholy business of watching the decline of standards in human behaviour we had never visualised.

I spent seven months in Boei Glodok, roughly one sixth of the time I was to be a prisoner of the Japanese. It was a curious period because being as it were still connected with the unbroken series of events which led up to my being captured, I did not so much regard it as a new way of life but as an interruption of the old. When I considered freedom, I did so in finite terms as indeed, did the majority - even amongst the pessimists a year was about the limit put on our captivity. Psychologically this was important for it led to most of us almost automatically conducting ourselves as we would have in normal life and being concerned with what others thought of our behaviour. But once the idea of a finite period had been replaced by uncertainty, conventional pressures slackened and the true character of individuals began to manifest itself and by no means always to their credit.

A Voyage Beyond Belief

I was fortunate in being able to share a cell with Lambert and Healey. We had come halfway round the world together, we had fought the Japanese in Singapore and Sumatra, and having all three of us drawn low cards on that vital morning on the stoep of the Hotel der Nederlanden in Batavia, we had gone on to fight them in Java. We had seen close friends killed and wounded and said goodbye to others who escaped to Australia and Ceylon. And in the end after more death and injury we had been the last three of the original squadron to fly against the enemy. And then with no aircraft left we had tried to escape together, failed to do so, shared the same native hut and entered Glodok side by side.

In a normal civilian life we would not necessarily have chosen each other for company but circumstances had so arranged things that it did not occur to us to look elsewhere and naturally we stayed close in Glodok. The effect of this was blinkering. We were not unaware of the suffering around us and did not entirely escape it, but we did not apply the possibility of dying to ourselves. When we felt depressed we escaped by strolling the courtyard together, looking at the cumulus longingly, reminiscing and deluding ourselves that we would one day fly again. Fortunately we were equally poor and thus there was no risk of envy creeping in and, importantly, each of us, because of the other two, was obliged to maintain his self-respect. As fighter pilots we had counted ourselves rather special and if this speciality was to be retained then we could not have anything to do with being unshaven, unwashed, unkempt nor with begging cigarettes from our captors or toadying to those who were by prison standards rich men. We felt moreover a sort of responsibility to those around us which sprang from the automatic but very positive respect which groundstaff always gave to aircrew. After all pilots are what air forces are all about.

So we were a little apart from the hundreds of men about us and to a degree sufficient in ourselves. This was to end abruptly. The 'we', so far as I was concerned was to become 'I' and Bertie and Pip, as I knew them, were to go out of my life and I was not to see them again until after the war was over. On October 21st, 1942, almost exactly seven months after entering Glodok, I left

A Voyage Beyond Belief

as one of a batch being transferred to Japan. When 'A' Squadron was with scarcely any notice 'posted', I had to go with it. Thus one day life was pretty much a routine business shared with two friends who had become very close and the next I was parading at the gate and they were saying goodbye.

I was sad to leave them but young enough to be glad that the pointless stagnation of life in Boei Glodok was at an end. Without the least idea of our destination, blessedly unaware of what the next few months would hold, I felt once more the tingling of adventure. And I was fortunate; if they chose to, both Lambert and Healey (who were subsequently sent to help build an airfield on the island of Ambon) would have a grimmer tale to tell.

At readiness in Java. Author and Lambert.

2

We embarked at Batavia's port, Tandjeonpriok, on *S.S.Yoseda*

A Voyage Beyond Belief

Maru, a very small ship packed as were all Japanese ships in a manner unimaginable to Western nations. The space between decks was subdivided horizontally so as to provide layers of men with just about enough head height to be able to sit up but who were so close side by side that when one turned his neighbour was more or less obliged to do the same. One travelled thus in the steaming equatorial heat in, as it were, an open fronted chest of drawers; it is fair to point out that the quarters of the many Japanese soldiers travelling were only marginally better. The ability of the Japanese to land surprisingly large invasion forces from a small collection of modest ships is easily explained.

The Yoseda Maru took us to Singapore and although it was of course uncomfortable, I have always looked back on that voyage with pleasure. We were given good food and freely allowed on deck and all we could see was fantastically beautiful. There simply are not words adequately to describe the loveliness of the sea close by the Sunda Straits which lie between Java and Sumatra. We have our visions of the perfect South Sea island, palm-fringed, girt with coral over which the surf breaks dazzling white, cooled by trade winds under a clear blue sky. If a man could take a handful of such islands and with a sweep of his arm scatter them irregularly over a great expanse of ocean so that here were clusters of four or five or six, here another of larger size, here one of horseshoe shape, here one like a sailing ship with a hundred palms as masts, here one so small that really it is a bare golden rising turning the sea around it a dazzling turquoise - if a man could do that he might create beauty to rival what we saw. I had flown over the Sunda Strait quite a number of times for it lies between the luxury of Java and the forbidding primeval jungle of Sumatra where there is no sand but the sea comes in under the mangrove swamps merging land and water, and I had thought it magical - but it was still more magical as we picked our way northwards for there were islands everywhere, misty mirages floating on a tranquil sea and holding out a heart-catching promise of freedom from life's problems.

The feeling was far different when we docked in Keppel

A Voyage Beyond Belief

Harbour, Singapore. Here was the evidence of a shaming defeat which would change for ever the opinion of the Orient about the British: scuttled ships, deserted gowdowns, piles of scrap. For two days we lay by the quay before we were filed ashore for inspection and disinfection. The inspection was by means of a glass rod thrust dedecoratingly up our anuses; the disinfection was as unforgettable. There was a ship which had been especially converted which had a curious wooden structure like an endless sheep dip along which we progressed naked into a warm bath which smelt of lime and was of the colour of mashed potato. In this we were required totally to immerse ourselves until, presumably, rid of germs and then we returned to re-dress ourselves in the same germ-ridden clothes. It was puzzling but in its way encouraging, for it followed that if it was required we should be cleaned so hygienically before being allowed to enter Japan (which we had by now discovered to be our destination) our quarters on the ship to take us there would be to match.

The vessel to which we were to be transferred was the ancient, rusting, decrepit *S.S. Dai Nichi Maru* and it lay just along the quayside from the Yoseda. From its sides ran four separate gangplanks and up three of these a seemingly endless kit-laden stream of prisoners was slowly filing and was to continue to do so ceaselessly through the afternoon; the fourth, the unused gangplank was, we discovered, for us.

How it came about that I should have been chosen as one of two men to accompany a Japanese officer aboard ahead of the rest to inspect and approve our conditions I can no more remember than how it came about I was to accompany old Wigram to Garoet but elected I was and up we went to inspect No 2 Hold forward. Our inspection took a matter of moments only, for the conditions were patently absurd and we advised the Japanese officer to this effect. He did not in the least disagree and undertook to have something done about them and we remained ashore for several hours while this, presumably, was being carried out.

At nightfall we went aboard. Nothing had been done. The hold measured sixty feet by eighty feet and was two decks down; it had an open hatch about twenty feet square roughly central to

A Voyage Beyond Belief

it. The floor was a consignment of wet iron ore which had been levelled immediately below the hatch opening and then sloped down at an angle of about thirty degrees in all directions until it met either the ribs of the ship sides or the bulkhead of the adjoining hold. Lighting was by means of a single electric light bulb hanging on a flex in the hatch opening which cast illumination little farther than the levelled patch beyond which gloom merged into Stygian blackness. The place was alive with rats, flies and cockroaches; access was by means of a single vertical iron ladder; furnishings consisted of a few dozen planks and straw mats. This was intended to be, and was to be, the home for two hundred and sixty-eight men in moderate health dressed for the tropics for a journey of thirty days into the Japanese winter.

In the beginning all was chaos. The two hundred and sixty-eight prisoners having made their way down the flights of stairs serving the two decks and then one by one down the iron ladder, their kit was simply pitched in from above becoming an ever-mounting pile on the levelled ore while they, to avoid the bombardment, took refuge on the slippery wet sloping sides. Above, the two decks having been subdivided in the manner of the Yoseda Maru allowed four layers of Japanese in a 'U' on three sides of the hatch opening to peer down on these proceedings. Indeed, having come aboard ahead of us and already bored, almost to a man this is what they did, kneeling, lying on their stomachs, laughing, calling, pitching down sweets and cigarettes, a sea of Oriental faces, shaven heads and glinting spectacles in a cacophony of gibes, good humour and unintelligibilia.

When the bombardment ceased the kit was slowly sorted out with items being held up, claimed and passed down to owners hand over hand. Taking into account the levelled portion, which had to be left unoccupied, theoretically there should have been sixteen square feet of sloping iron ore per man - which is about the size of a normal door; in practice it was significantly less because the lowest depths were utterly dark and none prepared to take them. In the event each man occupied about enough steeply sloping space not to touch the man on either side or above or below him on which he laid his kit, and,

A Voyage Beyond Belief

if he was fortunate enough to own one, his groundsheet, while the planks were set out to form duckboard pathways and the flat central space kept clear as a communal area.

An hour or so passed in a state of numbed disbelief during which the enthusiasm of the Japanese spectators ebbed steadily and one by one their heads disappeared from view as they turned their attention to whatever were more normal methods of amusing themselves in their chests of drawers on a troopship. At about eight o'clock a meal was lowered by ropes in enormous buckets. It proved to be the ubiquitous rice and a thin, milky-coloured soup with a faintly fishy flavour; this, with the occasional addition of a few sliced, dried potatoes, was to be our daily diet for the next thirty days although additional to this we had some small stores which consisted of a little sugar and tea and some tinned food working out at about one tin per man. Except as a kind of practice operation into the method of distributing food and organising two hundred and sixty-eight men crammed into a sepulchral hold with sloping sides of loose wet gravel, the meal served little purpose with minds far too occupied with adjusting to conditions unimaginable, unbelievable and unacceptable.

For my own part with the exception of another Hurricane pilot with whom I had played bridge on the way out on the *Indomitable* and one other also from another squadron, I knew only a number of men aboard by sight and none even as acquaintances. My possessions were my macintosh, two thin blankets and my wickerwork attaché case whose contents were so sparse in quantity as to slither around within. I wore a white towelling short-sleeved shirt and khaki drill slacks and sandals. And I owned, quite comically, a pith helmet too big to fit within the attaché case. Within the basket was my Pilot's Flying Log Book, a novel and a wallet, a razor with a single blade with a nick out of the cutting edge, a khaki drill jacket, a set of pyjamas already wearing thin and presumably an odd shirt or two and socks and underpants.

With this equipment I selected a random space on the sloping ore aft of the levelled space and by good fortune near enough to it to enjoy the benefit of diffused light yet not so near as to affected by light rain. I cannot recall who were my neighbours for all that one at least was to die before the voyage ended. I spread out my macintosh - a black oilskin kind of thing which was a good deal cracked and worse for wear - as a groundsheet and placed the attaché case behind my head to serve as a pillow but where on earth I put my pith helmet I cannot imagine although I must have hung on to it religiously for I was wearing it in the snowstorm which was to greet us on arrival in our camp in Japan.

3

We sailed next morning and, being allowed on deck took stock. The Dai Nichi, which was as cracked and as worse for wear as my old macintosh, was transporting in addition to its crew some one thousand soldiers and about one thousand two hundred prisoners all in holds such as ours. Sanitary arrangements for both captors and captives consisted of wooden structures built along the deckside each with three compartments over a trough which, until blocked, spilled into the sea. The prisoners' latrines were on the starboard side, the Japanese to port. There were nine for the prisoners, three forward allocated to serve five hundred men and six at the stern to serve the balance of seven hundred; the Japanese were proportionately better supplied having a dozen to serve one thousand. For washing there were no facilities beyond buckets of water hauled aboard but fortunately with the ship in such disrepair its steam pipes leaked so badly that a man with the patience, and the will, could collect a mug of hot water with which to wash and shave himself - a long drawn out operation only possible when permission to go on deck was granted.

We were part of a convoy of four small freighters painted grey and with black markings on their funnels which I have been informed, although I do not recall this myself, were later painted out and replaced with new markings. Initially we were protected by a very small and outdated destroyer but later we were to lose her and in fact also the balance of the convoy and sail on alone at the mercy of any American submarine.

The first few days were, I suppose, tolerable, apart from the

A Voyage Beyond Belief

nuisance of occasional tropical downpours which sheeted down unchecked into the holds driving those nearest the flattened area tighter against the rest who resisted being driven further into Stygia. But things changed as soon as the tropics had been left behind as we sailed northwards. The temperature fell and the warm rain became cold rain buffeted by winds which swirled it round in the vortex of the hatch opening wider and deeper, driving the men in the holds even farther from the light, farther down the wet and shiny slopes, farther towards the ribs where the rats were based. Then the rain turned to snow which floated down in impressive petals and, caught by the strange wind eddies, whirled deep into the gloom.

On November 4th we anchored off Saigon for a few hours (and some of us saw to our chagrin a very smart motor launch with uniformed white sailors manning it and a French tricolour flying from its stern) before continuing northwards through the China Sea towards what was then Formosa and is now Taiwan. *En route*, so I have been informed, although I have no recollection of it myself, we were attacked by a submarine and a torpedo passing through the centre of the convoy caused it to scatter. We arrived at Takao, Formosa's southernmost port, on November 11th, stayed for a few hours to take on some American prisoners who had been working in stone quarries and to disembark some of our own (although none from my hold) and, presumably, supplies before continuing on our way. After a few hours sailing by which time the weather had appallingly deteriorated, the Dai Nichi suddenly stopped. The feeling in the hold was very strange. The light, poor as it had been, went out and we lay in utter darkness hearing a tempestuous sea beating against and forcing sea water through the ship's rusty sides - for such was the condition of the ship that it was also possible to see the coal in the bunkers through the bulkhead which separated us from them they were so rusted through! The comforting sound of engines had ceased and most macabrely a guitar someone had hung up on some high projection twanged interminably and infuriatingly with every pitch and roll. We were a sitting duck for any allied submarine which happened to be in the area and in our minds was the suspicion (which such

A Voyage Beyond Belief

sinkings as that of the *Lisbon Maru* were later to confirm) that if we were torpedoed the first thing the Japanese would do was batten us down to drown like rats.

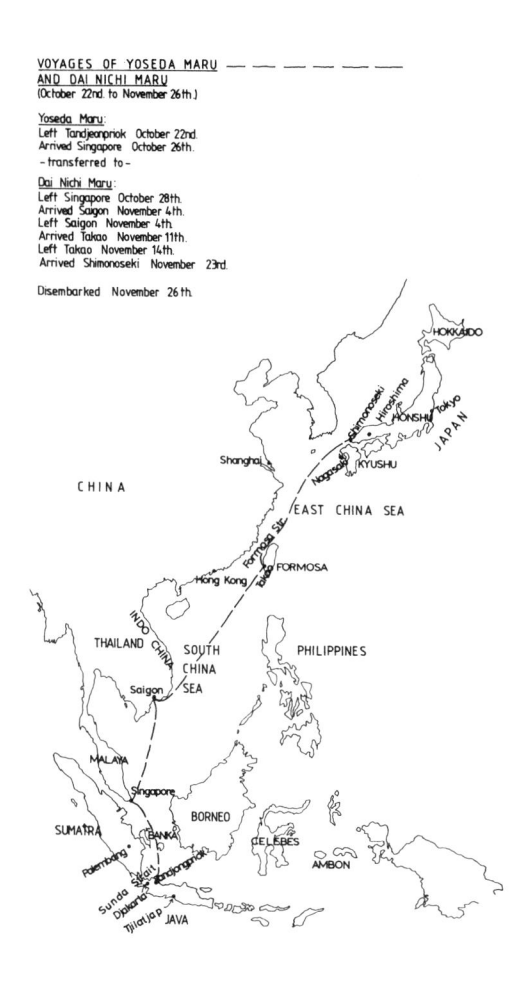

```
VOYAGES OF YOSEDA MARU
AND DAI NICHI MARU
(October 22nd to November 26th.)

Yoseda Maru:
Left Tandjeonpriok  October 22nd.
Arrived Singapore   October 26th.
- transferred to -

Dai Nichi Maru:
Left Singapore      October 28th.
Arrived Saigon      November 4th.
Left Saigon         November 4th.
Arrived Takao       November 11th.
Left Takao          November 14th.
Arrived Shimonoseki November 23rd.

Disembarked November 26th.
```

The map above shows the voyages on Yoseda Maru and Dai Nichi Maru from Java to Japan from October 2nd 1942 to November 26th 1942.

For three days we lay anchored in a bleak, windswept bay until

A Voyage Beyond Belief

some bodged up repair could be made which permitted the patched, leaky, worn out, rusting, Dai Nichi Maru with its iron ore and its two thousand odd souls aboard to limp on again towards Japan at about four knots, juddering and vibrating fearfully each time the screw came out of the water. We had lost the convoy and were quite alone.

By now a dreadful sickness had broken out manifesting itself in diarrhoea which as day succeeded day became increasingly prevalent. Conditions in the hold became chaotic. Weakened men were soon unable to climb a vertical ladder, or even have *time* to climb a vertical ladder and then two flights of wooden stairs through the racks of Japanese. Soon many were passing their stools into convenient utensils: tins, billy cans, plates; soon they were passing their stools where they lay. The wet iron ore became smeared and slippery with faeces, blood and mucus. The stench became appalling; morale fell steadily. Everywhere was stink, the cries of men in pain, the filth of soiled clothes, blankets, kitbags, bodies. Even those yet to succumb soon found their possessions tainted. Day by day the virulence of the disease increased, day by day more were struck down by it, soon those unaffected were in the large minority.

One had to do what could be done; it was important to persuade as many as possible to make the effort to climb the ladder and pass their urine and their stools in the proper place. For all the hideousness of the holds it was worse on deck where the wind screamed, and the rain beat, and the cold was biting on naked arms and legs. There was a huge temptation to succumb to indolence; by comparison with the empty, desolate, windswept deck and the tossing, dreary, foam-flecked waves there was warmth and companionship in the gloomy hold. Up above the troughs of the latrine soon began to be choked and once they ceased to function an adequate excuse would have been found to stay below, morale would have finally collapsed, and deaths frequent as they were becoming multiplied beyond all proportion.

I decided to take on myself the responsibility of keeping the latrines functioning. I have never properly analysed my reasons for doing so. Three times each day I picked my way

A Voyage Beyond Belief

around the hold calling for volunteers and it was then, because of my white towelling shirt, a bright patch of light in that dark and hellish hold, I earned the curious and quite inappropriate nickname of "Flash" by which I am to this day, more than fifty years on, invariably addressed by all of those who shared those days with me. It was not always easy to find those volunteers but then again I never failed to find them. Up we would go out of the relative warmth, hand over hand up the rusty iron ladder, past the two racks of comatose Japanese who appeared curiously unaware of the drama going on below and seemingly untouched by the disease, up the two wooden flights of steps on to the hard, cold, wet and shiny deck to the terrifying, huge, gale-swept seas. I shall never forget those seas in which we lurched and wallowed - one moment they were mountains rearing up above us threatening to crash down and send the ship to oblivion, the next, mysteriously, they had vanished and the Dai Nichi Maru seemed poised on a scummy precipice and there seemed nothing to prevent it slithering down into a valley which had no end. Sailors will understand, sailors can relate to tremendous seas just as pilots can relate to horizons which do what are to others remarkable things. But I was not a sailor.

We slid and slipped our way across the pitching deck, pausing when the slope was too much against us, grasping at anything to hand to hold us back when too steep. To sluice out the troughs we used buckets on ropes which we hurled over the side and hauled up, swaying wildly, crashing against the rusty sides and losing half their contents. We threw the water into the troughs to sluice them out. The troughs were hideous. Everything was choked together: blood and slime and excreta bound by bloodied paper and bloodied rags. It resisted shifting and was evil beyond words being not just the remnants of what men had eaten but part of men themselves. It was abominable and obdurate and it stank of death. We threw the water at it and the water was contaminated and picked up by the wind and whipped into contaminated spray which drenched us. It was a long, cold, unpleasant job sluicing out those troughs three times a day.

But at least afterwards, such as it was, there was the

A Voyage Beyond Belief

relative comfort of the hold while to others there was no such comfort and would never be again. These were those who were too sick to climb the ladder and join the queue which, day and night, never diminished. For them what went by the name of a hospital was rigged up on the deck. It was not a hospital; it was a staging post for death. These men, a clutch of them, under a flapping awning, moaning in despair and pain, were there because they were passing stools every ten minutes or so which is at the rate of a hundred and forty-four times a day. For all the biting wind they wore only their upper garments and as often as not these were only shirts and even these were bloodied and slimed. These men were dying and there was nothing to be done for them but to position them in some place convenient to their illness: within a few yards of the group of three latrines reserved for them. It was an unchanging scene: the leaden sky, the bitter wind, the tossing sea and the faint cries of men now incapable of walking unassisted in their last conscious moments of self-respect seeking to be half helped, half dragged with filthed and bloodied shanks at intervals of ten minutes towards the lavatory - as like as not to cry it was too late and pass more bloody mess across the iron deck. Their deaths were awful and without dignity.

The first man who died on the ship was given an impressive funeral which I attended. I have notes of the occasion made by another Dai Nichi traveller, an officer of the 41st Fortress Company, Royal Engineers who was taken prisoner in Singapore, which I quote below verbatim. Unfortunately I do not have his name and cannot therefore give him the credit he ought to have. The name of the man who died was Peter Glenister who obviously would not have been in our hold but I can confirm from my own quite strong recollection that the funeral was very much as my unknown correspondent describes.

'On November 11th, Peter Glenister died. When I look back I think how awful it was, such sordid conditions and with such a

A Voyage Beyond Belief

bleak outlook and at the mercy of a people of an alien culture. I do not know who made contact with the Japanese but a board was made available and also a Union Jack. A most impressive ceremony followed and some of us, myself included, were allowed on deck to make our farewells. The weather was fairly calm with grey skies except that it was warm it could well have been an Armistice day in England, which took my mind back to Armistice day services at Blundells School when the last post was sounded from the tower of Big School and my thoughts went back to my eldest brother who died in France in October 1918 and whose name was inscribed in the school chapel and on the entrance wall of the Main school building. In war how differently one can die.

The corpse was lashed to the board with the Union Jack wrapped over and presumably suitably weighted. Some well turned out Japanese officers appeared wearing white gloves and swords, together with some buglers. At the rear of the procession soldiers carried trays with rice balls, fish and sweets. The burial service was read by one of the senior British officers (I cannot remember if it was Tom Moore my O.C.), the Japanese officers saluted, the bugles sounded and the corpse was made to slide from the deck into the China Sea, finally disappearing below the surface.

The following day, November 12th, we were allowed on deck for short spells and during that day reached Takao, in Southern Formosa (Taiwan) where the weather was noticeably colder. We were anchored off shore that night and the following day our party disembarked by lighter at 1930 hours.'

It will be noted that we have a slight disagreement on the date of arrival at Takao but November 11th is the date written in my Log Book.

I have the feeling there may have been some sort of funeral service and ceremony for deaths following that of Peter Glenister but before long as they became frequent and commonplace, there were none and the men who died were pitched into the sea like rotten carcasses.

4.

There were many dreadful voyages which had to be endured by

A Voyage Beyond Belief

Allied prisoners of war of the Japanese and for those with an interest in statistics, details can be found in a manual by Sumio Adachi, professor of the National Defense Academy of Japan titled 'Unprepared Regrettable Events' first published in September 1982. However it may be sufficient to say that of those whose destination was Japan, Adachi states there were ten shiploads in 1942, twelve in 1943, seventeen in 1944 and six in 1945. Altogether some 34,000 prisoners were transhipped. These figures exclude the many voyages made between conquered territories such as from Singapore to Sumatra and Java to Ambon which were equally unpleasant. I have been informed that the voyage of the Dai Nichi was classified as amongst the worst three such voyages but I have no knowledge as to whether or not this was so. In passing, it may be interesting to note that out of all the vessels on which prisoners were transhipped, twenty-five were sunk by Allied action and (again according to Adachi) of the 18,901 carried on them there were 8,048 survivors. No doubt it was inevitable that some would be lost this way but many were drowned because, far from trying to rescue them, the Japanese took pains to make sure they would not survive.

The case of the Lisbon Maru (which was sunk on October 1st, 1942 in the East China Sea) is well documented and confirms this deliberate decision to have the prisoners drown rather survive and possibly escape. Not only once it was clear the ship was sinking were the prisoners battened down but many who managed to break out of the hold were machine gunned on the deck and in the sea itself. The East China sea lies just to the north of Taiwan, in other words relatively near to where we were when the Dai Nichi was wallowing helpless and unprotected and the machine gunning of prisoners on the Lisbon Maru had taken place a mere six weeks earlier. There seems little doubt that had the Dai Nichi Maru been torpdeoed (as, by then renamed Dai Niti Maru, she was by the American submarine Gurnard off the north-west coast of Luzon in the Phillipines on October 8th, 1943) there would have been few, if any of us who would have survived.

A Voyage Beyond Belief

Even without knowing about the Lisbon Maru, I think we all accepted this but such was our discomfort, so appalling our conditions and so dreadful what was taking place that it was an eventuality to which we gave comparatively little thought. Equally we gave little thought to the presence of our captors and for my part (as notes made shortly after arrival in Japan make clear) I did not apparently have, as I would have expected to have, a tremendous sense of hatred welling up inside me that men should be made to die so agonisingly and so shamefully. *'In an odd sort of way,'* I wrote, *'there were no Japanese on that ship. They lived their lives; we lived ours. We both accepted the others were there and there it ended. They neither mocked our deaths nor, apparently, regretted them. Our deaths were as far removed from the Japanese as would have been the deaths of the inhabitants of some previously unheard of island killed by earthquake, famine or pestilence. This is how it was to those Japanese comatose on their shelves. as the days and weeks went slowly by. They had their own problems.to occupy their minds, their own considerable discomfort. And they were after all theoretically heroes returning to their homeland.'*

5

On November 25th, we raised Japan. It was a dismal evening as we passed through the Moji/Simonoseki Straits to a vista of a sombre, congested and colourless town under cold, grey, lowering skies. The Japanese soldiery lining the rails showed little joy at its return from the warmth, colour and plenty of the tropics. There was, I still clearly recall, a most curious light which seemed to explain the strange, almost ethereal quality one finds in so much Japanese painting: a sense of unreality which has lingered through all these years of a town of heavy roofs which seemed to crowd together as if for warmth and comfort and to be dispassionate to man. Japan, the essential Japan, seemed to be in the ascendant; the slow moving ship with its expressionless soldiers and its mentally battered prisoners seemed of no account. I do not believe this reaction (which was by no means mine alone) was caused by what we had endured,

A Voyage Beyond Belief

but was simply brought about by the topography of unrelenting volcanic hills shrouded in murky, sullen clouds lowering over them be seen.

How different now was our state of mind from that which we had known when sailing past the sunlit Sunda Strait. There was not even a sense of relief at escaping from that hellish hold; indeed for all the deaths within it, for all its horror, or because of it, it had held companionship and become our home. In leaving it we would be exchanging something we had come to understand for the unknown; it was as if the gloomy vista which met our gaze was a warning that terrible though the past four weeks had been, what lay ahead would be even worse.

On the next day, having disposed of the latest fatalities, we disembarked and were again obliged to endure the indignity of glass rods shoved up our rectums only this time under the gaze of a bevy of girl office workers wearing the sailor suits which were their wartime costume. Then, savagely split into random groups (which abruptly parted friends, perhaps even brothers, from each other) each under the charge of an English speaking Japanese with an American accent whose principal instruction was to *"Right Face!"*, we were taken by ferry across the strait whence we straggled through seemingly endless wooden corridors which eventually deposited us on a railway platform. Two things I remember of that shambling march: men and women holding out photographs of their uniformed sons in the hope that passers-by would recognise them and women who walked holding out white scarves they were knitting, bowing and humbly asking for the contribution of a stitch.

On the railway platform it was very, very cold and we were dressed as for the tropics; most were ill, many very, very ill. There was a long, long wait. For all it was suffering; for many it was torture. Their stomachs writhed with pain and without even the energy to clap their hands or stamp their feet, their extremities were numb; they had even lost the warmth of hope. They were beings almost without existence. Even for the fortunate amongst us whose constitutions had, at least so far, resisted the plague which had swept through the holds of the Dai Nichi Maru, that time of waiting was a torment. We stood,

A Voyage Beyond Belief

or paced, seeing express trains roaring through at astounding speed, discovering that in Japan men and women shared the same common urinal.

Our train came eventually and as we boarded it we were given a ration which was our introduction to the kind of food we would henceforth be eating. The ration was known as a *bento* and consisted of a stiff straw box divided into two compartments: the one (the larger by far) filled with ice-cold steamed rice, the other with tiny pieces of seaweed and vegetables.

Through the whole of that night we roared through an unknown land. There was nothing to see of it but occasional near or distant lights, there was nothing to know of it - we could have been in any country which had the capacity to support an efficient, electrified railway system. It was a strange sensation.

At dawn the train stopped at a station and very much like a mail train unloading parcels, two batches of one hundred men were deposited on the platform before the train pulled out taking the balance to God knows where. The station was called Onomiti, which is a town on the north side of the Inland Sea of Japan which divides the main Japanese island of Honshu from its substantial (and in the southernmost parts semi-tropical) islands of Kyushu and Shikoku. It was a bitterly cold and windy morning. We were given another ice cold bento and then obliged to wait for five long hours during which the other group to ours (which included the man I had played bridge with on the Indomitable) left for a camp which we subsequently discovered to be named Mukaishima. Finally we, the second hundred, were transported by tugboat to the island of Innoshima which is in the *Ken* - of which the near English equivalent is 'County' - of Hiroshima.

The Inland Sea of Japan is very beautiful but we were not to appreciate the extent of its beauty until approaching another three years had passed for it was too cold a day for a hundred sick and shaken men to do anything but crowd into any chamber which shielded them from the sleet and biting wind. I found myself in the engineer's cabin which was warm and in which I

A Voyage Beyond Belief

met my first Japanese civilian, the engineer. He was a friendly man and he gave us all one of the tangerine style oranges which grew so profusely in Japan; in the galley below an aged Japanese was cooking himself some onions in soy and sugar which smelt delicious. There were five of us in that cabin - quite soon we would be carrying two, whose names were Durk and Poulson, on the first of the funeral marches.

As there was a jetty close by what was to become our camp the only possible reason for depositing us at the far end of the dockyard in which we were to work, was, I presume, to show us off as prizes to the workers. We were hardly an impressive lot and must have made disappointing propaganda: a shambling group, mostly in tropical gear, some even in shorts, many with hardly the energy to put one foot in front of its fellow, shuffling along laden with kitbags, attaché cases, parcels and bundles. I remember that first walk through Habu Dockyard. I can still see the skeletons of half-built ships, the flash of welding, the piles of wood and scrap, the curious faces, the dry docks and the slips. I can still see the dumpy travelling cranes and hear the harsh clang of hammer on metal plate and the woodpecker sound of riveting. But best of all what I remember is the weight of a sick man named Bowen-Jones I was assisting and the absurdity of wearing a pith helmet in a snowfall.

CHAPTER FOUR

ISLAND OF TEMPLES - INNOSHIMA

1

Long ago, according to the legend, a fisherman from Onomichi gave a travelling priest a lift in his boat dropping him off at the beach of Omaha on Innoshima Island. The boatman pushed off and then momentarily turning his head, saw to his amazement the priest turning into eighty-eight priests who were landing one by one. The story spread amongst many people and rumour had it that Kobodaishi (a high priest) had landed on Innoshima. So in 1908 all the villages held a discussion and decided to set up eighty-eight temples for pilgrimage and these were constructed by voluntary work of all the people on the island. The route of the pilgrimage is eighty-four kilometres in length and the pilgrimage is normally made around March 21st according to the lunar calendar. Each temple has its name and, curiously, no less than three of them are called Dainichiji (which is perilously close to the name of the ship which brought us to Innoshima, the Dai Nichi) and one of them is called Zentsuji - which was the name by which for quite some time our camp on the island would be named. But of this we knew nothing at the time for all that the roof of one of them was visible from the camp

Nor did we know that between the fourteenth and sixteenth centuries, Innoshima Island was the haunt of one of the three pirate families known as the Pirates Murakami who collected tolls from all vessels passing through the Onomichi Channel; had we done so, those of us who were to work for the best part of three years under the watchful eye of a Japanese of the same name, would have appreciated the irony of yet another coincidence.

Crayon drawing of the Oriko Gokei Jin Ja shrine by Geoffrey Coxhead. A small portion of it was visible from the camp.

Island of Temples - Innoshima

The temples remain on Innoshima as do the ruins of the pirates' castles but tolls are no longer collected and Innoshima Island is directly connected by a suspension bridge 1,270 metres in length (the longest suspension bridge in the Orient) to Onomichi. Visitors flock to the island which is exquisitely beautiful - a sightseer's paradise. But in the immediate weeks which lay ahead of us far from being a paradise, Innoshima was to be as near to hell as a man could get.

2

It may be helpful to explain briefly who were the hundred men who staggered into the camp and how I, a pilot from another squadron, happened to be with them. The majority were groundstaff of 605 Squadron which had lost most of its own pilots either in Singapore or because (for reasons which can be found in another of my books - *Hurricane Over the Jungle*) they had never arrived in the Far East. The groundstaff of my own Squadron, 258, had, happily, been diverted to Colombo, and when the fall of Java was imminent the rump of 258 pilots who had survived heavy losses flying in Singapore and Java were ordered away to rejoin them with the exception of six who were drawn by lot to stay behind of whom Lambert, Healey and myself were three. Serviced by 605 groundstaff we flew against the Japanese in Java until ordered to evacuate the island which was no longer possible for the reasons already given.

Thus did a hundred assorted men, a few of whom were strangers to each other, by a series of mischances find themselves in a camp in which with a few exceptions survivors were going to spend most of the next three years. The exceptions were the man I had assisted on our way through the dockyard, Bowen-Jones, who after some months was most mysteriously whisked away for reasons and to a destination unknown at the time and never discovered afterwards and five officers who were shortly afterwards shifted away to another camp.

There were two Warrant Officers in our hundred both of whom were to receive their commissions either during or immediately following the war. One was named Pritchard (a man of great quality) and the other, Cox - who was to prove of

Island of Temples - Innoshima

great value to the men on Innoshima.

A poor quality photograph taken by the Japanese showing the two Warrant Officers F.Cox & H.A. Pritchard in their working uniforms with identifying numbers worn on breast

Cox (left in photograph) was something of a rough diamond, but he very much busied himself in the affairs of the camp and the welfare of those within it. He had composed music and conducted orchestras in India. On Innoshima he got together a brilliant choir of approaching thirty members (known as Cox's choir) which gave us much pleasure and he stood up to the Japanese sufficiently to be punished by having to work for a period in the local dockyard - toil which those of Warrant Officer rank were excused.

Island of Temples - Innoshima

Nana bang ('nana' is a slang word for 'seven', the usual word being *schichi*) as Cox is affectionately enough referred to when old times are talked, was not everybody's cup of tea but he was to make a real and important contribution through the months and years which lay ahead of us.

3

On arrival in our camp on Innoshima we were welcomed by a staff who treated us more as if we were honoured guests than prisoners.

The camp consisted of a central administration quarters, cookhouse, bathroom and stores. It had been built on a narrow wedged shaped piece of land between on the one side the road which ran from Habu Dockyard to another smaller dockyard called Mitsunosho and on the other the Inland Sea.

Huts for prisoners had been built either side of the administration block, to the south where the wedge was narrowest a single-storied hut to accomodate one hundred prisoners, to the north where it was wider, two parallel rows of identical two-storied huts to accomodate four hundred. Beyond the far extremity of these huts at either end, under a projecting canopy was a row of ablution troughs and as separate buildings, lavatories the Japanese name for which was *benjos*. There were additionally various minor buildings used for storage of dry goods and the like.

Our quarters were in the single-storied southern hut which consisted of a continuous corridor off which were rooms, a small room at one end and seven rooms each large enough to take sixteen prisoners. The corridor was on the landward side and the view of the sea to the east was cut off by a continuous close-boarded fence.

This layout is illiustrated on page 58 of the chapter which follows together with a photograph taken from the hillside bordering the camp.

Island of Temples - Innoshima

Sketch of typical room by a unknown artist in the camp.

The huts were built entirely of wood which apart from windows was largely plywood fixed to framing and the ceiling was plywood as well. Along both sides of each room was a raised dais filled in with *tatamis* which are the black-edged traditional Japanese homes even to this day. The floor between these knee-high daises was wooden and supported tables to seat six with benches either side of them.

Central in each room was a wood-burning stove with a pipe which headed up and through the roof. Division walls between each room were plywood and the wall parallel to the sea and along the corridor was pierced with continuous sliding windows. Everything was brand new and there was a delightful smell of pine and an overall sense of light and airiness. Above each dais, behind the bedspaces, was a single shelf and on each tatami, with military precision, our clothing and bedding issue had been laid out. Again it was all brand new and as far as I recall, I believe accurately, it consisted of a pair of sheets, some blankets, a *futon* (which is a sort of duvet), boots, two pairs of white socks, two pairs of long white underpants which tied at waist and ankle, two dull green long-sleeved shirts and a standard Japanese army uniform of breeches, tunic, cap and greatcoat.

Captain Akiro Nimoto - Camp Commandant until a few weeks before the war ended when he was replaced.by 2nd Lieutenant Mori.

The Commandant, Nimoto, made a welcome speech similar to that which had been delivered by the Commandant in Boei

Island of Temples - Innoshima

Glodok, the staff were smiling and helpful and there was a further issue of all manner of minor things such as oranges, soap, lavatory paper, toothbrushes and tooth powder. And there was a splendid meal, one quite superior to anything we had had since being taken prisoner: great steaming bowls of pure white rice, a soup which was really a stew of meat and beans and vegetables and was thick enough almost to stand a spoon upright in it.

It was all really quite remarkable; unfortunately there were two things it did not address: the cold and sickness.

The rooms were open to the corridor and the stoves were unlit and the temperature within was therefore about the same as would have been found in a standard English summerhouse on a winter's day hovering around freezing point. And there was no medicine and although, theoretically we had a doctor, a man named Miki, his only interest was in declaring men fit enough to be sent out to work.

Dreadful though those four weeks on the Dai Nichi Maru had been, the weeks which lay ahead were, mentally at least, to prove even worse. The illness which was never defined but was akin to dysentry, was of the stomach and intestines which lost the capacity to handle the materials for life which now were being given generously to them so that once the illness had got a hold the food passed through the body almost unchanged in appearance. The disease spread remorselessly throughout the camp; I do not recall if there were any who escaped it, if there were they would have numbered only a handful. Each day, or rather every hour, was a struggle against dying. Correctly or incorrectly, once the diarrhoea struck, one believed that one's chances of survival depended on the length of time one could retain food following a meal. One thing *was* certain, survival depended on a will to survive, for the Japanese did nothing of any consequence. Death was preceded by terrible agony, the passing of pure green slime admixed with blood, and hiccups; I think it is accurate to say that no man struck by hiccups did survive.

So those eight or ten weeks before the illness had run its course were strange and terrible weeks. We lay on our tatamis

Island of Temples - Innoshima

fully clad in everything we owned including caps and boots, covered night and day with our blankets and duvets and still we were cold. We got up to eat, to excrete and, a few of us, the fitter or more determined, to march grimly up and down in the narrow space between sea wall and hut. Occasionally we tried playing cards or reading to pass the time but our hands were too numb with cold to hold them or concentrate. I have known far colder days on skiing holidays and once, at Goose Bay, a cold so intense that the air grasped one skin with steel pincers - yet I have never known such desolating cold as that cold on Innoshima seemed to be. One's mind and body was possessed by it, obsessed by it.

At first those most ill were simply scattered through the rooms but after a time the Commandant (who was clearly concerned that he might have the entire camp die on his hands) agreed that the worst cases should be shifted into one room which was dubbed a sick bay. For quite some time he obstinately refused permission for the stoves to be lit, but he agreed to the provision of two *hibachis* (which are circular earthenware pots in which on a bed of sand charcoal is burnt and are still the standard form of heating in modest Japanese homes) to be provided and later for doors to be made to shut the room off from the corridor.

The sick bay became in comparitive terms quite snug and the Commandant arranged for bowls of flowers to be provided in it. But we had no medicines and only a medical orderly with huge moon-shaped glasses who we dubbed 'Dim Joe' whose only interest in life appeared to be a fetish for giving injections of camphor in return for a bribe of cigarettes of which he appeared to have an unlimited supply.

Over the next few weeks, men died with savage regularity the worse case from a personal point of view that I remember being that of a man named Gibson whose head happened to be the other side of the plywood partition to mine. Gibson died on Boxing Day. Throughout the twenty-four hours before he died he alternately screamed and hiccuped. When he had died we carried his body to the small end room where we kept our pitiful luggage and doing the job of morticians plugged the orifices with cotton-wool and later twisted his body so as to fit it into a coffin too small for him. Another man who'd got hiccups kept calling out that he wasn't going to die; but he died. For some reason one man was actually shifted to the hospital in Habu where he died. A party of six prisoners (which included Harold Wade and Wilfred Batty, of whom more later) was sent to the hospital where they discovered the man, believed to be Gibbs, had died in a sitting position and rigor mortis was well advanced; it was left to them actually to perform the gruesome task of breaking his joints so as to be able to get him into the coffin. It is not clear why this party was sent to the hospital in the first place for the corpse was brought back on the sidecar truck affair on which vegetables were brought into the camp. With the coffin too small, the end broke open and his head was bumped to a bloody pulp on the potholed road.

In all this gloom there was one shining light, a Japanese guard named Luke who was a Christian. He was totally sympathetic to our plight and in particular assiduous in his attention to a man named Linnane who was desperately ill. Whenever his guard duties were over, he would come into the sick bay, hand round Players cigarettes he'd got from somewhere and comfort Linnane by the hour. Linnane was to recover and Luke, sadly, to be moved away from us.

As on the Dai Nichi Maru the first men who died were given a military funeral. This was a very moving and dignified affair.

There were three in this first funeral: Poulson, Durk and Gibbs - Poulson and Durk died on December 1st and Gibbs on December 3rd. We carried the coffins ourselves, six men to each coffin, the centre one of which was covered by a sheet on which a Union Jack was crudely painted. The crematorium was on the edge of a beach and to get to it we had to pass through the small village of Mitsunosho which more or less abutted the north end of the camp. It was night and very cold and the mud streets were ridged with frost. There was no real wind, only a gentle shift of air which quietly swayed the paper lantern which lit the head of the cortège. The only watchers were the silent villagers who gazed wih placid, faintly enquiring faces from the doorways of their hovels and the only mourners were Japanese soldiers who with arms inverted followed up behind.

Island of Temples - Innoshima

We, the pall bearers did not mourn - we were too much in discomfort from the weight of the coffins on our scrawny shoulders and the writhing in our stomachs of the same evil which had killed those we were carrying.

Thus we marched in the cold crisp night through the narrow, straggly village until the rough roadway changed to sand through which we plodded and the sound we made was less than the lapping of the surf. We didn't think that an inch or two from our own live flesh was rotting flesh but of the sharp edge of the coffin biting into the place where the shoulder meets the neck and the awful toil it had become with the soft, yielding sand grasping at our leaden feet. We had no idea and little thought of how far we had to go - it was become as all life had become, endless and unalterable. We saw the starlight on the sea and in the sky and the maize colour of the swinging lantern.

A priest was waiting for us, standing in the sand, an old, old man with a thin grey beard. Behind him was a furnace door, a red glow in the night. There were two brief services, one in English, one in Japanese. Then three shots fired across the Inland Sea.

It was an easier journey back with our only burden the sheet with the Union Jack saved for the next occasion and our spirits were higher because of the civilized manner in which the Japanese had played their part in the affair.

Far from being exceptional, we got off lightly with only eight of our hundred dying. In the nearby camp at Mukaishima, twenty-two of the hundred died and of one hundred and fifty in a third camp, thirty-five. The only reason I can put forward for our lower losses is the huge boost in morale which was given by the arrival of one hundred superbly fit men from Hong Kong who came to join us in January. But taking these known figures as being typical and adding to them the men who died at sea it would seem probable that of the twelve hundred prisoners who boarded the Dai Nichi Maru at Singapore between three and four hundred did not survive the voyage or the effects of it.

CHAPTER FIVE

THE H.K.V.D.C MOVE IN

1

On January 23rd, 1943 the second and final group of prisoners arrived and created a sociological situation surely without parallel. This group of one hundred men (apart from a spattering of regular soldiers) consisted of civilians who had been members of the Hong Kong Volunteer Defence Corps. They had no officers but amongst them was a Warrant Officer of the Army Educational Corps named Fabel who was to join Pritchard and Cox in a separate room.

While the backgrounds and standing of these H.K.V.D.C. men was varied, one could generalise by saying that the majority had been educated in British Public Schools, and in many cases in Universities, and had gone on to take up important posts in a booming pre-war British Colony and amongst their numbers were high-ranking executives in multi-national and private companies, civil servants, teachers, lawyers, bank managers, the Hong Kong magistrate, a University professor and a Hong Kong judge. Had they been in a regular service rather than volunteer soldiers the great majority would unquestionably have been commissioned. The 'Raffs', as the survivors of the first hundred soon came to be known, were on the other hand, almost without exception, regular Royal Air Force groundstaff or youngsters who had scarcely been out of their 'teens when they had either volunteered for the service or been called up. Thus it had been brought about that two groups of men almost exactly equal in number but of different ages, background, education, attitude, ways of speaking, experience and ambition

The H.K.V.D.C. move in

had been thrown together and would for nearly three more years be made, as dockyard hands, to share a life in which privelege, influence and rank would play no part whatsoever. By the decision of some unknown Japanese who saw the Allied prisoners only as a pool of available labour to be arbitrarily despatched in penny numbers here and there, a social experiment had been put in being in a place where the rules and guide lines would be made, and seen to be obeyed, by others.

The 'Volunteers' (as they came to be called) had been handpicked as amongst the fittest of 4,500 men in the prison camp of Shamshuipo on Kowloon, the mainland part of China held under lease as part of the Hong Kong colony. They had been whisked up in a matter of three days in the *Tatsuta Maru* which had been a crack cruise liner.

Unlike us, the earlier arrivals in Fukuoka 12 (as the camp was called at the time - it was subsequently retitled Zentsuji 2 and later again retitled, this time Hiroshima 5) they had not been landed at Habu town and been obliged to shamble through the dockyard but had been disembarked in the adjacent village of Mitsunosho from whence a brisk march of perhaps half a mile had brought them to the camp. They had wheeled in through the entrance gate, been counted off and were then dismissed to the quarters they were to occupy in one of the two-storied huts on the wider, northerly end of the camp. They were not to know who else, apart from the Japanese staff, was in the camp and probably judging by the lack of sound or activity assumed they were its first arrivals.

Such of the Raffs as were fit enough had been shifted a few days earlier from the single-storied hut into the southernmost rooms of the double-storied hut on the seaward side; the balance, numbering thirty-four, were still in their original billet or in the makeshift hospital and were later moved across in dribs and drabs. Of the fifty-eight in the double-storied hut only a proportion had so far been press-ganged into working in the dockyard; but as it was evening when the Volunteers arrived they were mostly, like those still too ill to work, lying on their tatamis and wearing practically everything they possessed even down to caps and boots.

The H.K.V.D.C. move in

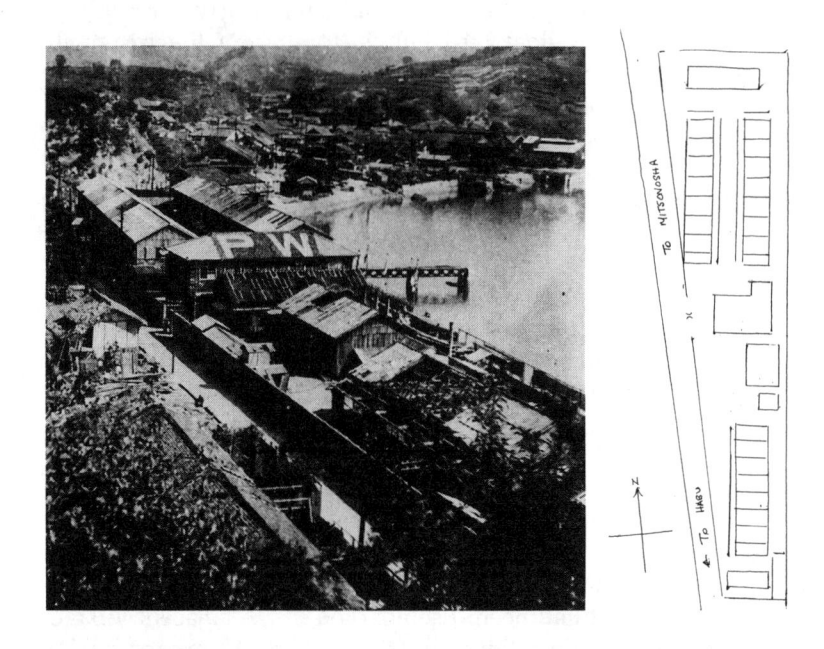

To the best of my knowledge the photograph above is the only one ever taken of the camp. It has a curious history. After the war had ended one of the prisoners noticed a Japanese with a camera passing by the open gates and decided he would take possession of it. Inside the camera was a film which this Japanese had used in taking photographs of damage following an air raid on Innoshima and as can be seen our camp, mistaken as a military target, was not excused. Other photographs showing damage to the dockyard are included in a later chapter. As the photograph is of poor quality I have included beside it a rough layout of the camp which I made at the time. The east side was bounded by the sea and the west side by the road running from Habu to Mitsonosha. The long hut to the south was the one the Raffs occupied on arrival and the eastern row of the pair of huts to the north the one they and the Volunteers later moved into. The largest central building was the Japanese administration, next to it the cookhouse and bathhouse. The small buildings at ends are benjos.

The H.K.V.D.C. move in

Four of the Dai Nichi Maru survivors whose lives hung on threads for several months. Rear row: W.Blow. Front row: L to R: L.J.Collis, G.Thompson, A.J.Brown..

A further group of Dai Nichi Maru survivors..

The H.K.V.D.C. move in

The two photographs on previous page and the two which follow give a fair idea of the variety of possessions owned by the R.A.F. and the Volunteers.. As will be seen the RA.F. men are wearing Japanese Army uniforms and in most cases thin greatcoats, whereas the Volunteers are largely in good quality British Army kit to which is given character by the addition of personal items such as scarves, pullovers and the like.

The photographs of the R.A.F. men were taken respectively in the Habu Hospital to which the four were, exceptionally, taken, and outside the camp bathouse. The photographs of the Volunteers were taken in the open space between the rows of huts.

In the upper photograph of the Volunteers the men on left and right of back row and the man in the centre of front row (Forrow, Bond and Low respectively) were members of The Genki Boys (of which more later) and in the following photograph Coxhead, for whom I am grateful for so much information and so many sketches, is in the centre of the lower row.

The H.K.V.D.C. move in

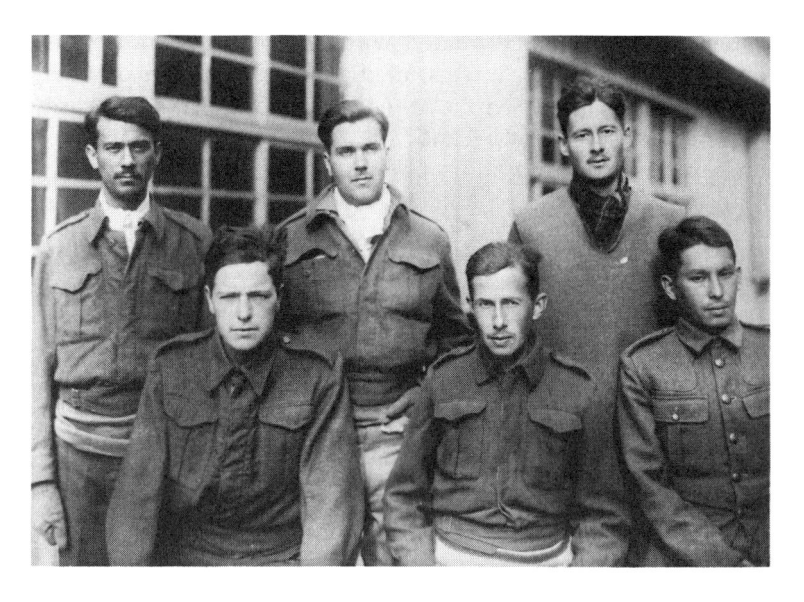

As may be imagined to both groups the moment of the Volunteers' arrival was not to be forgotten. The Volunteers hastening eagerly down the wooden passage with a year's prisoner of war experience reminding them that the choice of bedspace now could pay huge dividends later, were presented as they passed the first two occupied rooms with the spectacle of scores of emaciated men with shaven heads and staring, pain-filled eyes, all dressed in Japanese Army uniforms and many lying under their blankets with caps still on their heads and booted feet projecting. On the other hand the R.A.F. men, awakened to life by the vibration of running feet, the clatter of hobnailed boots and bursts of laughter and loud and cheerful conversation, suddenly saw come into view a stream of bronzed, fit men whose hair was long and decently cut, whose clothes might be varied but were of good order and whose possessions were astonishing.

For the Hong Kong Volunteers were, with only few exceptions, extremely well-equipped. They had between them expensive leather cases and lightweight grips, hand made shirts, cravats, shoes, bedroom-slippers, pyjamas, dressing gowns; pullovers, scarves and British warms; books and

The H.K.V.D.C. move in

watches; wallets which bulged with photographs and letters; mirrors, shaving-kits, towels, medicines and talcum powder; tins of meat, bars of soap, cartons of cigarettes. In some cases they had these things because they had been taken prisoner where they had lived and worked and their servants, and in many cases until they too had been interned, their wives and sweethearts, had been able to deliver such things into the camp.

Shamshuipo, which had been the headquarters of one of the infantry battalions on Hong Kong, was approximately square in shape and was bounded on two sides by the sea, on a third by the Castle Peak Road and on the fourth, the eastern side, by a row of Chinese tenement houses separated from the perimeter wire fence only by a narrowish road. Many women came to this fence to speak to the inmates and when the guards' attention was elsewhere or intentionally distracted, items of food or clothing could easily be thrown over or slipped underneath the wire - as an example David Bosanquet (one of the very few who successfully escaped imprisonment from the Japanese - by crawling with three friends through a drain which ran through the camp and issued into the sea) actually managed to get his shoes taken out, repaired and returned to him!

And apart from what could be supplied after captivity, it has to remembered that these were not raw young men who had suddenly been jerked out of the way of life to which they were accustomed and shipped out to a strange new world they could hardly have pinpointed on a map and where they had no connections, but were mostly mature, considered men many of whom had seized the opportunity in the several days between capitulation and capture to prepare themselves for a long captivity in an area they understood.

Amongst them too, were many with some knowledge of the Japanese, in some cases even of their language and their script; or if not of the Japanese at least of the Oriental way of life. Of this the Raffs knew nothing. Java, Sumatra, Hong Kong, even Singapore, had been names which if flung at them in geography lessons most would probably have been unable to place. In the pre-war days before package holidays the

The H.K.V.D.C. move in

average man's thoughts of overseas travel hardly extended beyond the Isle of Wight. Exotic countries were strictly for the movies.

The Japanese, as if to perpetuate the differences between these two groups of men for all that they would be working side by side in the dockyard, did two things: firstly, they had the Hong Kong Volunteers (apart from three who had to take spaces in the end, sixth room) live and sleep in different rooms from the Raffs; secondly, they issued them with a different uniform to work in. I am quite sure this was accidental; I very much doubt if it crossed the mind of our captors at that stage that there was any difference between the prisoners they took in Hong Kong and the prisoners they took in Java. I think they simply ran out of the working uniforms they had issued to the Raffs and had to look around for others for the Volunteers.

Be that as it may, the Raff working uniforms were emerald green in colour and made of a coarse wood pulp fibre from which you could extract small pieces of wood while those of the Volunteers, which were far superior, were of a pale green cloth. So distinction was perpetuated: in the dockyard the Volunteers (at least while their uniforms were new) were dressed like gentlemen and the Raffs as coolies; and in the camp the Volunteers were on the whole dressed as English Army officers taking it easy while the Raffs were dressed as Japanese privates.

The two halves of the camp were never integrated and I think that to a significant extent these initial differences helped establish this social separation. In any case the Volunteers, fit, energetic, self-confident, optimistic but not given to absurd wishful-thinking, found it difficult to relate to a group of young men averaging at least ten years their junior whose morale had been subjected to three months of appalling suffering. They listened in horror to accounts of a voyage they found difficult to picture and a few, only a few, passed round the odd packet of cigarettes. But this was how life was. The Volunteers had been taken prisoner in December not in March. They had had three months longer, and already a year in all, in which to discover that the first business of a prisoner is to look after himself. The

The H.K.V.D.C. move in

Raffs were jealous of the Volunteers' supplies but not in the least surprised they were not shared out.

There was in fact, to the Raffs as a whole, a strange unreality in the arrival of this group - a contingent dispatched from Mars could hardly have aroused greater surprise and disbelief. With rare exceptions their spirit was at its nadir with life reduced to a state of sheer existence. With recurring stomach cramps and diarrhoea a constant reminder that death was lurking in the wings, with bodies numbed by cold, with freedom lost and choice removed, in thrall to a strange, incomprehensible race and the only seeming variety offered for endless years ahead, hours of toiling in a drab, grey dockyard through which swept a bitter Siberian wind, hope had all but been abandoned.

The very fact that cold and circumstances forced all to dress identically, and that in the uniform of their captors, had a crushing effect, submerging individuality, repressing initative - it is not for nothing that convicts are made to wear prison garb. In Boei Glodok, Taber, untouched by disease, had lain down to die because living had lost its purpose; how many more of the Raffs in Habu, I wonder, would have died had it not been that the Volunteers by their example showed this to be untrue.

As part of the standard equipment of any Japanese barrack block a bath had been provided and this was to prove one of life's greatest luxuries. The bath was an oblong affair large enough to accommodate up to a dozen at a time and deep enough so that, when seated, the water was about halfway up one's chest. An efficient wood fired boiler was connected by flow and return pipes. The bath was located in its own separate wooden building and had a cement floor and the system for bathing was to scoop water out of the bath in one of the many wooden boxes provided, pour it over one's body, soap oneself, sluice off the soap and then get into the gloriously hot bath to soak.

I do not remember using this bath ahead of the Volunteers arriving but I suppose I may well have done because I was one of the limited number of those deemed fit enough to work; alternatively it may be that until they arrived it was only at the Japanese staff's disposal. Be that as it may, what I clearly

The H.K.V.D.C. move in

recall was watching some of these new arrivals clutching bars of soap, and even in one case a loofah, racing up along the corridor making the whole building shake and returning later, laughing and joking, their bodies boiled like lobsters, naked but for towels around their waists.

It was their nakedness which was above all surprising. For two months we had hurried our evening meal the quicker to get our hands back into our pockets and fully dressed down to caps and boots waited impatiently for the evening roll call to be over and allow us into the comparitive warmth of bed. Yet here were men who in identical rooms to ours, in identical temperatures, not hurrying their dressing, could actually sit around with their chests and legs still bare without apparent discomfort.

In this and in a dozen other ways the Volunteers by their example rekindled hope. It was not that they involved themselves in conversation with their less fortunate associates; on the contrary with only the rarest of exceptions they kept themselves apart as positively as a group of officers would have kept themselves apart from other ranks in an Army camp or on a Royal Air Force station. But they were perpetually on view. The benjos were at the far end of the hut and you had to go along the corridor which passed each room to get to them. Having quit a room, noteworthy for its uniformity and occupied by men dressed identically most of whom were lying on their tatamis, blankets drawn up to chin, staring gloomily at the plywood base of the rack of those on the upper floor, you looked into others amazingly over-furnished and bustling with activity, in which men dressed in all manner of civilian and military gear were puffing at cigarettes, seated at tables playing bridge, writing diaries, reading books, or comfortably chatting for all the world as if they were in their club or entertaining friends at home.

It had to rub off. Even the most sullen depressionists, the most gloomy pessimists were forced to accept that in spite of the cold, in spite of the fact of being a prisoner, in spite of the days of youth passing by wasted and unused, it was still apparently

The H.K.V.D.C. move in

possible to be amused and involved with living. And there were those amongst the Raffs, a few, who had not yet succumbed to the overall sense of hopelessness and despair who, some eagerly, some diffidently, some optimistically, ventured into these rooms of warmth and plenty to return later to their own, encouraged, and readied to uplift the spirits of those who slept beside them.

The result was magical and not merely in moral but also in practical terms. As if brought to life by the sudden changed atmosphere of the camp, or overborne by the demands of men accustomed to dealing with Orientals, the Japanese agreed that doors should be provided to the rooms and the stoves be lit. The billets which had been funk holds from cold and work became warm havens to return to; there was suddenly more than dying, shivering and working in a dockyard; purpose returned. The Raffs' recovery although it was still going to be slow, was sure and no more of them were to die. In fact all of the other prisoners who died before the war came to an end were from the Volunteers.

Yet, athough obliged henceforth to share identical ground rules of life, the same routine, the same work, the same food, the same privations, the two halves of the camp were brought no closer. One might have imagined that after a period approaching three years, differences would have broken down. They did not. Social mores, habits, prejudices and the simple preference of men being more comfortable with others of like background and experience triumphed. Each group was as distinct from the other on the day all marched out as on the day the Volunteers marched in.

There were it is true one or two amongst the Raffs who had had the same background and education as the Volunteers and could be at ease with them - even so, while they would occasionally be seen in one or other of the Volunteers' rooms, their visits were not returned except for some specific and exceptional circumstance, or where mutual benefit accrued.

Although the camp had been designed to accommodate five

The H.K.V.D.C. move in

hundred prisoners, only two hundred were delivered to it. The rooms in the single-storied hut which we had originally occupied were used for storage, as a sick-bay and as an occasional isolation unit. The second two-storied hut was never to be occupied but the Japanese gave approval for rooms to be turned into Anglican and Roman Catholic chapels which, by the skilful use of benches and tatamis was most effectively done and for concerts, lectures and the like; another was used as a place of rest for the few who were still to die.

Part of a sketch by an unknown artist which shows how limited was the space in which we slept and spent much of our time when not working. Only six full spaces are shown - the full row was eight. Space for possessions was limited as well but for most of us this was hardly a serious problem.

As can be seen from sketch reproduced in the previous chapter,

The H.K.V.D.C. move in

the rooms in the hut, in which we were to remain until one month after the war ended, were each furnished with tables, benches and a stove and planned as had been those of the original hut but were of double height permitting a second tier of sixteen men at the higher level. Originally the upper bedspaces were reached by climbing vertical ladders but following representations that the effort of doing so was excessive for men as sick as many were at the time, these two ladders were replaced by a single sloping ladder and the opposite end of what were in effect minstrels' galleries were joined by a bridge on the entrance side of each room thus forming a continuous 'U' at the higher level. Although this was not immediately obvious, the upper level was the better one to be in. Its occupants were shielded from the immediate view of passing Japanese and could for example smoke more comfortably at disallowed times.

A fine sketch of the administration block by Coxhead drawn four days after the war ended. The nearest building was the cookhouse and store and the buildings partially masked by it were the camp offices. The end of the unoccupied two-storied billet can just be seen.

Between the two double-storied huts was a reasonably wide

The H.K.V.D.C. move in

walkway which was used for exercise and for assembling prior to marching off to work. This was masked at one end by the administration quarters and at the other by the benjo. The administration block contained the Commandant's office, a guard room, sleeping quarters, a cookhouse run by the prisoners and some punishment cells known as 'Little Houses' which were so small a man could not lie down within.

The *Benjo* was a separate building with cubicles giving privacy to a man squatting over a long, wide, concrete trough about five or six feet deep which was always a reservoir of maggot crawling excreta. This had to be emptied occasionally and this was done by having a barge drawn up alongside the camp wall at high tide and a plank laid from barge to benjo. Men would then empty the sewage by hauling it out in buckets which they carried at both ends of a whippy pole and at some risk of losing their balance carted along the plank and emptied into the barge to be used as fertilizer for growing crops and vegetables. As can be imagined the stench given off from this operation was appalling and reluctant to disperse.

Not that our benjo was in any way different from all the other benjos on Innoshima and in fact everything provided to us was by Japanese standards of the highest quality, certainly of no less quality than their own barracks and, I imagine, superior to what was provided to the general labour force of Japanese and Korean workers drafted in to man the dockyards on Innoshima Island. As for location, this could hardly have been better. On the landward side hills rose steeply and in the right seasons were bright with orange blossom or blazing with azaleas; on the other side, no more than a yard or so from the windows of the huts, was a high stone wall and below it a beach with an old, defunct, iron jetty which reached out into that most beautiful of seas, the Inland Sea of Japan, island studded, swept by mountains, a protected sea, calmer than most and delicate in colouring. It was, moreover, a very busy sea on which one could watch by the hour the widest variety of craft: junks, ocean-going liners, merchantmen and tankers, hauled strings of barges, cockleshells of fishing boats and rowboats propelled by single oars, battleships, submarines and aircraft carriers - the variety was endless. It never palled, that vista;

The H.K.V.D.C. move in

the sun rose from it as did the moon, and at night it became magical with the yellow glows of fisherman holding oil lamps to attract their prey.

Geoffrey Coxhead, with whom I used to play chess regularly and with whom I have kept in close contact over the past fifty years, did a number of water colours or crayon drawings of both the camp itself and the view we were so fortunate as to be able to enjoy. The one illustrated below gives a splendid idea of the camp's idyllic location.

Innoshima   August 17th 1945   G.S.C.

Another of Coxhead's drawings was done looking directly out across the Inland Sea from the billets. After the war he most generously had this reproduced and circulated to us all. He included beneath the print a poem written by a fellow prisoner named Potter in Hong Kong describing the view seen from his camp there because it was in many respects appropriate to ours.

The H.K.V.D.C. move in

THE SEAWARD PASSAGE

Seaward from Innoshima   G. S. Coxhead

My prison window opens out
   Upon a vista wide ;
An island-studded harbour, set
   With hills on every side :
And right ahead and calling me
A passage to the open sea.

My prison house is fenced around
   With lines of knotted wire,
And weapon'd guards keep vigil there
   To foil my heart's desire.
'Tis nought—for fancy lets me free
Through yonder channel out to sea.

When morning breaks beyond the hills
   And floods the world with light,
I rise from my dream-haunted bed
   And straight direct my sight
Where morning tide goes flowing free
Through that blest channel out to sea.

And when the sun, a blazing ball,
   Stoops westward to his bed,
And Island Peak stands castle-like
   Against the flaming red,
The sunset streamers beckon me
To sail that passage out to sea.

When night enshrouds the silent camp,
   And slumber holds me fast,
'Midst all the dreams of distant ones
   That conjure up the past—
A constant vision comes to me
Of that near channel to the sea.

Though comfort small this place affords
   My constant joy is found
In all the sweep of hills and bay
   That ring the camp around :
And for supremest luxury
I have my passage to the sea.

                            A. Potter.

Except that we were not ringed with barbed wire and lacked Hong Kong's 'Island Peak' it was a very descriptive poem.

As well as being an accomplished artist Coxhead, who had been a teacher in Hong Kong, was a remarkable man. He was

The H.K.V.D.C. move in

for most of our stay on Innoshima obliged to work in a fearsome punishment party yet, as will be seen in excerpts from diaries which he kept, he accepted his lot philosophically and with astonishing good humour. He bore no hatred of the Japanese and after the war returned more than once to Innoshima and made it his business to re-meet Japanese he had known as prisoner.

CHAPTER SIX

HITACHI DOCKYARD

1.

The dockyard in which we worked was founded in 1881 by an Englishman named Hunter and later re-organised as *Innoshima Branch Yard* of the *Osaka Ironworks* who were its owners when we arrived. During our stay it was taken over by *Hitachi* and (to give it its full title) was renamed *Hitachi Zosen - The Hitachi Shipbuilding and Engineering Company Ltd.* After the war it was much expanded and became, I have been informed, the second largest shipbuilding dockyard in Japan.

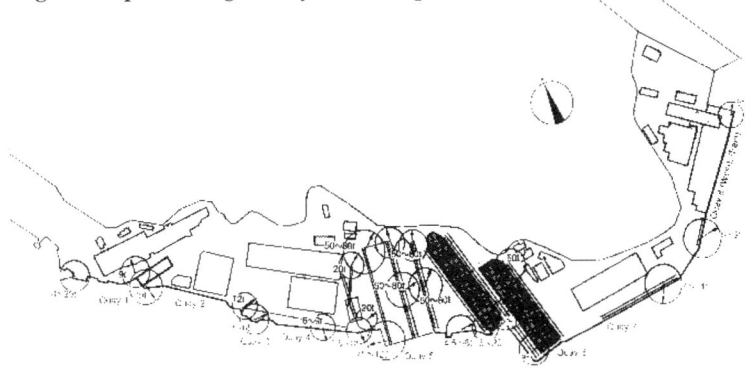

The above is a plan of the dockyard which has more or less the same layout as when we worked in it the major change being the addition of a second large dry dock (shown darkened) alongside the original Hachi (No 8) Dock. These docks are now known as Nos 2 & 3 Docks and are respectively 282.5 and 280.0 metres long, 46.5 and 56.7 metres wide and 11.3 and 11.1 metres deep. They can take ships up to 150,000 and 130,000 DWT.

73

Hitachi Dockyard

Built between steep hillside and the sea it was as can be seen a long straggling yard at a rough guess perhaps fully a mile in length from the woodyard at one end of it to the gateway into Habu town at the other. It had three dry docks:the original *Hachi Dock* (No 8 Dock) and two smaller ones (which post-war were joined together to make one) and several shipbuilding slips.

A fully equipped yard which the British had played a considerable part in building and designing, it possessed plate and machine shops, foundry and so on and was serviced by small travelling cranes which ran on internal railway lines and later by tower cranes. There was a work force of about two thousand men, mainly Japanese but leavened by prisoners and Korean forced-labour.

No doubt because there were far too many prisoners to be given the same sort of work, we were split into parties. Spelling of Japanese names and words used below (and elsewhere in this book) may well on occasion be incorrect.

    P.T.1. & P.T.2.   Cleaning out dry docks, ships' bunkers and slips. Coaling, unloading gravel and coke, barrowing coal, scrap metal and so on.

    T.1.   (My own) Known as 'Track' or 'Umpanko'. Maintaining or laying tracks for the travelling cranes, humping planks, hatch covers, poles, paint boards and so on. All work connected with scaffolding. Generally being available for odd jobs such as helping to swing ships' compasses and packing refrigerated holds with glass and asbestos wool.

    T.2.   Transporting metal on trucks and shifting wood in woodyard. T.1. often assisted in this.

    Sooko.   Shifting metal plates and girders.

    F.   Working on ships under construction, plating, bolting,

Hitachi Dockyard

and preparing plates for riveting.

C.P. Working in woodyard, shifting lumber.

Doko. Plumber's shop.

Denki. Electricians.

Foundry. Usual foundry work.

Machine Shop.

Bottle Party. Barrowing oxygen cylinders and humping on to ships.

Raffs and Volunteers were not as in the camp segregated and thus worked side by side. Depending on the party to which you were allocated your experiences, problems and advantages varied enormously. For example the Bottle Party run by a man accepted as unhinged who earned himself the sobriquet of "The Ape," was a punishment party and it is difficult to understand how the four unfortunates composing it (one of whom was Geoffrey Coxhead who in true Jean Valjean style had to put up with over two years excessively hard labour for stealing a single bento) survived. The cylinders were enormously heavy and it was a rule that even on steeply sloping gangplanks they must be carried single-handed - or perhaps one should say single-shouldered. The dockyard roadway was rough and ready, potholed, and booby-trapped by the travelling-crane railway lines which criss-crossed and stood up proud. It was a heartrending sight to see these four men, one, with a rope around his shoulder, in the shafts of a barrow laden with perhaps half a dozen bottles, the other three heaving and pushing behind, hurling themselves at the lines to surmount them while, urging on the proceedings was a screaming maniac. Very occasionally one of the men would be given sick leave against a volunteer taking his place, but on the whole these wretched men were going to have to face endless days of back-breaking toil, year in, year out and, towards the end, working

Hitachi Dockyard

twenty days out of every twenty-one.

A single example from Coxhead's diary gives an indication of the awful toil these wretched men had to endure and the spirit with which it was accepted:

Wed. 27th Sept 1944. Record amount of work - so we totted it up and found we had carted 103 bottles and carried 14 more: 117.

On the other hand an equal number of men in the plumber's shop had a splendid, easy time under the care of a kind, considerate and pro-Western foreman.

Between these two extremes C.P, the woodyard party (working in the northernmost triangle of the yard which is now largely occupied by buildings) was clean and its surroundings delightful with birdsong and the chuckling of wavelets against the sea walls rather than the clang of hammers and the rat-a-tat-tat of riveting, but with the foreman a Stakhanovite the work was fiendishly hard. 'F' was dangerous and for all Habu's 39 degrees of latitude, bitterly cold in winter when Siberian winds swept across the open decks of skeleton ships and men slipped off wet, sometimes icy plates and fell great distances. *Sooko* originally was hard but became light when Allied bombing brought the dockyard almost to a halt. P.T.1 and P.T.2 were heavy work but, as will be seen, carried their own particular advantages. The Foundry if hard was warm. T.1 and T.2. were more varied than most, occasionally excessively punishing but on average not unreasonable.

A number of the parties came to have Koreans as guards and the one allocated to us, after I suppose about a year or so, was a tall Korean named Watanabe, a sly sort of fellow who liked Western music and had the merit of being lazy - to many, perhaps surprisingly, this also was not at all uncommon amongst the Japanese workers in Habu Dockyard. Watanabe would sometimes disappear for quite long periods and hide himself away in some corner of the dockyard leaving us to our own devices; at other times he could be difficult and untrustworthy.

Our foreman was a remarkable and quite unforgettable

Hitachi Dockyard

character who, as mentioned earlier, had the same name as the family of pirates who at one time controlled Innoshima - Murakami. He could be a crusty old codger, dancing around on his little feet and shaking his arms in rage if you bodged your work; on the other hand he could have tremendous charm and he had the most beautiful smile I have ever known. There was not an atom of evil in Murakami who had worked in the dockyard since the British built it. He had never learnt a word of English and by the time he became our foreman he was too old to start. His shoulders were bowed, his eyes were rheumy, his hands cracked and calloused and his face was like a wizened apple - but when he smiled it was like the sun emerging from behind a cloud and lighting up the world.

We had a good relationship with old Murakami. He knew every inch of the dockyard and every hideyhole. We'd be working on a railway line, perhaps seven or eight of us, and of a sudden he'd nod imperceptibly towards an empty hut. We understood because we had over the months and years evolved a close association which had no need of words. He'd nod and we'd each unostentatiously pick up a piece of wood and slip quickly into the hut and Murakami would light a fire on the earth floor and we'd sit around it in a circle with the old man one of us and, if we had something to smoke, we'd smoke. Murakami never smoked cigarettes himself, only the fine hair tobacco of the older workmen. He had a long, thin, bamboo pipe with a metal bowl no larger than a fingernail and, hanging from it, a small, embroidered or bugle-beaded pouch which held the tobacco which was pale brown and fine as the finest hair. He'd fill the bowl and touch it to the blaze, take a puff or two, never more, then knock the burning dottle on to his leathery hand and, with it still burning there, refill the bowl with two spare fingers of the hand which held the pipe and relight it from the burning dottle. It was a fascinating thing to watch, an action done with extraordinary delicacy by hands as gnarled as pollarded trees from a lifetime's heavy work.

As for us, well we were fairly catholic in our smoking. A few used the Murakami type of pipe but they were the exceptions; the majority smoked cigarettes at the dockyard, even if it was a pipe in camp. Pipes are hard to hide at the sudden onset of a

Hitachi Dockyard

kempei (the black-clad Japanese style S.S. guard) and anyway tobacco was far too precious to waste. At the dockyard you never smoked whole cigarettes; at the most you smoked half of one and more usually a quarter. With a razor blade it is easy to create four cigarettes from one: you slice the paper twice along its length and re-roll the tobacco using the same paper thus making two cigarettes which you then cut in halves. Or again, using fine paper if you could find it (or even newspaper if you couldn't) you manufactured cigarettes out of your own dog-ends - and, there were those who would have to admit to it, also out of other peoples' dog ends picked up in the yard.

Smoking was a ritual carried out with exquisite care and great attention. When luxuries are few those which remain gather huge significance. One talked little when one was smoking and one didn't waste a shred of tobacco. Holders were *de-rigeur* and always burnt black at the mouthpiece. One knew when the smoke was at its end because the holder crackled with heat and the taste was of burning wood - then one blew and the burning stub, not a quarter of an inch in length, flew out. Or some managed even closer by using a pin which allowed them to continue smoking until the burning tobacco all but reached their lips.

Murakami would watch us in our antics of smoking, shaking his tired old head. Or as often as not he'd doze. You had to be very careful when he dozed for your break (or, to give it its Japanese name, your *yasumi*) was balanced on a knife edge. Outside might be the wet raw wind sweeping the sleet down from Siberia; inside, for all the draughts, there was a warm, snug, choking fug. And as well, and as important, every extra minute stolen was an extra minute won from the empty, endless, boring day, an extra minute not to have to be endured. And if one changed the volumne, the pitch even of the conversation, if one moved too suddenly, coughed too loudly, the old man might be wakened, or stirred from daydreams and his dread *shigoto!* (work!) would end it all.

Fifty years and more have passed since I first sat in one of those old rough, earth-floored wooden huts with Murakami but the atmosphere of it is as strong as if it were only yesterday. I can

Hitachi Dockyard

see the old man now, short, shabby in his patched and repatched working uniform, squatting flatfooted in his two-toed *tabis*, a tired old man of surprising strength - a kind old man, sometimes a waspish man, but never cruel if now and then unreasonable. I can see the others who with me made the ring, each crouching forward with their hands towards the fire, sitting in the dust, Volunteers and Raffs, a director next a van-driver, a professor next a postman, all, for the day at any rate made much the same. And dressed, apart from the working uniforms at the start, pretty much the same as well. Boots made of cardboard, mouthing at the welts and on the soles, sodden, steaming. Putteed ankles, ragged trousers turned to breeches, oil streaked and torn, the rents sewn up again with string extracted from cement sacks. Jackets with three figure numbers on the breast with missing buttons and pockets torn away.

A group of R.A.F. men in their working uniforms. Left to right: L.Warrington, G.Jackson, B.Hurst, W.J.Wood, J.D.Linnane, W.H.Sunburk, J.A.Sheer. Taken before the H.K.V.D.C. men arrived when the working uniforms were fairly new.

At work we wore caps of papery cardboard with peaks awry or

Hitachi Dockyard

even missing, banded with scarlet satin ribbon to show that we were prisoners, and the hieroglyphic of *umpanko* on them to show which was our party. Shaven heads, or heads that had been shaven starting to grow hair again, unshaven faces, hands calloused with fingers splitting open of their own accord, sharp nervous eyes, thinning cheeks and beri-beried legs, we were all made much the same as we clung on to our forbidden *yasumis* in the rough old huts of Habu Dockyard - bank managers and bookies, aircraftsmen and architects.

Such moments were to be savoured with a relish hardly known in normal times for to be a prisoner cleans the palate of living enabling its tiniest pleasures to be appreciated and to make one so jealous of them that a sudden tap from the old man's hand upon your leg would send a shaft of gloom into your heart. Only perhaps it might not be to tell you it was time to go out into the cold, or the blazing heat again - it might be that you would find that slow smile dawning and the old man would be pointing to a ragged vermilion circle like that on touch paper spreading outwards on your wooden fibre trousers where a spark had caught. And that was splendid because that kind of interruption far from ending things, amused the old man greatly and guaranteed more minutes by the fire.

He was a craftsman, Murakami San, devoted to his railway and with a surgeon's eye for it. We did many different jobs in 'Track' but largely our business was with the railway lines on which ran the puffing Billys of the travelling cranes. They were chubby, cheerful chaps these cranes and looked like ancient goods locomotives with a crane stuck up before their noses. They were old and antiquated and they groaned and wheezed and emitted great plumes of steam and scalding water from every joint.

We repaired old tracks, diverted them and ran new branches. We dug out the ground, carried and placed the sleepers, carried the lines and fixed them with spikes, gauged them and packed the sleepers firm and level. It could be hard work and it could be easy work. The sleepers were sometimes huge, great true square baulks of timber and sometimes modest, shorter, rounded. The railway lines were always heavy and you carried them four men to each, two and two, each pair with

Hitachi Dockyard

a wooden bow over their shoulders and a rope with a kind of clip which grabbed the flange and closed as you straightened and walked, with four of you carrying half a ton or so - and the curved rails were worst because they swung.

You packed the sleepers which meant that you stood on them and wielded what was called a *bita* which was a pick with one end blunt with which you thumped the earth until it was packed tight under the sleeper which rang sweet and true when you tested it; then you laid the rails and ran a gauge between them and fixed them with spikes which were massive nails with wide tops which you hammered in with sledgehammers so that the top edges of the spikes held the rails in place. As often as you dared risk it, you took care to miss the spike and have the shaft of the sledgehammer hit the rail snapping it, obliging you to take a leisurely walk to the far end of the dockyard to have a new shaft supplied and fitted. Curves were difficult because whilst the gauge had to be the same there had to be a different radius for the inner and outer rails.

It was here that the old man's genius was demonstrated. He would make a pile of wood around the rail at the critical point and light a fire to temper it and under his instructions we prisoners used a kind of claw called a 'Jim Crow' to bend them. This was a fearsome device, ungainly and very heavy, with two arms which bent over the rail like claws to grasp against the flange one side and a boss which pushed against it from the other. There were six holes in this boss and we had long iron bars we pushed in and out of these holes, three pairs working together, heaving down to turn the boss, all falling against each other, treading on each others' feet, mixed up with the fire, all flailing arms and Murakami, always excited when this was happening, shouting "Oisa! Oisa!" (or was it "Oisho! Oisho!"?) and clouting the rail with a sledgehammer and going along the line a little way with one eye shut and one eye open checking the curve was true. It was a strange sort of job with the ground red-hot under your feet and the bar ice-cold to your hands.

Another frequent job was pushing low trolleys made of rough baulks of timber bolted to a frame which ran on flanged

Hitachi Dockyard

wheels along the railway lines. These trolleys were laden with all manner of things, plates, sleepers, sacks of rivets or nuts and bolts and it wasn't a bad job really. You shoved out your arms and pushed, three or four of you in a line, body more horizontal than vertical, and you could get lost in thought as you watched the sleepers passing by beneath your feet. Often there'd be a halt and in summer, at least, this was a blessing. A crane might be off the line or manoeuvering in some complex shunting operation from one branch to another and there was nothing you could do but sit on the trolley and wait. The patrolling *kempeis* might look sour but you couldn't push a trolley through a crane.

In fact a crane coming off the lines was a frequent occurrence and when they did there was no one who could do anything about it but Murakami!.

And who knew where the old man was? Smoking his pipe beneath a slipway? Dozing in some hut? For he'd often vanish for long intervals. Maybe he'd decided he'd make the job you were doing spin out 'till lunchtime and he'd smile his beautiful, conspiratorial smile and chuckle *botchi botchi*, which I have never found in a dictionary but mean't 'look as if you're working but take your time'. And he'd amble off bandy, bowed, one man in Japan at least who didn't care a fig about the war and never spoke of it.

Then when a crane came off and got its wheels wedged in between the points there'd be a great panic while everyone looked for him. And when the old man finally came, never hurrying, granted dispensation even by the *kempeis* because he was old, respected, an Innoshima institution, and because they didn't impress him anyway, he'd size up the situation deciding which building to hook the crane to. Then we'd have to pull the huge shiny hook which was as big as a man's crooked arm out on its heavy, fraying hawser and hook it around a stancheon of the plate shop, say, and stand well clear to observe events. The crane driver would wind up the hawser taut, sparks would come shooting like a rocket trail from the crane's fire, steam would escape from every joint and the hawser would go tight as a bowstring as the driver in his cabin tried to haul himself back aboard the railway line by pulling against the stancheon. And usually it would work - but sometimes the stancheon would be

Hitachi Dockyard

pulled out and sometimes the hawser snapped and that was dangerous.

Aerial photograph showing Hachi Dock flooded and the new No 2 Dry Dock occupied. In our days the building to the left did not exist, this being an untidy, open area along which ran some of our railway lines. The travelling puffing Billys have gone and fine new roads have replaced the rough, broken surfaces along which we trudged for so many weary days.

During our enforced delays there was much to watch. There were the old crones, as old as Methusalah every one and all dressed alike in coarse, small-patterned blue and white combined coats and pantaloons called *mompes* and wearing *tabis* which were rubber shoes with two toes, one for the big toe and one for the other four. They seemed to have the same never ending job these poor old women who worked in gangs of perhaps a dozen having bows over their shoulders from which hung at either end wicker baskets filled with rusted nuts and bolts. They were tough and leathery because their loads were heavy and they'd been carrying them for years. They were short and squat, wore coolie hats and their pantaloons were full as babies' nappies. They would come jogging past in a sing song style, noticing nothing, going from one mysterious place to another, hands up to strings to stop the baskets swinging.

Then by contrast there were the dockyard executives who would sometimes be seen making their way on foot to the offices. (Through our entire stay we only saw one car pass through the dockyard, and that only occasionally and it was powered by a massive carbide bag like an over-inflated Lilo on its roof). These executives mode of dress was startling for they wore morning dress and green army caps and possessed shiny shoes which they carried in their hands to avoid them getting scratched. On their feet they wore clogs or, more often tabis and married their black striped trousers to the anklets of the tabis with puttees. In the summer instead of the black striped trousers they wore shorts and long socks which were held up by mauve suspenders and, swallow-tailed jacketed or not, they still wore their army caps.

Everyone wore puttees. The Japanese originally wore long puttees but the prisoners' puttees (which came from the Red Cross) were half puttees and after a while the Japanese cut theirs in half so that they would have half puttees like the prisoners. Many prisoners grew moustaches because of the agony it is to shave an upper lip with a year old razor blade; the Japanese are not a hirsute race and are normally clean-shaven but because the prisoners wore moustaches the Japanese tried zealously, and on the whole ineffectively, to grow them. The Japanese had compulsorarily shaven heads and so that the prisoners should not appear superior the edict went out that the prisoners should have their heads shaved also. This was done but the prisoners' hair grew much more quickly, and thickly, than did that of the Japanese and soon it was long again and the prisoners were looking superior after all. It was quite a game seeing how long you could let your hair grow and get away with it and it became a kind of interest in a life which didn't hold too much.

The Japanese, we found, were given to enthusiasms which were all embracing whilst upon them but inclined to be short-lived and but for Minahero in the camp (of whom more later) we

Hitachi Dockyard

might have gone back permanently to longer hair. But every now and again when hair had grown to a respectable crew cut length, Minahero would have a dozen in the guard room and run a channel with hair clippers through from front to back like a lawn mower cutting a single swathe and send them out again leaving them to choose whether to have the rest off or go around like a negative image of an Amerindian.

The hair and puttees were manifestations of the all-encompassing militarism of Japan and this influence was bolstered in Innoshima by the soldiers and sailors who were always swarming through the dockyard. These were the Gods and the highest executive walked warily in their presence aware that the lowliest private could have, had he chosen to, struck him with probable impunity. Each rank walked in positive fear and trembling of the rank above. It was a common happening for a non commissioned officer, a sergeant say, to revenge himself when strictured by knocking about one of lower rank and so on down the line with the lowliest private taking it out on any convenient dog.

THE CHAIN OF COMMAND IN THE GREATER EAST ASIA CO-PROSPERITY SPHERE!

1 WARRANT OFFICER / SERGEANT	2 SERGEANT / CORPORAL	3 CORPORAL / PRIVATE 1ST CLASS
4 PRIVATE 1ST CLASS / PRIVATE 3RD CLASS	5 PRIVATE 3RD CLASS / P.O.W.	6 P.O.W. / BEDBUG

FROM "RANGOON RAMBLERS" USA.

An amusing cartoon drawn by an unknown prisoner which, except perhaps in the sixth section, is no exaggeration.

There was irony in this for the Japanese ran their wars on a rota basis which returned servicemen back to civilian life and many who once been Gods were now nonentities. But they were

Hitachi Dockyard

proud of their service days and forever pulling out photographs of themselves in uniform much as an English serviceman pulls out photographs of female conquests.

In company with those who shared these days, I have always found it difficult to reconcile the Japanese who make our cars, our televisions, videos and so many things, and make them well, with the Japanese I knew on Innoshima Island. The Japanese whom we knew then, (and I do not mean only simple workmen), behaved with astonishing and continual stupidity, and completed work was often of the poorest quality - and after all it was a major dockyard, owned by Hitachi.

They were especially obtuse in the tasks they gave their prisoners. For example one of these was cleaning the bricks which were used as linings to ships' boilers. The boilers were huge cylinders with rounded ends with inlets and outlets for pipes with the result that the lining bricks had to be purpose-made and came in the strangest shapes and sizes like old-fashioned childrens' building bricks. They were made of fireclay and were very soft, very expensive, in very short supply and of vital importance. They were removed with scrupulous care from the iron boilers and deposited in a pile under the cover of the end of the steelwork shop and we were given the job of chipping away the cement (which was far harder than were the bricks) so that they could be re-used.

This was a pleasant job, particularly on cold days because the bricks retained their heat for an astonishing length of time and many a pleasant winter day did I spend sitting on a pile of warm bricks, selecting one at random, and knocking away the mortar with a little hammer while watching the rest of the dockyard hauling its barrows through the puddles of the unmade roadways, carting its cylinders, nuts and bolts and planks and all the rest, with the cold wind numbing hands and feet, or the swirling snow, or the unrermitting rain canting off coolie hats. We were never pressed when cleaning bricks and so we applied ourselves with the care of sculptors, daintily chipping until the last speck of mortar had been removed. Then a smart tap of the hammer would break the brick in half and we'd throw the pieces on the discard pile.

Hitachi Dockyard

Or again there was fettling castings in the foundry, where one would sit all day in the dust of years of fettling, knocking the rough edges off the castings and then again at the end snap them in two as you had the bricks.

There was the business of insulating ships. Our captors were busy looting the Dutch East Indies, Malaya and the Phillipines and for this they needed holds especially insulated for carrying perishable foodstuffs up from the tropics to Japan. The insulating material was glass wool or a powdery, fibrous substance which I have always, somewhat gloomily, been certain was asbestos. The Japanese who were fearful of tuberculosis which was endemic in the country loathed working with these substances and it was decided that carpenters would provide the framework behind which the wool would be stuffed by the *furyos* as we were called. The carpenters built an inner wooden lining against the metal ribs of the ship's hull which consisted of bearers bolted to them to which horizontal boarding was nailed and when a sufficiency had been done would retire up the ladder by which access to the hold was gained on to an upper deck where they would smoke, doze and chat, whilst we, exchanging places, would descend into the cold and clammy bowels.

With few exceptions the Japanese positively lacked the zeal of a Stakhanovite and there was an unspoken understanding there was no cause for us to hurry - so long as we were working with the wool or asbestos, so long could the carpenters doze and smoke the day away, protected even against the sudden materialization of a *kempei*. One of the things we did from time to time (and not merely on these occasions but on others when we were doing something or other on a ship) was to have someone go ashore, ostensibly to make a necessary visit to a benjo, and *en route* take care to catch his foot accidentally in the cable which supplied the ship's electricity. This was easily done for cables were run aboard up the gangplank from a junction box ashore and all ships under construction were festooned with smaller cables running from this main lead; a quick jerk and the entire ship was plunged into darkness, riveting stopped abruptly and bolters, welders, carpenters and prisoners were obliged to stop work until the fault was traced and repaired. This usually took quite some time as the leads were, like most things in Japan in those days, make and mend affairs, and anyway it was an electrician's job and one had to be sent for and found.

Any idea that the Japanese were all enthusiastic to put in a hard day's work for their country, ought to be dispelled - in fact I cannot recall anywhere seeing lazier men than some of the dockyard workers of Habu. You would find them everywhere: lurking behind the benjos, tucked away in dripping tunnels underneath the slips, hiding in the ironclad compartments of half-built ships - and all the time the black-clad kempeis (or, to give them their more accurate title *kempeitais*) were after them, searching the nooks and crannies, sniffing out fires, hauling them out, knocking them about and jumping on them. There were the odd Stakhanovites but these were rare and usually young. So no one minded all that much when the lights went out and no one was in a tremendous hurry to have them put on again, and we would lie back and doze in the insulating room and on the deck above the carpenters would be doing the same.

But all things come to an end and eventually electricity would be restored and reluctantly we'd set to work. The wool, which as I have said was of two kinds, the powdery kind, and a kind which was very much like the insulating material laid these days in lofts, was delivered in sacks which were pitched down through the hatchway. We didn't all work at once - for one thing there was hardly room and for another the likelihood of anyone braving breathing in the stuff to catch us slacking was remote. So we had half in action while the others rested. If the sheathing had reached that height, there might be a couple up on the scaffolding and another pair lifting up the sacks and passing up two or three feet lengths of offcut boarding which was everywhere and the occasional carpenter's tool. The tool was dropped behind the sheathing and thus lost for ever and the offcuts wedged horizontally and hidden by a sprinkle of the powder or a thin layer of wool with the result that spattered all around the hold were huge areas which were totally uninsulated. All this we did with huge glee but all the same it was a job we could have well done without. The powdery stuff which hung in the air was taken down into the lungs all day

Hitachi Dockyard

and the woolly kind got everywhere, under your nails, into your pores and through to everything you wore - there was at least a month of wriggling before you got rid of it.

It would, of course, be absurd to suggest that life was entirely filled by days such as those fettling castings or insulating holds; on the whole dockyard work was dull and wearisome, often punishingly heavy and every day was endless. But at least it had the merit of variety. We were better off than we would have been working in a coal mine or quarry and we were given the opportunity of studying the Japanese to a degree not offered to many for a dockyard hums with life and draws into itself men of different kinds and different experiences. There were, for example, seamen off ships who had travelled the world before the war, could speak some English and being quasi military and transient were less fearful of the *kempei*s and often eager to stop and chat; one of my most poignant moments as a prisoner of war was hearing one of them descending a gangplank whistling 'Santa Lucia'. There were sailors who were instinctively pro-British and not infrequently troopships whose passengers regarded us as being more akin to them than were the civilians. And there was the encouragement denied to others of seeing the steadily increasing numbers of holed and battered ships limping in to be repaired.

Against all this was the cold and wet. Spring and autumn were short seasons and summer was wearyingly hot but it was the winters which we dreaded. This may surprise those who know the Inland Sea for under normal conditions winters on it are pleasant enough with many brilliant cloudless days. That there are orange trees proves that temperatures can never fall too low. But, apart from in the first few months, we were underfed, and our clothing was seldom dry and held little warmth. With the exception of one Red Cross issue (which aroused both guards and dockyard workers to anguished envy) the boots supplied by the Japanese were rubbish. Within a week or two of getting them the soles were through and one was stuffing in bits of cardboard in the vain hope of mitigating the discomfort of cold, wet, clammy feet. The wind, which was sharp and gusty, Siberia-laced, cut through fibre working uniforms and there was no way of drying them after a soaking.

Hitachi Dockyard

The Japanese attitude towards us getting soaked was strange. They would keep us working in a downpour until satisfied we were thoroughly wet and then perhaps relent and usher us into the relative shelter of one of the tunnels under the slips. We were always pleased to go and yet from this distance one wonders why. One could hardly have been more cold and miserable nor could the passing time have been so long. Soaked through, one dare not move for fear of cold, wet clothing touching a drying area of skin yet all the while drip, drip, drip, water seeping through from above would be puddling on a knee or shoulder and the wind, howling through the tunnel as through a pipe, taking away any warmth one might be gathering in it. Such days were endless; nor did they end at nightfall. There was no way to dry wet clothes and so next dawn they had to be hauled on again still wet. Even the comfort of dried boots, if managed, was ephemeral. The sky might be crystal clear but the road was as potholed as if it had been under shellfire and every pothole was filled with water. Within one hundred yards of leaving camp an hour long turning of a boot before a stove was nullified, one's feet as wet as they had ever been and the day which stretched ahead a melancholy prospect.

Warrant Officers didn't have to work but they were, however, obliged to attend the dockyard so their days were as long, perhaps even longer, than for the rest and the cold and wet troubled them equally. All the same I would have much preferred to have been in their category and for a considerable portion of my stay in Habu, I should have been, for my own automatic promotion from Sergeant Pilot to Warrant Officer came through. I approached the Commandant and told him that I was now entitled to the same priveleges which Pritchard, Cox and Fabel enjoyed.

"Why should you be?" he enquired.

I showed him my latest postcard addressed with Warrant Officer's rank. He read it with interest, then handed it back to me.

"You get a letter from Mr Churchill confirming you are a Warrant Officer," he said, "and you won't have to work."

Foolishly, I didn't take up Nimoto's suggestion and send the

Hitachi Dockyard

card to Churchill, who, I am sure, would have co-operated.

A drawing by one of the prisoners, signed by most, if not all of them and by Churchill himself after the war.

CHAPTER SEVEN

THE STAPLE - FOOD

1

Many things occupied our minds: warmth, illness, work, tobacco, how the war was going and when we might be freed, but far exceeding all of these in importance was food. For our first year in Japan the camp was under direct Army control and our food was excellent both in quality and quantity with meat, fish, rice, fruit and vegetables in great variety; we had no reason to complain. We were being fed better than the civilian population and in fact at the time the dockyard took over the job of feeding us we were getting two thousand eight hundred calories a day which is only five hundred calories less than the 1915 Inter Allied Commission recommendation. My own weight having fallen disastrously in the first two months not only recovered but made me marginally heavier than I had ever been before.

In November 1943, the dockyard administration took over and immediately reduced the calorie intake for the next fifteen months to what was theoretically two thousand four hundred (but was normally less and frequently significantly less) and, more importantly, the quality to a lower standard. Further cuts followed in increasingly rapid succession and by the time Japan capitulated our calorie intake even by Japanese calculations was one thousand seven hundred which according to generally accepted standards is about one hundred calories less than the minimum a man lying in bed at rest can theoretically exist on. In the meantime working hours had been lengthened and we were now putting in eleven hours a day for twenty days out of every twenty-one. Towards the end my own weight, in common with

The Staple - Food

all but a few who, as it will be seen, had their own means of supply, was falling dramatically. By the time war ended we so lacked energy that we would walk around a girder thirty feet in length rather than step over it. A few more weeks would have wrought disaster.

The hunger of men given over a lengthy period insufficient food to satisfy their wants yet just sufficient to keep life going has curious consequences which vary according to attitude, character and sense of purpose. But in one way all are affected equally: the sex urge entirely vanishes. And not only does it become impossible to think of women sexually but extremely difficult to think of them at all. To pass the time one might try to conjure up sexual images but the result was dismal failure. You just could not hold in your mind the idea of a girl lying naked on a bed; the best you might do was imagine one in a pretty dress on a summer lawn with the chink of teacups rather more important than her voice; and quite soon you'd forgotten the girl and the teacups and your mind had shifted to steak and chips.

Obsessed by thoughts of food one struggled to come to terms with a problem beyond solution. The different approaches were many and varied and this may, perhaps, be most easily demonstrated by imagining the scene

There are, shall we say, twenty-nine in the billet who have returned from a long day in the dockyard which has ended with a weary slog back carrying on the shoulder a heavy offcut of rough and chafing wood for the cookhouse fire. Roll call (*tenko*) is over and the meal has been collected from the cookhouse. It consists of a mixture of rice (or barley) and the pulp of beans after the oils have been pressed from them (the resultant being termed *daizo*), a thin soup of carrot tops flavoured with soya and a few pieces of *daikon* which is a sort of overgrown radish which has been pickled in a dayglow saffron preservative.

Now whereas it is not too difficult to ladle the soup out reasonably equally it is no easy matter dividing a bucket of daizo into twenty-nine equal portions and even more difficult to divide, say, five pieces of daikon between five tables at four of

The Staple - Food

which sit six men and at the other five.

The daizo is served by paddling it into a small bowl which is knocked out on to each man's plate. But no one is allowed to eat. The server must first go round until all twenty-nine portions have been served; if there is a trifle left in the bucket, he then goes round again distributing a few grains to each; if on the other hand he has misjudged the other way and there is insufficient to fill the final bowl or two then he must go round and take a tax off those already served.

All this has to be carried out under the eagle eyes of the remaining twenty-eight men who need to be satisfied he is exerting similar pressure with his paddling to each and every bowl. And on each succeeding night serving must start at a different table for, although there is much discussion on the matter, no decision has yet been reached, or will ever be reached, whether a bowl made out of taxed portions is more tightly or more loosely packed.

Eating must still be delayed for there is still the infinitely more difficult business of the daikon to be solved. As there is no conceivable way in which five radishes (each of about the length of a banana but varying in shape and thickness) can be divided equally between twenty-nine men, chance has to come into it, chance regulated to avoid all possibilities of cheating. The solutions arrived at were numerous and complicated and at this distance in time seem difficult to credit.

Suffice to say that each radish having been calibrated as carefully as a thermometer before being cut into pieces of little more than the size of a ping pong ball, a complex system of card-cutting first establishes which batch of segments shall go to which table and the pieces having arrived there, further card cutting must be done to decide who shall have each piece.

It is only now that eating can begin.

Suppose we observe a table of six men, three on each side, who have sat facing each other through five hundred evening meals and will face each other for another five hundred before they are done:

The first has six plates, knife, fork and spoon. He divides

The Staple - Food

his meagre ration into six equal portions. One he will eat plain, one with salt, one with curry powder, one with soya sauce, one with water and one with carrot tops dredged from the soup. His is a six course dinner.

The second is a Genki Boy (of whom more later). He hardly bothers with his pitiful ration - he might even give it away, although this is most unlikely. Additional to it he has a huge bowl of steaming pure white rice quite twice as large as anyone else's daizo and perhaps a cut of salmon.

The third has a large flat plate on to which he puts his portion and, wetting a knife, smooths it out flat and very thin before drawing criss-cross lines which divide it into, say, sixty-four squares. With chopsticks he picks out one square and eats it, puts down the chopsticks, flattens out the missing space and redraws his lines. And so on. He is the last to finish his meal which gives him comfort.

The fourth who has a large spoon, polishes his meal off in a couple of mouthfuls and quits the table. He has made his point - but as he makes it every night, few notice.

The fifth has saved something from his breakfast, meagre though that was. He has starved himself all morning - or maybe brought home half his lunch and starved himself all afternoon. The portion he adds to his evening ration has by now developed a slimy look but the resulting quantity is respectable.

The sixth eats quietly and steadily trying not to glance enviously at the Genki Boy's repast nor at the sixty-four square man who looks as if he will go on for ever.

All this may sound flippant and exaggerated but it was how it was. And it is how it would have been had the one hundred and eighty odd Raffs and Volunteers of Habu been exchanged for any other one hundred and eighty average Britishers put into such a situation. For food was all important - the essential pabulum of mind as well as body. Geoffrey Coxhead's diary underlines the point. It is a fascinating document which covers every aspect of prisoner of war life with sensitivity and humour: punishments, disasters, triumphs, the progress of the war, amusing incidents - all get their turn; but in the margins of each page he faithfully records

The Staple - Food

the constituents of each and every meal down to the smallest detail.

2

From the day the dockyard administration took over, there was never enough to eat apart from unusual occasions such as the arrival of a Red Cross parcel or barrels of rice or beans intended for some ship required suddenly to sail which, although probably already a little sour, or often rankly so, might just as well be sent to the camp as left to go entirely bad.

For the last two years that nagging ache of hunger never left one and the unsatisfying meals merely eased what was almost physical pain. Thinking of food became the paramount interest and talking of food the paramount conversation. Very many collected menus; one man in my billet collected maggots which he kept in a small bottle and fattened up on green stuff; he maintained they were high in protein. Some, fortunately not many, succumbed to an unbridled food mania and became dreadful to look at, their faces taking on a haunted expression, becoming oddly hawklike and their eyes sharp, staring, shifty. Such men bartered clothing, books, cigarettes, eveything they owned for food. Their entire waking hours were spent talking, contemplating or looking for food and the judgement of their fellows became not of the least account. They had crossed a line into a world where there were other rules and standards.

One of the men who succumbed in this way had held one of the highest and most respected posts in Hong Kong and one would forever see the poor fellow folorn, wretched, disgraced, with staring eyes and cadaverous face poking amongst the rubbish heaps and picking through slops. Towards the end of the war in desperation he was made a cook. After the war he went back to Hong Kong, got back his post and filled it with distinction until retirement. How he had behaved on Innoshima was not spread about; he was a very decent man and anyway there were perhaps not too many entitled to cast stones.

With food of such importance, there had to be occasions when it provided light relief. There was, for example, the case

The Staple - Food

of the *Sato Maru*.

Sato is the Japanese for 'sugar' a commodity in such short supply that it was not even on the ration for the civilian population and to the best of my knowledge the only men who had any on Innoshima were the prisoners who got it in occasional Red Cross parcels or looted it off the ships.

I have no idea what was the *Sato Maru*'s proper name. She had come from Java or some such place and, having been badly bombed *en route* had been diverted to Habu for repairs. Heavy rain pouring through the rents caused by bombs or shelling had damaged the sacks of sugar which had been part of her cargo causing them to split open, whereupon the sugar, liquefied by water and heat, had run across an iron deck, later to be frozen to a sheet as the ship sailed northwards.

I cannot remember who put it around in the 'Canteen' where we ate our miserable midday ration that the ship was loaded with sugar for the taking, but the room was soon buzzing with the news and plans were hastily being hatched. It may seem strange that prisoners of war should have the freedom to go aboard ships on which they have no business but fortunately the Japanese were both astonishingly naïve and slaves to symbolism. Like the red tabs worn on a general's uniform, a red armband manifested power; and a basket on one's shoulder was acceptable proof that the man carrying it had been sent by someone to go somewhere and have it filled. And a man walking up a ship's gangplank had obviously been sent aboard to perform some task, else why was he walking up the gangplank? And a need to visit the benjo was always an easy excuse for quitting your party.

Thus within an hour after our return to work I was one of several viewing that deck on the Sato Maru with disbelief. Discrediting the rumour I had slipped aboard as much to check the story as for any other reason only to find myself offered a bonanza; there for the taking was a veritable skating rink of inch-thick frozen sugar. Others, less doubtful than I had been, had come prepared and were already mining gold.

It was a opportunity not to be missed. But where was I to put the stuff? I could think of only one solution - in my socks! So I took them off and finding a piece of wood joined the scrapers. It

The Staple - Food

was astonishing how much sugar my socks could take - they expanded until they resembled truncheons! Having all but filled them, I tied them together and concealed them by hanging one down each trouser leg.

It proved to be a memorable afternoon. *Umpanko* was working in the woodyard, loading hatch covers on to a trolley and then transferring them on to a pile on the edge of Hachi Dock. There was snow on the ground but a warm sun was melting it - *and* my sugar. I had to accept three hours of it oozing down my legs. But never mind - by the time I got back to camp quite a quantity remained, the stoves were roaring well, the billets warm and there was a hot bath from which to de-congeal while contemplating the joys which lay ahead.

The sugar had got fearfully mixed with bits of sacking, straw and other impurities best not pondered too deeply on and clearly had to be refined and this it was generally decided was best done by boiling it up and sieving out impurities. The stoves were by now peculiarly suitable for this purpose. They were of the fat bellied type often found in barrack blocks and we had made two rows of iron collars around them to act as shelves on which to place tins which had contained powdered milk in Red Cross parcels in which to cook windfalls and which came to be known as *Klim Tins*. As far as I can remember there was room for about half a dozen on each of the shelves and for a further four on top. Refining was soon in progress, the Klim tins being filled with sugar with a little water, put by the almost red-hot stoves and boiled to a treacle which was then sieved through whatever might be available, vests, shirts or pjyama coats and the process repeated once or twice with as a result a tin of syrup rather black in colour but of quite excellent quaity.

That first evening there were only a few refining but by the next all the stoves were fully charged with filled double rings whilst other refiners impatiently waited for empty spaces worried lest they shouldn't complete before lights out at nine. There was pushing and jostling and continual calamity as an overfilled tin boiled over and the ignited treacle sent yard high mauve flames roaring towards the ceiling while a lava flow of burning treacle spread across the floor. The room was filled with the glorious smell of molasses and thick with

The Staple - Food

smoke and there was tremendous activity as other refiners played snapdragon grabbing at their tins. But so soon as the flames died down the tins were back and others were wafting the smoke out with waved blankets through open windows and scraping the charcoal from the floor.

"Make way for a Klim tin pie!"

Even now it seems to me quite remarkable that although refining went on for three days we were never interrupted by such accidents. Look outs were of course posted to watch for the guards who occasionally patrolled the passage and presumably the arrival of none coincided with a major conflagration. But there was no attempt to hide what we were doing, there was tremendous and unusual activity and the pungent smell could hardly have gone unnoticed. But there it was - the refining continued unhindered. Equally remarkable were the subsequent scenes on the Sato Maru. The Japanese do not use sugar as do Europeans. Their tea is green tea, unpolluted by milk or sugar and the idea of sweetened rice, anaethema. Nor generally do they eat puddings. Nevertheless they like sweet things and to have the opportunity of securing a luxury so denied was not to be resisted. There were not only prisoners on their hands and knees scraping the sugar from the iron decks of the Sato Maru but Japanese as well. It really was the most astounding sight, scores of Japanese and prisoners elbowing each other aside as sharp eyed as miners seeking the richer veins which still remained.

It all ended abruptly. On the fourth day when we returned to the Canteen preparatory to marching back, the Commandant, Nimoto, was there. I crossed to the flimsy apology of a greatcoat with which we had all been issued and tapped the pocket to reassure myself the tin containing my morning's loot was safe and sound. But the pocket was empty. Looking up I caught the eye of Nimoto, standing near. *"Sato nai,"* he said. That was all - *"Sato nai."* He could have said the same to everyone for not one container of sugar was to be found. And there were no unpleasant consequences - no punishments, not even a mention of the exploit. I often wondered if, when we had gone to bed, they were refining sugar in the guard room.

3

There are one hundred sen to a yen and privates or aircraftsmen got ten sen, non-commissioned officers fifteen sen and warrant officers twenty-five sen for each day's attendance at the dockyard. There was a daily issue of two cigarettes and additional to the pittance paid each man got a further three cigarettes for every full day's work. If he worked a full month without a day off sick he received an extra fifty sen. In addition if his ganger reported he was a good worker he became

The Staple - Food

a 'good percentage man' and was paid an extra five sen a day. At the time ten sen was worth a little less than a penny. While initially this pay was quite useful and you could buy from a small stock of items available in the Canteen (or have bought for you by the cooks who were allowed to shop when they went in with their barrow to Habu to collect supplies) curry powder, green tea, fruits in season, jam of a sort, biscuits, soya sauce, tooth powder and so on and, importantly, cigarettes, later it became another matter and money became all but valueless.

There was nothing to buy: nothing for the Japanese, nothing for the prisoners. The shops were empty. A diligent worker might get a voucher enabling him to buy a new peaked cap made of material hardly superior to cardboard. That was about the whole of it; not even a one sen bamboo cigarette holder was for sale and of course no food of any kind. So with tobacco being of such importance and in such short supply, it provided a yardstick by which to judge the value of different foodstuffs. The currency of exchange is not always money - cowrie shells were used abundantly as money in parts of India and Southern Asia and on Innoshima the currency came to be cigarettes.

In our three and a half years we received the approximate equivalent of nine Red Cross food parcels per man and a few bulk supplies. The parcels contained a wide variety of items such as coffee, sugar, powdered milk, meat, paté, puddings, butter, cheese; the quantities of each was of necessity small (there is a limit as to what can be put into a box about fifteen by ten inches and six inches deep) but they were of inestimable value not only for their food value but psychologically because of their variety and because they contained so many things which simply did not exist in Japan.

Each item came to be valued individually in terms of the cigarettes contained (of which there were six, or sometimes eight, packets of twenty). There were, for example, two bars of chocolate, each of which could be broken into six cubes. Each cube was initially valued as being worth one packet of cigarettes; later the market in tobacco firmed and the going rate went down to four packets, that is eighty cigarettes, for a bar. The cigarettes were of well known American brands such as Old Gold, Camel, Chesterfield or Philip Morris and were far

The Staple - Food

superior to the Japanese *Kinshi* which we normally smoked. You could always get two Kinshi for a Camel. Thus it can be seen that even at the lowest rate of exchange it was possible to swap your two bars of chocolate for one hundred and sixty Camels or three hundred and twenty Kinshi which when sliced and re-rolled gave you guaranteed smoking for about three months! For just two modest bars of chocolate!

Red Cross parcels put the authorities in difficulties. Ill feeling could easily arise amongst a large and deprived labour force existing on bare essentials if it was (as it was to be) presented with the sight of prisoners enjoying luxuries such as lumps of chocolate which it had all but forgotten existed or saw them smoking cigarettes of a size and quality which made the local brands look mean and pitiful. When a batch of parcels arrived (on one occasion no less than eight hundred were delivered) Nimoto understandably shilly-shallyed before issuing them. There followed, so far as we were concerned, a frustrating time of waiting. We knew they were there, stacked in our original hut, neat, pristine cardboard boxes packed with ambrosia - Tantalus reaching for the clusters of fruit just out of reach hardly suffered more than we did; and for that matter Nimoto must have heard the song of the Sirens in his ears at the thought of the Lucullan banquets there for his taking. Although many said he helped himself, my own belief was that he didn't and if so is very much to his credit - or a testimonial to Japanese discipline.

The all-absorbing interest in the parcels' contents is well-exemplified by quotations from Coxhead's diary:

"Friday Movember 24th, 1944:

'An interview between Pritch (Pritchard) and C.C.(Camp Commandant) concerning the Red Cross parcels. The latter's line a thoroughly oriental twist: he understands that Christmas is a festival day when Englishmen give presents to their friends! Now he has been very good to us in the past and will give oranges and minerals on the next holiday to celebrate the beginning of the camp. This of course leads up to the inevitable request for a parcel. Pritch replies that he "doesn't know." Another preamble about the large quantity of cigarettes possessed by the prisoners - when the parcels come - and their abuse trading with Nippon workers for food: angling for a reduction of cigarettes from 5 to 2 1/2 a day. C.C. seems keen just now to get hold of

The Staple - Food

our cigarettes; this latest attempt follows two others: a call for non-smokers, to whom a vague promise of oranges is extended - unsuccessful; and a threat of camp stoppage for a fortnight if anyone caught smoking out of proper time and place. At present, general feeling in the camp is definately against giving C.C. a parcel.'

And then a few days later:

'In an interview on 28th November, C.C. asked Pritch for a box of parcels, and Pritch agreed: one for himself (C.C.), one for Smiler (a permanent guard), one for the Dock Captain, and one between Minnie and Sakimoto. Pritch then extracted certain promises: plenty of fresh veg would be forthcoming during the next months; sick men with malnutrition and fevers etc, would not be required to do fatigues; a holiday on Christmas Day could not be promised - but we might finish early.'

When issuing of parcels finally took place (normally on a *Yasumi* day), the complexion of life entirely changed. Of a sudden one was no longer a pair of hands at the beck and call of an oriental conqueror, but an unlucky member of a race of entirely different and altogether superior substance. Quite apart from the gastronomic joys which lay ahead, the possession of these superbly packed and presented luxuries which by their very quality showed up the shoddiness of the nearest Japanese equivalents - where indeed there even were equivalents - gave a huge fillip to morale and reassured one that the notion the Japanese could win the war was laughable.

Now thoughts of food took an entirely new direction and one could actually consider what one would choose to eat tonight and for many nights. Conversation descended from vague clouds of misty impossibilities to the earth of positive preferences. Menu gathering ceased to be the province of the suspect few but to be a perfectly sensible occupation: there was, after all, far more that one could do with liver paté than spread it on a piece of toast; and even a few mouthfuls of *daizo* was elevated to an interesting course when a knob of butter was placed on it and allowed to melt golden, fatty and delicious through its contents.

And everywhere was bargaining. As Coxhead wrote:

'An interesting list could be compiled of current exchange rates of parcel merchandise - a very busy market inded.'

The Staple - Food

There were those who calculated that to scoff a pudding which could be exchanged for enough cheese carefully husbanded to flavour twenty bowls of rice would be an unforgiveable extravagance; there were those whose idea of supremest luxury was to lie abed on a *Yasumi* morning (when one didn't have to get up till seven) and be handed by a friend a cup of sweet milk-laced coffee and sip it while smoking a Philip Morris right through. There were those who calculated vitamin contents; and those who took an accountant's pleasure in organising their affairs so that with a bit of luck they wouldn't have a gap before the next parcel came.

There was, as Coxhead indicated, something akin to a stock market in operation. Values of items fluctuated according to circumstances; if the cigarettes earned by working were not dished out on a Yasumi day because they had failed to arrive in the camp, then a man with a spare packet of Chesterfields was better placed for supper than he had been at breakfast time. Then there was the case of the Cornish wafers. There had been much criticism of these biscuits which were of the lightweight kind, large in diameter and occupied space which could have held at least four more of the four ounce tins of butter. Moreover they had little food value, disintegrated in your mouth and were gone in a trice. Their cigarette value was minimal - until an ingenious fellow discovered that if you placed one in a saucer of water before you left for work, by the time you got back it had swelled to the size of a three egg omelette.

Fortunes were made and lost out of Red Cross parcels. To succeed in transferring the lather of the soap issued to us by the Japanese to your face your hands had to move at lightning speed and in any case latterly the ration was half a bar every other month. There was a man who calculated he could make himself rich by stagging Red Cross soap. He bought many bars and possessed himself in patience. Sadly, some mysterious gel (a handful of which when put with a Yasumi day's washing fetched out the dirt as effectively as any modern biological washing powder) was discovered in the dockyard and soap crashed in value. And there was the case of a man in another camp who wrote and sold share certificates in a factory he

The Staple - Food

owned in Canada in return for food from Red Cross parcels - I have often wondered how the courts ruled when the owners of those certificates presented them for payment!

A poem was written about using Red Cross parcels and I include it because of the indication it gives of the importance which was attached to them. The boys who liked their grub in a tub and those who took no risk, existed - and the poem was written to send them up. The word *legge* or *leggy*, is a bastardization of the Malay word *lagi* meaning 'more'.

'Legge' was adopted into our prisoner of war language equally by R.A.F. and H.K.V.D.C men and became a word of considerable consequence. As written earlier when any meal was being served out no one was allowed to start eating until the server had satisfied himself (and so informed the gathering) that there was neither a tax to be collected or *legge* to be distributed.

<u>Parcel bashing - for and against</u>

We are the boys who like our grub
And when we have it, it's in a tub.
If for a snack you have a yen
Gather round boys, here's the gen.

First for bulk you need it seems,
About eight bowls of rice and beans.
And we hardly think it rash
To use our milk in one big bash.
For sugar we use every dot
As for butter? All the lot.

And for fruit? Well why not whack it
Why mess around with half a packet?
And while you're mixing, it's rather natty
To throw in your bully and Rose Mill paté
I say you chaps, that was very nice
Has anyone got any legge rice?

We are the boys who take no risk
We eat our parcel sixth by sixth.
We're sad our Camels do not grate

The Staple - Food

And ration our butter eighth by eighth.
If you want something really nice,
Gather round - here's <u>our</u> advice.
First you take a single prune,
As for butter - half a spoon.
For sugar a single dot will do,
Oh! Can we afford it? Make it two!
Now cream is really quite a cinch,
Use your Nestles - just a pinch.
Mix it well into a basin
And add the juice of a single raisin.
I say chaps, that's a lot that's gorn in!
Better save half 'till the morning.

Although food was always in short supply in Japan and towards the end of the war desperately so, ships that were actually in commission and had a resident crew were usually well stocked and it followed that all those whose work took them aboard were on the look out for provender. Two parties in particular - P.T.1 & P.T.2. - had opportunities the others lacked because one of their jobs was coaling and it is only ships that are in commission which need coal. They seized these opportunities gleefully and their exploits were so remarkable and so successful as to merit the separate chapter covering them which follows.

CHAPTER EIGHT

THE GENKI BOYS

1

P.T.1 & P.T.2 were, as were most other parties, composed of both Raffs and Volunteers. After so many years I cannot remember how many there were in each party nor the names of all their members and in fact I believe their make-up varied from time to time. I should say that the two together numbered several more than a dozen with possibly a slighter larger preponderance of Raffs than Volunteers. Amongst the members of P.T.1 were Forrow (Volunteer) and Henderson (Raff) and amongst those of P.T.2 were Batty (Raff) and Bond and Halsall (Volunteers). Other members included Warrington and Spink amongst the Raffs and Low and Goldburne amongst the Volunteers. In the earliest days no doubt its members had lucky finds and even useful hauls when, for example, a careless seaman had forgotten to lock the galley store. Then at some stage, probably when the cuts in our rations had begun to make living distressing, it occurred to one or other of the parties that a more positive view should be taken of their opportunities and that rather than rely on good fortune they ought to take matters into their own hands.

This they proceeded to do so successfully that before they were done they were to earn themselves the sobriquet of 'The Genki Boys' and not merely to be the envy of us all but to leave such an indelible impression on our minds that even now, fifty years and more afterwards, no meeting of ex-Innoshima prisoners takes place but that quite shortly their deeds will become a part of the discussion. For myself, seeking a subject for my third novel I was moved to base it on their exploits.

In 1966 Macmillan published my "The Genki Boys" which was well enough received to have subsequently been issued in

The Genki Boys

paperback and large print and has been dramatized. My Author's Note in the first edition read:

> *The Genki Boys is a book of fiction based on fact. On the island of Innoshima in the Inland Sea, nearly two hundred prisoners lived from November 1942 to September 1945, and worked in the island's dockyards. These prisoners were drawn chiefly from the R.A.F. and the Hong Kong Volunteer Defence Corps and were as dissimilar in their backgrounds as are their characters in my story.*
>
> *Against this backcloth I have placed my prisoners who are entirely imaginary; it is important to stress this as there were men in more than one camp who were titled 'Genki' because of their exploits; there were Genki Boys at Innoshima who would themselves confirm not only that my characters were fictional, but also that the events described in this book could well have happened. The meaning of the word 'Genki' is indefinable, but I hope in this book its use will become as clear as it was to those scores of thousands of men during the long drab years of imprisonment.*
>
> *San San, Jamaica. February 1965. Terence Kelly.*

So what does 'Genki' mean? Well my small dictionary sees it as a noun meaning 'vigour', 'energy' and 'pep'. But in Innoshima it was used by the dockyard workers much more as an adjective, had a far broader meaning and embraced almost any quality which was enviable and to be respected. To us a 'genki' bowl of rice was one filled to overflowing; to the Japanese (who evidenced an abiding interest in such matters) a *chimbo genki* was an outsize penis. A man who was well was *genki* but a man who couldn't turn a rusted valve was *'genki nai'*. Until the day of the Japanese surrender. America was *'yowai'* (which means weak or feeble) and Japan was *genki*; on the day following capitulation the Japanese were quite cheerfully explaining their defeat by:*"Nippon yowai; America genki'"*

For the last twelve months, or for even longer, you could always pick out a Genki Boy for he was a man with a well-made body and rippling muscles who stood out amongst his fellow men like

The Genki Boys

Atlas among those ladies of Lynn, so uncommonly thin, that when they essayed, to drink lemonade, they slipped through the straw and fell in.

The only people you might have confused the Genki Boys with was the cooks - but if you looked closely you would have seen that the cooks were merely fat. You might also have noticed another difference between cooks and Genki Boys and that was the difference which is seen between men of mere position and men of power, between men living on the income from inherited wealth and wealth creators.

For all their protestations the cooks lived well, while the Genki Boys made no attempt to hide how well they lived; in a word one flanneled, the other flaunted.

The Genki Boys became rich mainly through looting ships and were rich in the fullest meaning of the word. They were powerful, mighty and exalted; they had large possessions; their dress was the most superior and their furnishings the most valuable in the camp; their meals were banquets. They were as millionaires to paupers, as lapdogs to alley cats, as fattened pigs to church mice. And whether or not one could morally justify such flagrant inequality, there is not the least doubt they added contrast to a dreary scene and gave it life.

Every man looked for ways to increase his ration. On the march back at night with every spare foot of usable soil under cultivation, there was a great temptation to dart from the line and steal a peasant's pumpkin. On the whole this was still regarded as a despicable thing to do but there was no compunction in reducing an unattended sack of sweet potatoes and a tax on a merchant seaman's rice was fair game; equally, food barrows passing through the dockyard were ripe for pilfering and food stolen by a Japanese could be hi-jacked from his cache. And in fact it was quite astonishing in what strange places food turned up and there were few who didn't know, individually, their day or two of glut. But it was only the Genki Boys who organised things on a truly professional and substantial scale.

The Genki Boys

'Chick' Henderson

Manual coaling of ships is a long drawn out process. From some shore dump, sacks have to be humped up a sloping gangway and their contents then upended into a chute leading to the bunkers. It is not a job which requires much supervision and as the P.T. foreman, a man who was named Mori, was neither Stakhanovite nor madman like the Bottle Party's 'Ape', he soon fell into the role of dockyard aristocrat and spent a fair amount of his time chatting, smoking and slumbering in odd corners while his charges were left to get on with things. So long as the correct tonnage went aboard within a stipulated period, so long as there was always one man jogging, sack on shoulder, up the gangplank and another one returning, everyone was happy. It was easy enough, with the crew on shore leave, for the party to organise things so that a couple were free to roam on the look out for throw outs from the galley or split sacks of rice and from this petty pilfering, with occasional hauls from

The Genki Boys

unlocked galley stores, there was steady progression to organised robbery.

The Genki Boys following the advice of Francis Bacon that a man must make his opportunity as oft he finds it, soon developed into very professional thieves. There were four problems to be overcome: access to galley stores; avoidance of discovery while looting; transportation of loot; and smuggling loot through searches before leaving the dockyard and on arrival back in camp.

The first problem was classically dealt with by manufacturing skeleton keys. I handled the keys they used. They were very simple: thin pieces of metal of different sizes and thicknesses threaded on a string and worn round the lock-picker's neck under shirt or working uniform. I have no idea who designed these keys - perhaps there was someone with peacetime experience - but it seems it wasn't one of the group who actually made them for one of the Genki Boys, 'Chick' Henderson, told me that they had to pay ten bowls of rice for each of them. But it was a good investment - they were so well fashioned that no lock could defeat them.

The second problem, avoidance of discovery, was simplified by the design of the average merchantman of those days which had companionways running both sides of the ship fore and aft which were joined by a cross passageway (thus forming an 'H') and galley and galley stores were located off this passage. Close by the junction points on both sides of the ship were the coal bunker chutes. As it was explained to me, at each of the junction points and at each of the coal chutes a man would be stationed, a fifth would be posted outside the galley store, and a sixth, having opened it, would go inside. Meanwhile there were spare men carrying coal. All points of the compass were now covered and in the event of sudden alarm the form was either for the man inside the galley store to be temporarily locked in it or for the robbery to be abandoned or put off. If all went well, the man in the store having sized up the alternatives would make his choice. This might be many things: a sack of rice, barley or beans; a barrel of *miso* paste (which was a soya bean concoction used for flavouring and vitaminizing soups and stews), sugar, fish, pickles, ship's

The Genki Boys

biscuits, salt or fat and even occasionally eggs, meat, tinned food or saké.

Whatever was chosen was passed out to the passage man and thence to whichever of the junction men indicated he was unmarked. He would take it or throw it to the coal chute man who dropped it down into the bunkers. Then, in turn, the Genki Boys would go down to the bunkers to split the haul, or possibly return to do so at their leisure on a following day. This they did into what were known as 'scrounge bags' or 'gloat bags' which were threaded on string which was around the neck with the bag lying flat against the chest or belly. On the Micawber principle, many men in other parties carried scrounge bags as well although their chances of filling them were remote. It may be that the scrounge bags which all the Genki Boys used were of superior design - Ken Forrow tells me: "the ones we used were life jackets with the stuffing taken out of them with straps put on to go around our necks and the main bag rested in the apex of our tummy when loaded."

The scrounge bag of course went a long way towards coping with the fourth problem, discovery by search. This raises a point which I have never solved to my satisfaction: how the Genki Boys could have carried on for as long as they did without being found out. The very fact that we were searched sporadically indicates that it did at least occur to the Japanese that we might steal from them and one would have thought it had to be obvious even to this most myopic of races that something was going on when amid a camp of scarecrows there was one party with such splendid bodies.

It is a puzzle to which none of the seven surviving Genki Boys I have spoken to within the last year or so have given me a totally satisfactory answer although. Forrow has given me a partial one. It seems that on one occasion early on having lifted some rice and partially removed it to safety they returned to the scene of their crime to find their foreman helping himself to what they had left behind. Thenceforth he became an accomplice and in return for their silence in not reporting him and his co-operation in looking the other way, he was always rewarded with a share of the loot. Forrow also told me that they were usually aware when a search was likely. "I found."

The Genki Boys

he wrote, "the Japs on the whole were rather predictable. For instance if there was to be a search on return to camp the guards had fixed bayonets."

While this goes some way to explaining how at least while they were looting his party was partially protected, it does not explain how P.T.2 (which usually worked quite separately from P.T.1) could carry on looting month in month out and never be discovered doing so. There was little co-operation between the two parties. Forrow wrote: "we were wary of each other and did not communicate our activities so there would be no poaching and a possible cock-up" while Batty, Bond and Halsall to whom I put the question baldly recently were communicative on the point only to the extent of saying that they were - unlike the members of P.T.1 who they considered took absurd and unnecessary risks - scrupulously careful.

I used to wonder sometimes if there was collusion between the kempies and the Genki Boys and of one thing I am absolutely certain: that the Commandant, Nimoto, who was an educated man and no one's fool, by the time the Genki Boys' physique was so unmistakeably at variance from that of the balance of his charges, must have realised what was going on and decided to leave well alone.

To keep their foreman happy, the Genki Boys worked as hard as the most enthusiastic Japanese. One would see them hauling a line of coal barrows around the dockyard which were loaded as heavily as those of the bottle party, unaccompanied by any ganger, sweat pouring off half naked bodies, sinews taut as whipcord, muscles bulging, putting every last ounce of energy into their task; or as black with oil as the inside of an engine sump after furiously emptying out some bilges; or, most terrifying of all, one would watch them dripping blood, flailing with a kind of pitchfork at great mountains of trimmed steel swarf, vicious, curly stuff which sprang back and slashed the skin.

There is no doubt that amongst the reports which had to be sent regularly to Zentsuji from which all the Fukuoka camps were run, the P.T. parties would have stood out glowingly, reflecting handsomely to Nimoto's benefit. But had he allowed them to be caught red-handed he would have had to mete out

The Genki Boys

the sternest punishment and while this perhaps would not have bothered him too much, news of their crimes would have reached the ears of his superiors in Zentsuji whose wrath at a Commandant who had been so lax, would have been fearsome. At the very least he would have lost a job which gave him an easy way of life and kept him free from the rigours and dangers of war; most probably his punishment would have been far greater. It is perfectly conceivable that he let it be known that these splendid men who set such an example not merely to their fellow prisoners but throughout the dockyard were *persona grata* so far as he was concerned and with a Japanese officer being a God to both soldier and civilian alike, the point was taken.

At all events they were never caught out and went on looting to the end on a truly massive scale. A whole sack of rice was unexceptional and I remember on one occasion standing beside one of them, Wilfred Batty, as we were put through one of the occasional searches knowing, because he'd told me, that the wicker basket pulled by its rope hard against his back was filled with eggs!

In the camp itself there was a curious conspiracy of silence so far as the Genki Boys were concerned. They were not at all averse to recounting their exploits and anyway the proof of them was there for all of us to see, for they didn't eat their mouth-watering extras skulking in corners, but openly. And what they did not consume themselves, they sold. I cannot answer for what happened in other rooms, but in my own sales took place upstairs in the billet, usually against the camp currency of cigarettes and as an example my own fifty year old notes state that the price for a raw kilogram of rice was eighty. Stock was stored under the bed spaces. The dais on which we slept was an open timber framework on which the *tatamis* were laid and, because these were of a standard size, to fill the space at the bedhead a narrower piece of tatami was laid and this could be lifted out and things hidden below. (This was where I hid my Log Book and some raisin wine I brewed). When a sale took place, the purchaser, bowl in hand like an Oliver Twist, would pay his cigarettes, whereupon the Genki Boy involved would pull up his hidden sacklet, untie the string around its neck, dip in his own measuring bowl and fill it, wipe off with a

The Genki Boys

ruler anything surplus above the rim back into the sacklet, transfer the rice, beans or whatever it was into the purchaser's bowl, dismiss his customer and nod to the next in line.

Although I am now informed that on occasions surplus loot was distributed to the camp generally, and odd items such as eggs given to the very sick, I do not personally recall a single instance of a Genki Boy giving any of his loot away except to a chum who he kept ticking over. Objections were seldom raised for the camp was basically divided into two groups: those with too much pride to do business and those who were eager to trade or hopeful of crumbs from the rich men's tables.

Such objections as were raised were met by an argument it was difficult to counter: that if an objector wanted food to give away all he had to do was go aboard a ship and help himself. The reply to this that he didn't have the opportunities the Genki Boys had, was met by the unanswerable response that when there was no loot on the ship they were supposed to be working on, the Genki Boys went on ships where there *was* loot they were *not* supposed to be working on. And this was so: on one occasion they made a haul from a troopship swarming with more than a thousand soldiers on which they had no business whatsoever. Whatever your views about the Genki Boys you had to admit they had enterprise and courage and out of this naturally followed a further reason why objections to their behaviour were so muted. They were speaking from strength. Weakly positioned people can rarely do well against the strong - the more so if jealousy and need are the real motivations of their anger. If further indication is needed it can be drawn from the fact that the Genki Boys were never robbed. Rich as Croesus, still accumulating wealth in kind, buying soap, books, shoes, socks and the very clothes off others' backs, their sacklets of rice and beans and miso paste were left untouched even though the billets were largely empty through the day with no one about to check what a man excused work for accident or sickness might be up to. I always thought it strange that a man would collect maggots to eat with his rice yet never think of stealing from the Genki Boys. Envied they might have been, but their courage and enterprise overawed many around them.

I received a letter recently from a fellow prisoner named

The Genki Boys

Cyril Moulstone - nicknamed 'Swede' because he was a country born lad - who, liking the look of Australia when being repatriated through it, decided to stay and make his life there; it exemplifies the point.

'You know, Flash,' he wrote, *'when one thinks back to those days in the camp, the break-ins into ships' stores and general stealing from the Japs, it makes one's hair stand on end. The leaders like Batty, they were as cool as cucumbers and as skilled as locksmiths. I'm afraid I went on only a couple of break-in operations, I just didn't have the nerve that these sort of fellows had. I went on one such break in to a ship's store. Opening the door was child's play. They had a look inside then stood in the doorway and said: "There's a good variety in here. What do we need?" You would have thought they were in a supermarket, picking up the week's grocery list.'*

And he goes on to recount, a break-in in the smaller Mitsunosho dockyard, when it was decided to raid a Japanese Naval vessel for all that there was an armed guard on the gangway. They went on board carrying a pole and a 5 gallon can with just sufficient rubbish in it to provide cover over the intended haul, broke into the store and discovered a huge quantity of eggs, theirs for the taking. They made several trips on and off the ship collecting them and hid them temporarily in the nut, bolt and rivet store ashore and then, (with Moulstone carrying one of them), took them back into the camp in the three buckets which had brought the rice and soup lunch ration to the dockyard!

Quite recently, at a Far East Prisoner of War Reunion, I remet 'Chick' Henderson (with whom I had had no contact for getting on for fifty years) who regaled us all with stories of his exploits as a Genki Boy of which I include the following two taken down verbatim.

"We went on to this ship, the Ile de Francee" "Henderson recounted. *"She'd come up from Indo-China. We walked into this refrigerator room and there was this half a pig. There were four of us, me, Bill (Sunburk), Vic Bond and I can't remember who the fourth one was. We were digging coal away from this bulkhead and I said 'let's have*

The Genki Boys

this half a pig." So we got a basket we were carrying this coal in and we put this half a pig in it and carried it into the benjo and I cut it into four and I'd got my bag on so I stuffed it in. This was about half past eight in the morning and Bill went in and got his quarter and I said to Vic :'Look, you're the biggest - he was six feet two - so you take the knuckle end' and he said 'right' and went in and got it. But when the fourth bloke went in, can't remember who he was, there was no pig left. We never found the fourth bit. And the funniest thing I ever saw was Vic digging this coal away from this bulkhead after that because every time he pushed the shovel in the knuckle of this pig came up sticking out of his shirt!'"

And his other story went this way:

"We got on deck and it was an Army ship full of soldiers. Anyway we broke in, we'd got our skeleton keys, we got in there and pulled out this whacking great crate full of cigarettes, 'Crossed Flags' and we prised the top off and it was chock a block filled with these fags and I thought, God, I'm never going to be poor again!

But there was a noise and obviously some Jap was going to come through the door and who was with me? I forget who it was now. But it was unbelieveable. He actually dived through this bloody ventilator and he went clean through the ventilator and he finished up in the boiler room! And there wasn't a scratch on him!

And here's me, sitting like a burk, sitting on the edge of this box, and I heard this noise and a soldier came in and, you know, "yakity, yak, what are you doing here?" And I made out I'd hurt myself, you know, groaning and all that and my hands up to my head. 'Oh,' I said, 'I fell. Hurt my head, you know.' But they didn't believe me; why should they with the bloody doors wide open?

So they brought me up, two or three soldiers, there was a sergeant and, you know, he knocked me about a bit and then he stood me in front of this brazier, put more wood on it, it was a cold day, and I had to stand right in front of this thing and I started singeing and burning, and smoke was coming up. I don't know what was burning, but something was. And I was coughing and spluttering.

And Cox came across. He tried to sort of say something. Then Bill Rowe came along and he started yammering at them in Japanese. And there's me still standing in front of this fire. Burning! And then they pulled me away from there and the sergeant hit me again, knocked me about a few times, yelled at me as they normally did. Then he gave me twenty fags and told me to clear off. But I was reported when I got back to the camp. Yamamoto had me

The Genki Boys

in. Smiled at me. But they made me kneel down, usual thing, they put the bamboo rod behind my knees, told me to sit on it. And after a bit I kept falling. You know how it is. No circulation."

These are remarkable stories and even my credulity was a little strained by them but in fact they were largely confirmed By Forrow (who has never met nor spoken to Henderson since they were both separately repatriated). In the first story the man with the knuckle end of pig was in fact him, not Bond. (The confusion in Henderson's mind is understandable - 50 years is a long time in which to carry accurate memories and Forrow, like Bond, was very tall.)

Forrow (photograph on page 60) writes:

"We were scouting round in the cookhouse of this large French liner the Japs had probably captured from French Indo China and opened a large refrigerator door and there, hanging all on its own, was a whole side of pork. We found a toilet nearby with cubicles and took the side of pork into the toilet and promptly cut the pig into manageable pieces. I ended up with the whole leg with the trotter resting in my neck and the end of the leg in my belly and carried on working for the rest of the day. Now I know how a pregnant lady feels."

As for the second story, he writes:

"We were on a large military transport and at Yasumi time Chic (sic) and I went to the toilet, ostensibly, but to scout around for the store. We wandered down a flight of wooden stairs and at the bottom was a heavily padlocked door which we opened with our lock picks. It was the main store filled with all the goodies, tinned stuff, cigarettes etc. and Chic kept watch while I went into the store to load up.
Whilst I was in the store Chic said the Japs were coming. I scurried to the back of the store and found a two foot square manhole with no cover on the floor which I promptly leapt into and dropped about fifteen feet into the propeller shaft tunnel. I made my way up through the engine room to join the rest of the PT lads around a fire still on Yasumi. I had no sooner settled down than there was a lot of military activity and a guard came over and

The Genki Boys

apparently asked our foreman if any one of us had been absent to which he answered 'No'. Our foreman was one of us being elderly and we always gave him some of our loot. Chic eventually joined us having been bruised up."

After this passage of time even to me it seems almost unbelievable that two small groups of European prisoners could, under the very noses of their captors, for so long run rampage through their ships and I find it quite inconceivable that had roles been reversed, had Japanese prisoners been working in a British or American dockyard they could have got away with one tenth of what the Genki Boys achieved.

Such accounts as Moulstone's and the two given above by no means exhaust examples of the Genki Boys looting exploits which could be given but out of a fund available I have limited myself to them for the reasons which follow. In Moulstone's case his stories were committed to writing and he was himself a participant and in the case of Henderson and Forrow I have selected them amongst others they have told me, because they are the only ones I have where two men, both regular Genki Boys, who have not spoken to nor met each other since the war was over, basically confirm what each has said.

Incidentally an amusing sidelight on these two remarkable men is that Henderson after the war became the North Shields Housing Manager and Forrow worked in the Hong Kong Treasury and was awarded the O.B.E. for his efforts; he now lives in England in a house named *Din Fong* - which, translated, means, he tells me, *Mad House!*.

I would very much like to have recounted stories which involved P.T.2 but I have resisted doing so because although, when I met some of them together recently at a Far East Prisoner of War Reunion held at Stratford on Avon, I begged members such as Batty, Bond and Halsall, to send me dictated or written accounts of their own exploits, and left them believing they were going to, subsequently they were to a man unwilling to respond and I think it would be wrong, after a lapse of more than fifty years and clearly against their wishes to rely purely on my own memory or on the memories of others. It is perhaps

The Genki Boys

sufficient to say that the experiences of the Genki Boys in P.T.2 were every bit as varied and hair-raising as those of their compatriots in P.T.1 and the risks they took as fearsome.

To close this saga of the Genki Boys and put their conduct towards their fellow prisoners into a proper perspective, the extent to which the thought of food filled our minds must not be forgotten. No topic occupied so great a proportion of conversation, no diary gave greater space to any other subject, no object compared with it in importance. Our minds were as haunted by it as are those of the libidinous by lust and the power-hungry by ambition. It stood apart with a mystical existence of its own which influenced behaviour within its own field much as does religion to the devout.

No doubt amongst the Genki Boys who are still alive there are some who, when they look back on those days and remember how well-fed and equipped they were compared with their compatriots, feel a twinge or two of conscience - but they were after all only a cross-section of members of the camp, itself a cross section of society, and there is no reason to believe that had a different dozen or so men been drafted into the P.T gangs instead of them their behaviour would have been all that different.

CHAPTER NINE

LIVING WITH THE JAPANESE

1.

Day began with Reveille at 5.15 a.m, roll call at 5.20, physical training from 5.20 to 5.30, breakfast at 5.30, fall in for work 6.20. and we left for the dockyard at 6.30. The march took about twenty minutes, the first part of it being along the edge of the sea. With the camp being on about the 39th parallel (roughly equivalent to Lisbon) the variation in sunrise was not particularly marked and my constant recollection is of looking from our island across to another whose skyline was sparse trees etched against a lightening sky. It was very beautiful. About halfway along the march the so-called road, undrained, unsurfaced, boobytrapped with potholes, turned inland through a cut in a low outcrop of hills which had until then bordered its western side and we saw the sea no more but skirted a foundry and casting shop known as Karoto before passing the *kempeitai's* guardroom and entering the dockyard. Ahead stretched the massive length of Hachi Dock, to the left and bordering the road the extensive woodyard and to our right the Canteen buildings and the main thoroughfare continuing into Habu the only town of consequence on Innoshima.

Having entered the yard we made our way to the Canteen where we had to rid ourselves of greatcoats (thin affairs hardly deserving of the name) if worn and then fall in again for *Taiso*. Taiso, which can be translated as 'gymnastics', was a set of physical jerks which never varied from beginning to end of war and, I understand, still continues in factories and so on to this day. It was done to music (the tune, quite a stirring one, runs through my head as I write) which at 7.00 a.m. blared out from

Living with the Japanese

loudspeakers through the length and breadth of Japan. It is a mind-bending thought to imagine the best part of one hundred million Japanese, men and women, young and old, hale and not so hale, swinging their trunks, bending their knees, whirling their arms in unison all the way from the northernmost tip of Hokkaido to the southernmost tip of Kyushu. (In a recent television programme on China, I discovered they do something of the same sort there and there are a *thousand* million Chinese!)

Every month we were, like all other workmen in the yard, issued with a work card which was stamped with an orange hieroglyph for each day's attendance. Wages were based on these cards as were also punishments for non-attendance. On the following page there is an example of one of these cards owned by Ken Forrow reproduced on to a sheet of paper with comments and signed by the Camp Commandant and the interpreters.

After Taiso, we handed in our working cards (which in the evening were returned stamped to prove we had worked that day) and were marched off by a guard and our civilian ganger. At 12.00 a.m. we were marched back to the Canteen for lunch and sat at both sides of very long tables with either an interpreter or a guard at the head of each. Food was brought from the camp on barrows by the cooks. At 12.40 we went back to work, finishing in the early days at 5.00 p.m. (The length of the day was continually being extended until towards the end of the war it finished at 7.00 p.m. or even later). We returned to the camp carrying on our shoulders offcuts from logs for the cookhouse fires in time for roll call at 5.45 p.m. (later this was taken at 7.00 p.m) a meal at 6.00 p.m. and lights out was at 9.00 p.m. Apart from three extra National holidays a year, there were originally two holidays each month but latterly we had only one day off in twenty-one. Theoretically there was no official rest during working hours but most foremen allowed fifteen minutes morning and afternoon for smoking and some, as has been explained, considerably more.

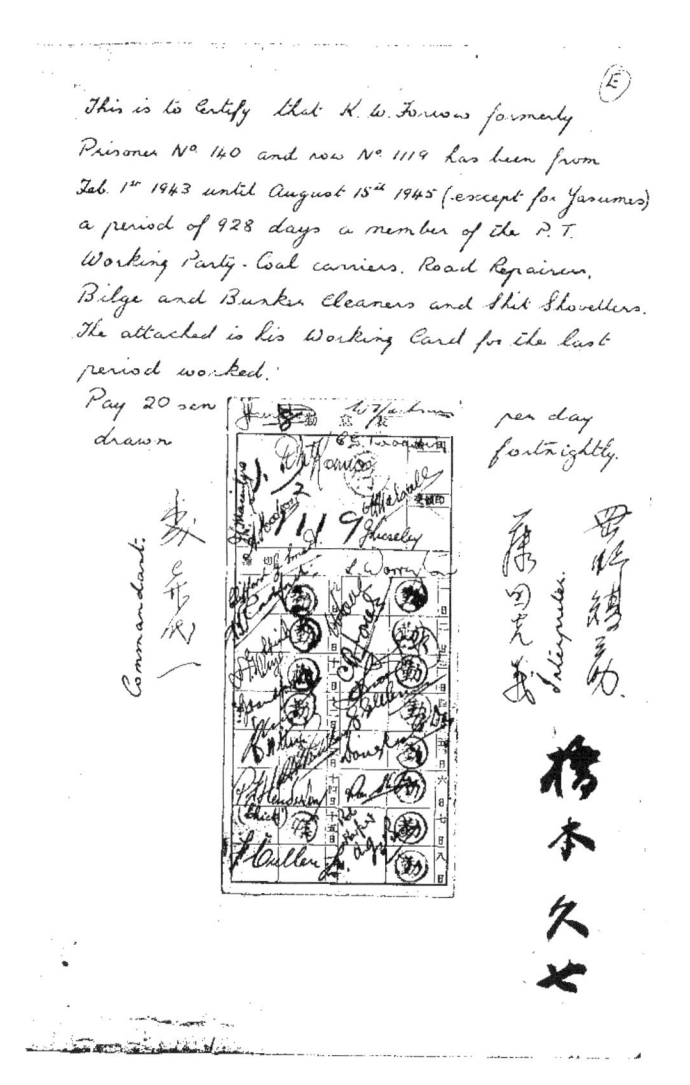

Ken Forrow's last work card.

On holidays, *(Yasumis)* Reveille was at 7.00 a.m. followed by roll call which was normally taken by one of the permanent camp staff supported by a bevy of temporary guards who were changed at monthly intervals and whose approach was

Living with the Japanese

signalled by a loud initial shout of Tenko! from the end of corridor. It was then the job of the 'Room Leaders' (I was Room Leader of Room Two) to see that 'all men' (a favourite Japanese expression) assembled in a 'U' around the room and, when the posse arrived, call the room to attention with a cry of *Chutski!* (more accurately *Kiyo tsu kete!*)and order them to salute: accurately, *Keirei!*. After the salute had been returned you ordered them to be as they were - *Nauri!* - and then number - *Bango!* This was a performance which greatly appealed to the Japanese and it was meant to be done loudly and at lightning speed. So at the call of *'Bango'*, off we would go starting with the man nearest the door across from me and travelling like a fusillade around the room: *Ichi! Ni! Sang! Shi! Go!* etc all the way round to me - *Sang ju ni!* (thirty-two) or some lesser number if any men were sick *(Byoki)* or in the cookhouse, which I would explain. This performance was of course not only carried out on Yasumis but twice each day, morning and evening. Having checked against a list, the posse would continue along the passage to all the other rooms.

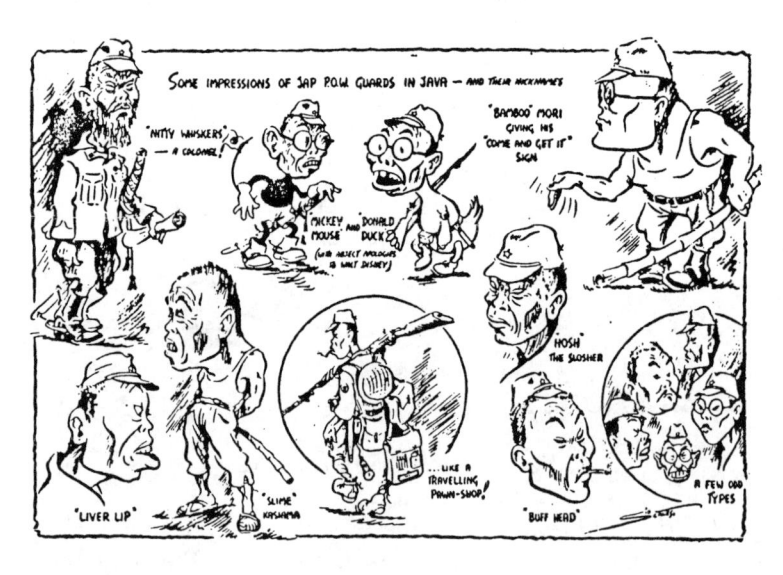

We may not have had these particular guards, but we certainly had look-alikes!

Living with the Japanese

Generally speaking after the first year or so through which hale and hearty men left presumably to serve as cannon fodder, the permanent staff were not changed greatly through the whole time we were on Innoshima. Except when taking roll call, carrying out searches, making proclamations or punishing offenders, they left us alone whereas the monthly intake used their spells of duty wandering up and down the passage. Initially these men were soldiers, often wounded, some even one-armed or one-eyed, who had served their active time; latterly we had others employed by the dockyard who were dressed in a quasi military uniform whom we called *jeeps* for whom the official title was, I understand, *gunzoku*.

On Yasumi Days one never knew when the Japanese would take it into their heads to have us all out working on some job in the camp, doing taiso, parading to witness a punishment or the awarding of prizes to good workers, having our fingernails and toenails ('tunnels' the Camp Commandant called them) inspected, listening to a pep talk or enduring some endless announcement. But it is fair to say that on the whole we were left alone to do laundering as best we could without soap, to cobble up disintegrating clothes, to bring out the year old razor blade and sharpen it up on the inside of a tumbler, to de-flea our beds and de-louse our uniforms - in a word to utilise the rare day off to mitigate discomfort and restore a degree of self-respect.

It was on Yasumi Days that the difference between the two groups in the camp was most apparent. A visitor glancing in a Hong Kong billet, on say a cold winter Yasumi Day with the stoves as yet unlit, would have seen a group of well-dressed and often well shod men mostly between thirty and forty years of age wearing good khaki battledress, or cardigans perhaps, often with some sort of choker at the neck, many with woollen gloves or mitts and with forage caps or balaclavas, lying on their tatamis reading books or newspapers, writing up diaries, sketching, seated at tables playing bridge or chess or engaged in earnest conversation. Had he not known he was in a prison camp he might easily have assumed that here were temporary quarters for some officers awaiting the completion of their mess. A few strides along the passage would have presented him with quite a different picture. Here the men would, with only a few exceptions, be youngsters in the earliest twenties for the most part wearing the dull green padded breeches of Japanese Army uniforms, tunics buttoned high up at the neck and Army caps. They would have no gloves, or at best the remains of working gloves made of layers of waste materials roughly stitched together. A book would be an exception and card games if played would be hearts or solo. There would be a general feeling that this billet was far less active and far less furnished for the shelves above the Raffs sleeping spaces bore little while those of the Volunteers being better filled hid more of the plywood while their tables prior to meals had more homely and varied touches from the bowls and cups they had brought with them.

In summer, or if the stoves were lit, the differences while less marked would still be apparent for the variety of lightweight wear the Volunteers could boast: shirts and shorts and even bathing trunks, a towel thrown carelessly across a shoulder, imaginative touches which made each man an individual, contrasted with the dull uniformity of men who at best could choose between a Jap issue shirt or some ragged remnant which elsewhere would not even have been pressed into service as a duster. And if when it was warm the contrast in activity was less this brought with it no increase in communion between the two sections of the camp; men who had worked beside each other for days on end in the dockyard, kept themselves apart.

For all that they were eagerly anticipated, winter Yasumi days were disappointing. If left alone there were fourteen hours punctuated by three meals between Reveille and Lights Out to be filled. Fires were only allowed for two months of the year and in any case when permitted were not to be lit until approval had been given, fuel, like every other commodity in Japan, being in short supply. And although there were the essential jobs of mending and dhobying to be done, there was little pleasure doing these with fingers numb with cold and stomachs crying out for food.

But in summer it was another matter. In summer one could take a torn shirt into the woodyard abutting the north end of the camp and sit on the stone sea wall while one cobbled up the rents with twine drawn from paper sacks. Immediately to the left would be the dockyard of Mitsunosho, a friendly little yard with one small, dry dock; it would be still and silent for Yasumi Days were common throughout the whole country; to the right, (as can be seen from the illustration below), the line of billets, two-storied, pine-planked with sliding windows, half masked by a fence whose evenness was disfigured by blankets and sheets hung over it to air; in front of the huts, central to them, a set of wide, crumbling, stone steps tumbling on to a rock-strewn sandy beach which had once given access to an iron jetty, its three spans supported on stone piers but now unusable, all rusted through, the first span quite collapsed; below the fence a high sea wall with orifices for drainage from the rough road passing by the camp, which spouted water hugely when the rain was heavy; ahead tranquil beauty - a shimmering sea, backed by overlapping heat-misted mountains between which were wide twisting openings which gave the impression this was the open sea; in the foreground, green and yellow islands and the jetty of Mitsunosho village.

A sketch of the camp by Coxhead done from Mitsunosho direction.

Living with the Japanese

Even on Yasumi Days the Inland Sea was busy. Big ships would come into view starting as splodges of distant smoke which steadily developed into aircraft carriers, liners, battered cargo ships - nearly all heading for the Habu Dockyard. And as well as the big ships there were the smaller craft, scores of them near and far, mostly square-sailed with the canvas stiffened by horizontal spars giving a fan effect. These were the fishermens' boats or ferries plying between the islands. Except when a warship passed, this was a peacetime scene and it was good to be in the comforting sun with the essential things one had to do no longer chores but pleasant occupations.

2

Mail was of course of huge importance and all but a very few of us received some during our stint with the Japanese, some, including myself, a very considerable amount in both postcard and letter form. Whereas most probably the majority of relatives of the Volunteers had from the very beginning a fairly good idea what had happened to them, this was not so in the case of the Raffs who had simply vanished off the face of the earth.

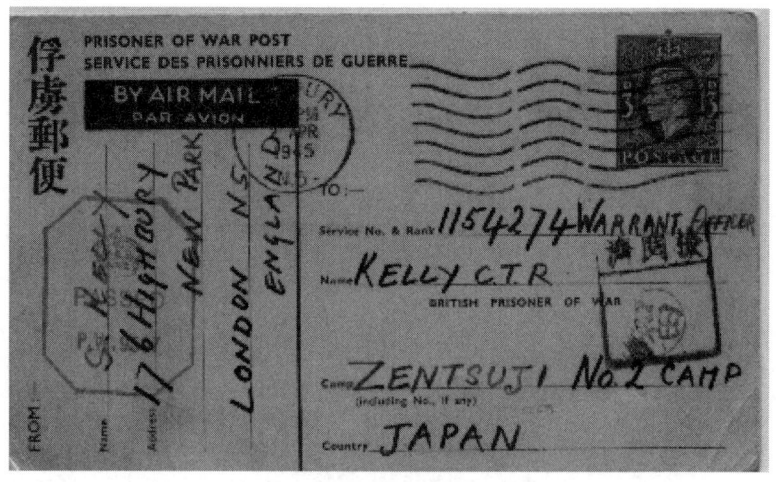

A typical lettercard.

Living with the Japanese

My parents, for example, had no idea whether or not I was still alive until well into 1943 and probably learnt I had survived and was a prisoner at about the same time the first card our captors allowed us to send arrived with them. This was a stereotyped affair which said: *'I am fit and well and working for pay. My health is (blank). Please see that (blank) is taken care of.''*- followed by a signature. You filled in the blanks as you chose and as you thought appropriate to make sure the card was sent. Return mail started to arrive early in 1944 and sometimes came in huge batches with lucky recipients perhaps receiving half a dozen cards or letters at the same time.

Forming as it did a bridge between the life now being lived and the life one had once lived and hoped to live again, even to those who were unlucky, its arrival was always a tremendous tonic and contents were exchanged and discussed at length. There was a certain amount of censoring (both by British and Japanese authorities) but not overmuch.

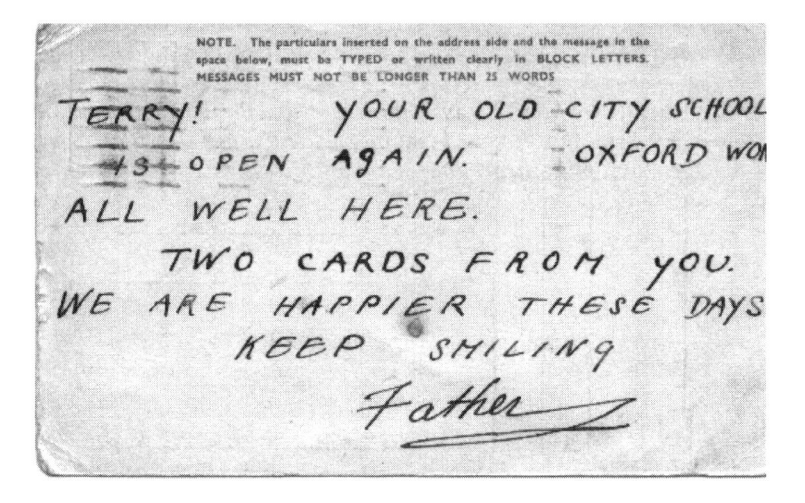

> NOTE. The particulars inserted on the address side and the message in the space below, must be TYPED or written clearly in BLOCK LETTERS. MESSAGES MUST NOT BE LONGER THAN 25 WORDS
>
> TERRY! YOUR OLD CITY SCHOOL
> IS OPEN AGAIN. OXFORD WON
> ALL WELL HERE.
> TWO CARDS FROM YOU.
> WE ARE HAPPIER THESE DAYS
> KEEP SMILING
> Father

Photographs were sometimes included and attempts were of course occasionally made to convey news of how the war was going but on the whole writers were sensible enough to realise that doing this put the whole card or letter at risk and that

Living with the Japanese

anyway news of the family and life at home was of more importance.*'Your old city school'* refers to the City of London School where I was educated and has obviously been mentioned to convey that the war was nearly won and London was getting back to normal.

One very amusing letter arrived within a sweater which was part of a small consignment of American clothing received in midsummer, 1944:

>July 29th, 300 Park Ave, Freeport. N.Y.

Hallo, there!

Just dropped in to say hello for a minute. I've just finished this sweater and though I didn't mind knitting it, I'm really much happier about the whole thing now that it's over. It's not the sweater I mind so much as the sweltering, and I do mean hot, weather that makes me feel that nobody in his right mind would ever wear the thing. However, perhaps it's a slight bit cooler where you are - and please don't think I'm as much of a picklepuss as I sound. Now that I speak of it, I wonder where you are and what sort of a time you are having, where you're from - all that stuff. Please don't think me rude when I say that if you'd like to get letters now and then - well, I'd love to write them and maybe this sweater could be an introduction,

>*'Bye now,*

>*(sgd) Catherine Eddy.*
>*(I'm still a Miss and just 21)*

I don't know whether the man who drew the sweater in the lot, ever wrote to thank Miss Eddy for it but receiving this information only fairly recently, I tried to contact her. But not surprisingly, nearly fifty years having passed, she had long since married and moved away, apparently to Massachusetts. The current resident of 300, Park Avenue, Lorraine Harwood, most kindly went to immense trouble to pass on my letter but unavailingly. Yet I was almost lucky for it seems that Miss Eddy, hoping to come in and have a look at the house in which she grew up, had actually called about a year before unfortunately at a time when the present occupant was away. So the trail has gone cold - but who knows? Perhaps one day she may make another visit to Freeport - or perhaps someone who reads this book may be able to advise me where to contact her.

On Innoshima, books were almost as prized as letters and one of the few specific purposes which brought Volunteers into a Raff billet was to exchange one. To be the owner of a book (or for that matter a pack of cards) was to lift you above the general rut; you were in demand. Books were priceless; even the most inveterate smokers resisted selling them for cigarettes. When I left Java, I had a book. I have no idea how I came by it and it was a trashy novel I thought so little of that I lent it to someone, on the Dai Nichi I suppose, and promptly forgot all about it. Later I often saw it as it made the rounds; but it had passed through so many ownerships by then that there was no question of claiming it as mine. Lending that book and not taking care to get it back was the most extravagant thing I ever did. I had cut myself off from reading for the rest of the war. I had torn up my library ticket.

No obstacles were placed in the way of practising religion. Protestants and Catholics were allowed a room in the unused double-storied hut in which to erect an altar. Japanese staff were supposed to be present at services but never came until our Thanksgiving service for Victory! On the next page a sketch is included of the Catholic chapel. The Protestant chapel was a simpler affair, the altar being a table with a sheet draped over it. It served another purpose, doubling up as a structure under which illicit cooking could be done. One of the Volunteers, Lamb, spent a lot of his time on his knees before it, seemingly in contemplation of the life to come but in fact lost in anticipation of more immedaite joys - the meal he was busy cooking at the time. Sadly he got caught by a guard when parting the sheet to see how the pot was doing and, as Forrow puts it: "That was the end of the altar and nearly the end of Lamb!"

The Catholic chapel of St Francis Xavier.

Generally speaking one worked through Sundays and days of religious festivals unless they happened to coincide with dockyard holidays but even so within their limitations Christmas Days were taken as having the same significance they would have had elsewhere as can be seen from the excerpt taken from my Log Book covering Christmas Day, 1943.

Living with the Japanese

<u>Xmas Day 1943</u>

By far the best day in nearly two years of prisoner of war existence. Our billet decorated with small Xmas trees laden with brass turnings and candles, with branches and greetings festooned around the walls looked very pleasant. On Christmas Eve the choir put in some carol singing outside and the rooms were humming with activity as trifles, cakes and pies were made from the Red Cross parcels that came so opportunely.

An extraordinary difference in atmosphere from last year when there was so much sickness. Up to then so far as I recall seven out of our meagre hundred had died miserably and Gibson lay in agony shrieking horribly to pass away thankfully on Boxing Day.

Unfortunately the 25th was no holiday and we were obliged to go to the docks to work but the Xmas spirit was so prevalent that our spirits were not a whit dampened. On return a service was held to a very good attendance. The church, fashioned with raised forms covered with sheets as an altar with brass candlesticks someone had managed to save from the wreck, with inverted tatami carpet and pews of forms covered with the same material was very peaceful.

My morning menu:

Soup (only cabbage, I fear)
Rice and sardines
Prunes and cream
Tea (with milk and sugar!!!)

Quite unparalleled in 21 months!.

We astounded the locals with carol singing at the docks. (See later) Two years of this miserable existence have not so far broken our spirits, thank God! Perhaps the dock people, Takizawa in particular, realised what Christmas meant to us for our old man, Murakami, packed us up shortly after ten a.m. for the morning and we did little in the afternoon, sitting by a fire (for it was very cold) leisurely sawing through a rail.

Lunch was no great feast, merely carrot tops and daikon soup and rice - but with visions of an orgy ahead we were not depressed.

Back at last, a wonderfully hot bath awaited us and, thoroughly warmed, we prepared for dinner. Our tables, resplendent with

Living with the Japanese

white sheets and trees and photographs looked inviting.

My Christmas dinner - without peer since March 8th, 1942:

Soup. (Just vegetables with a slight salmon flavour)
Fish and rice.
Cottage Pie. (Sweet potatoes, bully and M & V par excellence)
Milk Pudding. (Self-made: rice, cream, butter, raisins, orange juice and peel and sugar)
Raisin wine.brewed for nearly four months out of the last parcel - excellent and quite heady.

The Japanese gave us all a very generous Christmas present:

50 Cigarettes, a bar of soap, a dozen oranges, toilet paper, curry powder, boot blacking and dry green tea

After dinner, feeling full, we turned the lights out and lit the candles and had a sing song followed by a game of House! ('Bingo') The room looked very pretty and albeit the evening was very cold and fires had made no appearance, it was I think to all a most pleasant and memorable Xmas.

I hope our people and friends of whom we were all thinking so much had relatively as happy and cheerful a Christmastide.

With regard to the carol singing at the docks mentioned earlier, this was preceded by carol singing at 4.30 a.m. in the camp led by Cox's choir and on arrival at the docks the choir at a pre-arranged signal stepped out astounding the Japanese guards, foremen and workmen around us and led us in a rendering of 'Silent Night.' which was not inappropriate for at 7.00 a.m. it was still quite dark. It was certainly a very moving, and inspiring moment.

3

Cox's choir was a splendid group culled equally from Raffs and Volunteers. Their repertoire was of necessity limited and perhaps all the more appreciated because it was so. Particular favourites were 'When the foeman bears his steel' and 'The Soldier's Chorus' from Gounod's 'Faust'. There were two excellent singers whose solos became the recognized camp songs. One (written by a prisoner of war in Hong Kong and invariably sung by John Furnell) was unashamedly sentimental:

John Furnell who it was believed had been accepted by the Japanese to become one of our medical orderlies because of his fine singing voice.

That Distant Day

Strange things may happen as the world comes and goes
The heart of the world whispers warning
Like the stardust at night with its deep purple light
Brings an echo of that distant dawning.

That distant day will come my sweet
And bring you close to me
The sky is a rapture
Of gold tinted hue
The birds will sing a melody

Living with the Japanese

For me - and for you.
Night brings an ache, but patiently
I look for that dawn and always say
The hours that pass so blue
Only bring me closer to,
That distant, that certain distant day.

Edward Tandy - who wrote both words and music of the second song 'Roll on that Boat'. He was a brother of the well-known English actress, Jessica Tandy.

The second song, 'Roll on That Boat', was written towards the

Living with the Japanese

end of 1944

<u>Roll on that Boat. First Version.</u>

There's a ship that plies the ocean, she's a ship of mystery,
For there's nobody knows her tonnage or her crew
Or her port of registry.
She may be an ocean liner,
Or she may be an eight knot tramp
But to me she'll be, the finest ship at sea
When I walk up her gangway plank.
Roll on that boat,
Roll on that boat,,
Roll on the day when we hear the captain say
Full speed ahead and our ship gets under way
Roll on that boat,
Any old tub that will float,
For our troubles will be over, and life have just begun
When we sight the cliffs of Dover, gleaming in the sun
Roll on that day, when we're on our homeward way.

In the following year after intensive bombing by American Super Fortresses (or B. 29s for which the Japanese translation is B Ni Ju Ku). - the words were revised!:

<u>Roll on that Boat. SecondVersion.</u>

Ships may ply the ocean, but a ship's no good to me.,
For on the day we win the war and they open up the door,
I shall want to be home for tea!
You can go by P & O or by Cunarder,
Lounging in a deep deck chair,
But I've set my heart, on a flying start,
And I'm going home by air!
B Ni Ju Ku,
B Ni Ju Ku,
Need you be curious to know
Why the fastest ship afloat will be too darn slow,
And a B Ni Ju Ku,
Is the only kind of transport that will do,
For we'll set off in the dawn,
And by dusk the following night,

Living with the Japanese

We'll see london stretched beneath us
In a gleaming pool of light,
B Ni Ju Ku, we are waiting here for you.

As one of the only means remaining through which feelings could be expressed and a life suddenly brutally denied reached out for, composing poetry was a common exercise and it would not be difficult to compile a substantial anthology dealing with prisoner of war emotions for even those who did not compose, if they had any sort of notebook, almost invariably collected.

In the early days following the arrival of the Volunteers, concerts were not infrequent but latterly they were rarely staged. Free time was precious, there were chores to be done, energy was lacking and whether it be from dockyard injuries, beri beri, skin disorders, stomach troubles or what have you, there were few not nursing some complaint. All concerts were held in one of the empty rooms to which benches were moved across for seating on one side with the raised tatami dais on the other acting as a stage. The Japanese sometimes attended and indeed most of the sketches relied for their humour on lampooning our captors who were extraordinarily dense when it came to comprehending the gales of laughter which followed lines or jokes in which slang Japanese words or expressions were contained.

I had written a few sketches and so on and in 1945 I was prevailed upon not only to provide further contributions but also to become an impresario and organise a concert myself. I designed and prepared a programme which I still have and although it was badly stained by someone spilling something on it, it remains legible and I reproduce it below. The most remarkable thing about this programme is the date "Yasume Day, Aug 14th 1945" **(the very day before the war ended)** and the statement on it: "Positively the First and Last Performance!"

INNOSHIMA
PRISONER OF WAR
CAMP
PROGRAMME

POSITIVELY
THE FIRST AND LAST
PERFORMANCE.

YASUME DAY
AUG 14th 1945.

There was an opening chorus of 'Roll on that Boat' followed by 'Sigh no more, Ladies', 'Ye Banks and Braes', 'In old Madrid',

Living with the Japanese

'Because' and of course 'That Distant Day'' These were shared between one of our medical orderlies, John Furnell and another Volunteer, Kenneth Keen.

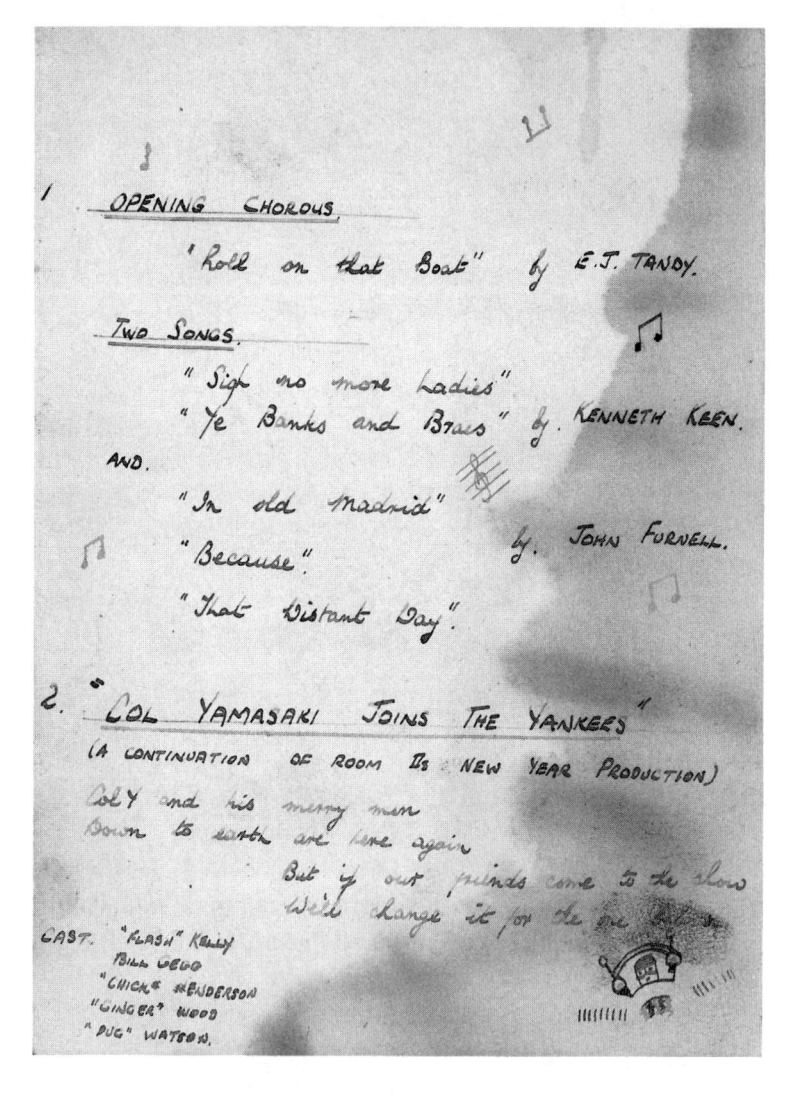

Part of the programme

Living with the Japanese

The opening sketch *'Colonel Yamasaki Joins the Yankees'* had a note beneath the title in parentheses: *'A Continuation of Room 2's NewYear Production'* followed by some doggerel:

Colonel Y and his merry men
Down to earth are here again.
But if our friends come to the show,
We'll change it for the one below.

(The one below was entitled *'Culbertson to Love Time'* which was a bawdy sketch based on a couple making love on their honeymoon night who are separated only by a thin partition from a bridge four with their words overlapping with consequent reactions - there were, I see, three Volunteers and three Raffs taking part) It is clear from the doggerel that I felt that even our dozy captors could hardly miss the points made in the Yamasaki sketch. The piece was performed in two halves the first at Xmas 1945 with the three principal members of the cast (both R.A.F. and H.K.V.D.C.) seated in line astern on a bench.

The sketch is appended below, not with any claim of literary merit but because it does encapsulate several things: the morale of British prisoners of war even after three and a half years loss of freedom, (in the Volunteers' case nearly four years), the shortages and the shoddiness of almost everything in Japan by the time the war was drawing to a close; the contempt in which we held our captors and our disbelief in their high-flown claims of loyalty and courage.

Colonel Yamasaki Joins The Yankees

Scene: Japanese fighter station operations' room.

Telephone rings

Operations: Hallo Station XXX, to this there's no preamble,
              Those dirty Yanks are on the way,
              Get ready for a scramble.
              They're coming from the east and west,
              Heading for Japan,
              With about 100 fighters and 200 *bakudan* (bombers)
              What is your squadron status?

Living with the Japanese

        How many aircraft have you got?
        You'd better get them mobile,
        You're going to need the lot!

Col Yamasaki: This is Colonel Yamasaki, we did have quite a few
But the Yanks paid us a visit and left us only two.
Now my riggers came from dockyards and so did every fitter
So they went and lit a fire, because the day was bitter,
They went and lit a fire and the petrol tanks got hot,
And then one kite exploded,
And now we've only *stot!* (Slang for 'one')

Operations: Well get into your aircraft, *speedo* get away,
Sing Banzai for the Emperor, today is Rescript Day.
                                           (Note 1)

Col Yamasaki: Corporal Yamamoto, *asmaré* (fall in) my crew,
We'll have a *Bango* (numbering) quickly,
We've got a job to do.

Cpl Yamamoto: Asmaré!

Enter Sergeants Yamaguchi and Fujiwang

Col Yamasaki: Sergeant Yamaguchi and Sergeant Fujiwang,
   Chutski!   (stand to attention)
   Kiri!   (salute)
   Nauri!   (as you were)
   Bango!   (number)

Sgt Yamaguchi   *Ich!*   (one)

Sgt Fujiwang: *Ni!*   (two)

Col Yamasaki: *Sang!*   (three)

Col Yamasaki: Sergeant you're my nav man, give me all you've got,
The wind speed and the ceiling,
Where there's cloud and where's there's not.

Sgt Yamaguchi: Well Ops are on a *Yasumi,* (holiday)
So there isn't any griff
But there isn't any cloud about,
And the wind is just a sniff.

Col Yamasaki: Fujiwang, my gunner, have you bags of ammunition?
B Ni Ju Ku's (B. 29s) are on the prowl
On this hectic expedition.

Sgt Fujiwang: We used our ammo yesterday, so ersatz must suffice,
But don't despair, Commander,
We've *genki* balls of rice!   (Note 2)

Living with the Japanese

Col Yamasaki:
: We've got a squadron scarmble,
We're leaving right away
Here's your *hara kir*i daggers,   (Note 3)
In case we boob oday.
Corporal where's my fitter?

Enter Fitter

Col Yamasaki:
: I want my aircraft quick!

Fitter:
: (slowly) Well I've got to find the prop, Sir,
And I've got to fix the stick
The tailplane's fallen off, Sir,
And the engine isn't there,
But by dint of nails and hammer,
You soon shall take the air.

Fitter hammers on various parts. The Colonel and his crew climb aboard the form and make exaggerated motions of taking off.

Col Yamasaki:
: Hallo, Station XXX, we're fllying o'er the sea,
At a height of near 2,000 and a speed of 83.

Operations:
: Steer a course of 45,
Keep your eyes skinned on the blue,
They're using Lockheed Lightnings
And *taxan* (many) *Ni Ju Kus* (B. 29s)

Col Yamasaki:
: My gunner and observer,
Scan the skies with might and main
And for Pete's sake let me know quick
If you sight a single plane!

Sgt Yamaguchi
: Colonel Yamasaki, I see them in the sun,
Ich, ni, Hirohito save us! 500 if there's one!

Col Yamasaki:
: Sergeant Yamaguchi, why that dismal wail?

Sgt Yamaguchi:
: Dismal wail, Gor blimey - there's fifty on out tail!

Col Yamasaki:
: Well don't despair my comrades,
Though things don't seem too hot,
The Emperor is with us,
And the Yank's a rotten shot.

Sgt Fujiwang:
: Colonel please excuse me, his shooting's not so rank
The dirty bastard's got us,
In our *migi* (starboard) petrol tank,
Propellor's fallen off, Sir, and the engine's holed a bit,
You can tell your bloody Emperor,
We're really in the shit!

Col Yamasaki:
: Well draw your daggers comrades,

Living with the Japanese

                Slit your bellies with a smile,
                We all will be promoted,
                Like those on Attu Isle.   (Note 4)

Sgt Fujiwang: What slit out guts? Not likely!

Sgt Yamaguchi: That looks alright in print
But what the hell does it get me
If I make myself extinct!

Sgt Fujiwang: That old Bushido spirit, is a lot of Tommy Rot,
Tojo didn't slit himself,
When he got in a spot!   (Note 5)

Sgt Yamaguchi: I'm going to join the Yankees,
Of that there is no doubt,
I'm going to leave this aircraft,
Where's my bloody parachout?

Sgt Fujiwang: I'm going to be a *furyo*, (prisoner)
And watch my body swell
For they've lots of Red Cross Parcels
And *taxan* meat as well!

Sgt Yamaguchi: To the land where there's no *Bango!*
No *Asmaré* to fear,
So *Sayonara!* (Goodbye!) Great Japan,
I see my future clear,

Col Yamasaki:: I think that you've got something,
In fact you make me ponder,
I think I'll jump out with you,
To that great land over yonder,
I too will feed on parcels,
I too will swell my guts,
And you can stick your Fujiyama   (Note 6)
Where the monkey sticks his nuts!

(This ended the sketch at Christmas 1945. What follows was the second part of the sketch which was performed the very evening before V.J.Day!)

Col Yamasaki: Remember the instructions we learnt at flying school,
When you juimp, count *ich, ni, sang*,
Before you make the pull.
You know the squadron saying,
If it don't open get a swap,
But in Japan there's *taxan nai* (Nothing)
So I guess we'll simply drop.
Well best of luck my comrades, remember *ich, ni ,sang*
Let's hope for better fortune,
Than those at Palembang!   (Note 7)

All bale out

Living with the Japanese

Sgt Yamaguchi;   I'm falling mighty *speedo*
                 That sea looks hard as rocks,
                 I wish I had the paper brolly,
                 I used in Habu Docks.

Sgt Fujiwang: Banzai! Mine has opened.
                 Tho' it's mighty hard to tell,
                 It seems the *haikyu* (rationing) must apply
                 To parachutes as well!

All land in sea.

Sgt Yamaguchi: This sea is mighty *samui* (cold)
                 This really is a shocker,
                 I never thought I'd meet my end,
                 In Davy Jones' locker.

Col Yamasaki: Scan the horizon comrades,
                 Or shortly we shall sink,
                 Unless some Yankee doughboy,
                 Can save us from the drink.

Enter sailor in boat

Doughboy: I looks to starboard and to port.
                 Say what's that on the lee?
                 Looks like three doity bundles, floating on the sea!
                 But jeeze, I see they show some life,
                 A shipwrecked crew perhaps?
                 Well damn my soul and blast my eyes,
                 A gang of doity Japs!
                 I guess I'd better rescue them, that old *esprit de corps*,
                 Is something that we're suckers for,
                 In times of peace or war.
                 So up your come you blighters,
                 It's lucky that I saw you,
                 I'll take you to our admiral,
                 He'll have some questions for you!

Sgt Yamaguchi: I'm Sergeant Yamaguchi

Sgt Fujiwang: I'm Sergeant Fujiwang

Col Yamasaki: I'm Colonel Yamasaki,
                 The aircraft *ichiban*! (Number one)

Doughboy: (Hauling them aboard) Cut out all that bullshit,
                 You're just three doity Nips,
                 Your rising sun won't rise no more,
                 It's heading for eclipse.

Enter Admiral.

Living with the Japanese

Doughboy: Admiral, here's three prisoners,
Tho' somewhat doubtful booty,
Yamasaki, Fujiwang
And Sergeant Yamagooti.

Admiral: Now, Colonel, you're a fighter pilot,
So will you please explain,
Why when we saunter o'er Japan,
We see no fighter plane?

Col Yamasaki: I see our tactics fox you,
But orders are today,
That if your planes are in the west,
We head the other way

Admiral: Well Colonel Yamasaki, tell me what you do,
When you hear the *keikaikeiho* (air raid warning)
And spot the *Ni Ju Ku*. (B 29)

Col Yamasaki: When we spot the *Ni Ju Ku*
And hear the bombs'commotion,
Why then you see the Nippon man
 Jump smartly into motion.
You see him running here and there,
You never see him still,
And like a mole he takes to ground
Or burrows in a hill.

Admiral: Well what about your rationing?
From all the tales I hear,
In Japan there's *taxan nai*,
And what there is, is dear.

Sgt Yamaguchi: We`ration boots and shirts and hats
And rice and beer and socks.
The only thing the *haikyu* misses,
 Is working in the docks.

Admiral: Ah, working! Yes! Well let me see,
Your men of course are keen,
They work all day from dawn to dusk,
And shirking's never seen?

Sgt Fujiwang: You've got the wrong conception of how we go to war,
If ever you are in the docks you'll hear a mighty roar,
But don't let me deceive you,
That's not of busy slips,
That roar's the snore of countless men,
Sleeping in the ships.

Admiral: What then are Nippon's chances
Of winning in this fight?
Have you the ships, the planes, the men

Living with the Japanese

                Against the Allied might?

Col Yamasaki:	Of men of course we had enough until you bombed a lot But now they're thinned like cabbage seedlings In Smithy's garden plot! (Note 8) Our ships are few and short of oil And what we have aren't good, Since '44 we've had no iron, So we've built them out of wood. But most of all we feel the dearth in the aircraft stakes, We've got some wooden biplanes We keep for old time' sake. Our Navy 0 (Zero) we think would do If the wings would stay attached! (Note 9) And bombers? Well, we had a few, But they've all been body-crashed! (Note10)
Admiral:	Well thanks for all the gen you've given, You've put my mind at rest, And when the war comes to an end, You'll come off second-best. So here boys, take these daggers, And so avoid disgrace, But do the deed away from here. Don't clutter up the place.
Japs together:	What slit our guts, not likely, We've got saner views We want to go on living, So we simply must refuse.
Col Yamasaki:	No, please to take us prisoner, We'll work hard to a man., If you give us Red Cross Parcels Like those in Great Japan.
Admiral:	Just as I thought! You've got no guts, You haven't got a bit, Here give 'em spades and shovels, And make 'em shovel shit! And if you catch 'em slacking, No mercy to the swines, Cut their tobacco ration And SEND THEM TO THE MINES! (Note 11)

<u>Notes</u>

Note 1: The Imperial Rescript. This was the Japanese explanation of their reasons for declaring war and a statement of war aims. It was read over the radio on the eighth day of

Living with the Japanese

every month, the eighth being the monthly anniversary of the commencement of hostilities.

Note 2: This business of throwing rice balls at enemy aircraft to bring them down when ammunition was exhausted was continually repeated with all seriousness in *The Mainichi* and in *The Nippon Times*.

Note 3: *Hara kiri* can be translated literally as 'belly cut'. While accepting it was a method of committing suicide practised by zealots, on the basis of our experience of the average Japanese we were very doubtful as to whether the vast majority of them would have contemplated doing so.

Note 4: Attu Island was the most easterly island of the Aleutian chain of islands and was the first occupied territory to be taken back by the Americans. After a fierce naval bombardment it took 20,000 American troops and three weeks of fierce fighting to subdue 2,000 Japanese, not one of whom was found alive. All were posthumously elevated two ranks.

Note 5: This is correct. In spite of being disgraced and his honour therefore irredeemably impugned, General Tojo did not commit *hara-kiri*.

Note 6: Fujiyama with an all but perfect conical shape is not only the best known of all Japanese mountains but has an almost spiritual significance.

Note 7: The attack on Palembang in Sumatra was preceded by a Japanese paratroop drop which has been covered in detail in author's *Battle for Palembang* (published by Kimber in 1985 and in paperback by Arrow Books in 1991 under title *Hurricane in Sumatra*.) Many of the paratroopers were killed.

Note 8: Late in the war, a man named Smith conceived the idea of growing vegetables in a patch of waste ground adjacent to the camp. Unfortunately his seedlings were killed when in an air attack bombs straddled the camp and sea water was thrown over them.

Note 9: The Navy O (better known to the general public as the Zero) was poorly built and if overstressed in the habit of losing its wings as I myself observed during a low level attack on Palembang.

Note 10: It was claimed that rather than allow themselves to fail (or to be taken prisoner) Japanese pilots would 'body crash' their machines - a claim taken by us all as being highly suspect but to a considerable degree supported as we were later to discover by the numerous *kamikaze* attacks on Allied naval vessels. It remained a matter of doubt with many who were inclined to the view that most at least of the pilots who killed themselves in this way were either locked into machines with insufficient fuel to do more than reach their objective or threatened with death if they returned.

Note 11: This was the constantly repeated threat as to what would happen to us if we failed to work hard enough!

5.

The diversity of skills displayed in prison camps was remarkable. One found amongst our one hundred and eighty odd men, any number who could play a part in a sketch with competence and many who were very good indeed while the choir, numbering about thirty, was superb. We had composers and artists and those with the ingenuity to invent complicated mechanical contraptions to assist men who had been injured and for whom the Japanese provided no equipment. Most found themselves capable of carving such things as pipes and a few discovered an ability they had not realised they possessed and made the most delightful objects with the most basic of tools - for example a model submarine, perfect in all its details from a lump of wood and pieces of metal picked up in the dockyard. The chess set Coxhead and I used was hand-carved.

Anything that might conceivably be of value was retained.

Living with the Japanese

Flotsam cast up on the beach was collected as was the string which closed cement sacks. Powdered milk tins (Klim Tins) from Red Cross parcels were kept to serve as cooking pots and the best parts of disintegrating shirts to serve as flannels. Clogs were carved out of bits of wood, socks whose legs had parted from their feet were sewn together, woolly caps fashioned from remains of pullovers.

Making these things helped pass empty hours. One yearned for Yasumis, yet when they came faced the problem of how to fill them. It is perhaps not surprising that men without cards or books collected menus which there was not the least hope of enjoying until the war was over. One could set oneself tasks such as learning rudimentary Japanese grammar and the fifty-one syllables of *Katakana* and *Hiragana* but, thinking only in terms of leaving Japan as far behind them as possible, few availed themselves of the opportunity. Many fell back on reading and re-reading the two or three letters, sometimes of scant importance, they had found themselves with when taken prisoner. When newspapers started arriving they were of tremendous value but from D Day onwards they abruptly ceased; fortunately for many the hole was plugged by the coincident arrival of mail which came in ever increasing quantities so that by the end only four men had received no communication of any sort. The most unfortunate were those whose relatives were in Hong Kong or Shanghai as very little mail was received from these parts; on the other hand remittances of money through the International Red Cross came to a few from Hong Kong and from nowhere else and although of little value, by its reminder that another fuller world existed, boosted morale.

In the dockyard, where the greater part of the time was spent, faced with ten hours ahead for up to twenty days in a row, one fell back on continually repeated experiences, endless discussions on how the war was going and when it would end, on the merits and demerits of the latest batch of guards or the comparative food value of beans compared with rice. Or one would invent subjects for discussion. There was a man named Humphrey Knight, a Volunteer, who was ten years my senior who, after the war, was to live in Tokyo and be Managing

Living with the Japanese

Director of perhaps the largest expatriate import/export organisation in Japan at the time. He used to make occaisional visits to England where his son and daughter - who used to come and stay with us for quite long periods - were being schooled. I remember now so clearly the warnings he used to give us in the late fifties and early sixties about Japan's resurgence as an industrial power and his anguish when, as he so often did, he warned industrialists at home of the tremendous competition which was going to lie ahead for them and they scoffed or at best refused to take his warnings seriously. How accurately he prophesied our present days.

But this was to be in the years ahead. Our thoughts on those long drawn out days in Habu dockyard were of the present and how to pass those endless hours more quickly. Many times Humph and I would sit perhaps sawing a rail taking it in turns to recount such an absurdity as to how if let loose in the morning in, say, Piccadilly, with one's pockets lined with money, one would spend the day; and we would do this in the fullest detail perhaps starting with coffee in Fortnum's through to ending up in a Swallow Street night club!

Humphrey Knight of the H.K.V.D.C. who was to become a very close friend not only in Japan but after the war. Having lived in Japan he spoke competent Japanese while his wife, Phyliis, who died a year or two ago was fluent. After the war they returned to Japan where Humphrey was managing Director of Dodwell and Co and remarkably he launched a ship built for Dodwells in Habu Dockyard!

Living with the Japanese

It all sounds so unlikely now but somehow the dragging hours of those long days had to be killed. One smashed pickaxe handles as much for the half hour of the day it wasted getting them replaced as for any other reason; and *ima nanji desu ka?* (what time is it?) was perhaps the question most frequently asked by prisoners of dockyard workers. With the end of each working day there was a sense of achievement because it meant there was one less day of a wretched life to be endured and ahead were a few hours through which one knew a kind of freedom.

This was especially so on 'first bath' nights. The system was that once the Japanese had used the bath no new wood was to be added to the boiler and it was declared available. It was soon discovered that after three rooms had used it the water was too cool and soiled and it was agreed that Volunteers and Raffs should have the use of it alternately with each of the rooms taking it in turn to have 'first bath', which thus came round on each sixth day. This was huge luxury, the more so on the by no means infrequent occasions when the Japanese disdained their rights and a pristine bath of clear and steaming water met the first arrivals.

Those 'first baths' were unforgettable joy. The dreary dockyard day was over and tomorrow a long way off; aching limbs were soothed, numbed bodies warmed, gloom was dissipated. No rugger fifteen splashing in its changing room after a match was more re-invigorated and restored. The room was as filled wih laughter as the bath was filled with bodies, all packed in like pickles in a bottle, cross-legged on the base, seated on the shelf which ran around it, bodies against each other, necks, legs, arms protuding; thin men and well-built men, Genki Boys and cooks; Volunteers or Raffs.

And afterwards there was no compulsion to fight for a place around the stove if lit for it is surprising how long the body retains warmth after a bath taken scalding hot; on first bath nights one could relish the meal such as it was and the essential cigarette which followed it and afterwards enjoy sitting around through the time remaining before lights out and instant sleep.

'Instant sleep' is no exaggeration. Within five minutes of lights out except for men with serious physical discomfort all

Living with the Japanese

were asleep and would remain almost in a state of catalepsy until reveille. For it was not that they didn't wake. They woke frequently - a diet based on rice sees to that. All night long the corridor rang with the clogged feet of men making their way towards and back from the benjo. Most men made several trips - but in a trance-like state and returning would lean against the knee high dais, fall forward, turn over, pull themselves up and the coverings over them, and be instantly asleep. Insomnia did not exist on Innoshima; when life is ruled by others and come tomorrow, next week, next month, next year most probably, there is no decision of importance one has the chance of making, the mind is strangely emptied of anxiety.

About once in every three weeks or so one had a broken night. With their long history of devastating holocausts which swept through towns of wooden and paper houses packed close against each other, the Japanese were understandably afraid of fire and we had to take it in turns to act as night watchman (the Japanese term was *fuchinban* - or at least that is how it sounded - I have failed to find it in a dictionary). For one hour we had to tramp up and down the wooden corridor. We were never alone on this duty for the corridor was never empty. But the men tottering half asleep past the *fuchinban* at best would grunt a recognition but mostly were more like zombies than companions.

If there was no insomnia neither, with thirty-two men sleeping on door width bedspaces, was there silence. Grunts, snores, teeth being ground, mutterings, the passing of wind, even the sound of heavy breathing orchestrated into an uneven flow of sound which never ceased.

The Japanese required us to sleep alternately head or feet towards the centre of the room and I suppose this made good sense. As it happened I slept with my head towards the partition while my left hand neighbour, a man named Rangeley who was an inveterate snorer, slept with his towards the centre of the room. I had a broom which I laid beside me and whenever his snoring disturbed my sleep, I would chuck him with it firmly under his chin which would cause him to gasp and cease his snoring. In seconds (if either of us had really wakened) we were both again asleep. How many thousands of times I must have pushed that broom under poor Rangeley's

Living with the Japanese

chin, I cannot imagine, but in the morning it was always the same, he expressed the hope he had not been too bad and assured me that he had not the least objection to my doing it.

The point was that both of us had had a good night's sleep.

'Sleep that knit's up the ravell'd sleave of care
The death of each day's life, sore labour's bath,
Balm of hurt minds, great nature's second course,
Chief nourisher in life's sleep.'

How true that was on Innoshima!

CHAPTER TEN

THE SECOND BLESSING

1

"Look to your health; and if you have it, praise God, and value it next to a good conscience; for health is the second blessing that we mortals are capable of; a blessing that money cannot buy."

Izaak Walton 1593-1683

After the initial deaths resulting from the Dai Nichi voyage only four more prisoners (all Volunteers) died on Innoshima and all within three months of each other at the end of 1944. One of these was Professor Ashton Hill of the Hong Kong University,

I knew Ashton Hill reasonably well and attended a few discussions or debates in which he took a part. One of these, I remember, was on the proposition that a woman's place was in the kitchen, on a pedestal or in the bed. This must have been quite early on for Bowen-Jones, who was to be so mysteriously whisked away from us, took part, espousing a woman's proper place as being on a pedestal. I cannot remember who put forward it being in the kitchen, but I recall that Bowen-Jones, who was a very good speaker, was eloquent. The last word however was with our Professor. In short terms dismissing the kitchen claims, he dealt succinctly with the remaining opposition by saying simply: "As for the proposition that a woman's place is on a pedestal, what nonsense that is; a woman's proper place is in the bed - that *is* her pedestal!"

Equally pithy was his contribution to a debate on whether prisoner of war life brought out the best or worst in a man. "It's like the benjo," he said. "It brings out everything."

The Second Blessing

Professor Ashton-Hill

Ashton-Hill died from pneumonia complicated by beri-beri. According to Ken Forrow the immediate responsibility for his death lies with Minahero. Apparently Forrow attempted to be excused work and attended early morning sick parade but 'Minnie' deciding he was fit enough to work yelled "you no sick" and struck him about the neck and one of his blows landed on a boil causing it to burst and blood to flow. Now the sovereign way to be excused work was to have something to show and Minnie, impressed by the gore and pus changed his mind said "you sick" and replaced him in the work party with Ashton-Hill who up to that moment had been excused. I do not remember this myself but Forrow informs me that Ashton-Hill collapsed in the dockyard and was brought back dead.

The other three deaths were those of W. Fleming who had been with the Blue Funnel Line who died from suspected stomach ulceration after, I understand, eating something from a barrel he had found left unattended in the dockyard which he had mistakenly taken to be food, J.M. Mackinnon of the Hong Kong shipping firm Mackinnon, Mackenzie and John Stirling Lee of the Hong Kong and Shanghai Bank who both, like Ashton-

The Second Blessing

Hill, died from pneumonia while suffering from beri beri.

I scarcely knew either Fleming or Mackinnon but in spite of his being many years older, our sleeping in different rooms and working in different parties, John Stirling Lee had become a very close friend and his death was the saddest loss I was to know on Innoshima.

John Stirling Lee

Lee, always known as Stirling Lee, was a proud and highly-principled man who carried his views to what was perhaps an exaggerated degree. Nothing would have induced him to open a conversation with any Japanese (whom he loathed with a hatred I have never known exceeded) and nothing would have persuaded him to accept a cigarette from one. When he discovered I was seriously setting about trying to learn their

The Second Blessing

language and the Katakana and Hiragana syllabary, he was bitterly disappointed.

He was man who was universally liked although there were those amongst his contemporaries who saw him chauvanistic and tunnel-visioned. For my part, young as I was at the time, able to compare his capacity to live by his principles when so many were abandoning theirs, I admired John Stirling Lee, seeing in him the qualities which had made Britain the great nation I still believed she was for all our shaming at our captors' hands. After he died, I went across to the hut where his body had been laid prior to cremation and wept for a loss which was irreplaceable.

Stirling Lee's ashes and those of Professor Ashton-Hill and the eight R.A.F. men who had died were subsequently taken to a Buddhist temple where they were laid on an altar and a Buddhist Service took place at which the Warrant Officers and Room Leaders (including myself) attended. One of the other Room Leaders, Flight Sergeant J. Price wrote a description of the occasion and I can do no better than include what he wrote at the time.

'On the morning of November 28th myself and the other Room Leaders and the Warrant Officers were told to attend the service dedicated to the laying up of the ashes of the late Prof Ashton-Hill and John Stirling Lee of the Hong Kong Volunteer Defence Corps; the ashes had been lying in state in the Church of England chapel in the camp.

'We fell in at 9.30 a.m. along with a few friends of the deceased. The little party then proceeded to the Buddhist Shrine at Mitsonosho. Before entering the building we were instructed to remove our boots and socks and leave them on the steps outside; after entering the building we were instructed to kneel facing the shrine.

'This shrine consisted of a main centrepiece with a recessed background, the whole set up being illuminated by electric candle fittings; in the middle of the arrangement was a stand which came into use during the ceremony. On each side of the main shrine were smaller shrines which did not appear to have any part in the proceedings. In front of the main altar were lying the caskets containing the ashes of the eight R.A.F. men who had passed away

The Second Blessing

two years previously. In front of the altar stood two baskets of oranges and still nearer to us a small low-legged table on which was lying a small book and a mallet.

'The ritual was opened by the appearance of the priest who bowed firstly to the shrine and then to the Camp Commandant and then to the kneeling Englishmen. The priest was attired in a vivid green kimono over which was worn a black apron figured all over with designs and patterns in silver; he also carried a string of glass beads which he continuously passed through his hands in a circular motion. He had entered from the right hand side of the shrine and knelt down beside a small table similar to the one in the centre. After placing a lighted taper in a centre stand, he commenced to sing or chant a dirge, frequently striking a small gong producing a sweet tinkling note. After he had been chanting for about five or ten minutes he was joined by a girl whose attire was a black kimono over which was worn a blue apron adorned with white.

'She too started to chant in a tone lower than the priest; she appeared to be making as big a discord as possible. During her chanting she was reading from a book and at intervals she struck a huge metal bowl with the mallet from the small table in front of her; the bowl when struck produced a deep booming sound in direct contrast to that of the priest. As the priest paused to take a breath the girl continued; when the girl paused, the priest continued. I have learnt later that the priest's chanting was for the souls of the departed and the girl, by her discord, was scaring away the evil spirits that were attempting to enter the soul.

'This portion of the chanting finished, the priest arose and, murmuring in a low voice, he disappeared behind the shrine and re-appeared with a bowl and a tray. The lighted taper was taken from the stand and placed in the bowl and the tray, containing incense, was was placed on the small table by the girl before the Englishmen who were required to sprinkle incense on the lighted taper, the Camp Commandant and one of the Nippon camp staff being the last to perform this part of the proceedings.

'After this the chanting was re-commenced, continuing for another ten minutes, the proceedings being brought to a close by the girl giving the bowl a hard bang. The priest arose and, making a deep obeisance to all present and the girl doing likewise, the caskets containing the ashes were placed in front of the altar. All the vases and stands on the altar were very small affairs and of a deep red wood with gold leaf designs.

'I believe there are very few Christians (Englishmen) who have been allowed to attend a Buddhist ceremony.'

The Second Blessing

2

Beri beri, which was responsible for these latest deaths, is a most curious disease. It is caused by a shortage of Vitamin B1 and has an enervating and dropsical effect. The body, filled with liquid, swells, and this swelling can be extraordinarily rapid particularly when resting. A man, thin as a lath can sit down to a game of cards and before he has got through a rubber of bridge or a few hands of solo his legs may have swelled until they are as tight as sausages. This is partly illusory for he can press his fingers into them and the indentations will stay there for a long time. Beri beri was not an excuse for a day off work unless it was coupled with septic conditions which it aggravated; wounds which might have healed in days, often took months to do so if they healed at all.

Apart from the Genki Boys and cooks, almost everybody in the camp suffered from beri beri but although it was unpleasant, disturbing, wearying and sometimes painful through lung congestion, in our case it proved only to be a killer when coupled with pneumonia. It responded swiftly to a change in diet but in our experience only slowly to a concentrated intake of vitamins in pill form - it was as if the body knew the way to extract vitamins from natural sources but found difficulty when they came out of a bottle. Of the few commodities available in Japan almost to the end were *Wakamoto* and *Ebios* tablets which were reputed to be rich in vitamin B1. With little to spend pay on they were bought and eaten like sweets with, so far as could be observed, no noticeable effect - perhaps, like many things available in Japan in those days, their substance was less in quality than their packaging suggested.

A cousin of beri beri is pellagra which is caused by deficiency of Vitamin B2 and was so far as our prisoners were concerned far more serious; it has the disadvantage that it can leave permanent damage whereas a good diet probably removes all the effects of beri beri. Pellagra was common with the Volunteers in Shamshuipo where it came to be known by its four Ds: dermatitis, diarrhoea, dementia and death. It may well

The Second Blessing

have been that the Boei Glodok *Strawberry Balls* was pellagra in its early stages. Fortunately, although there were those who suffered from it on Innoshima, the attacks were less severe than they had been in Hong Kong.

There were other unpleasant ailments stemming from a lack of vitamins: there were thigh rashes which itched abominably and there was a tendency for fingers to split open of their own accord and bleed - this could be very painful, particularly in the winter and with the rough and dirty work, healing was a slow process. And there was a mysterious ailment, never diagnosed and from which I still suffer occasionally, whose symptoms were a sudden painful and worrying affliction of the eyes which, filling with water, smart abominably only after a while for these symptoms to pass away.

The Japanese attitude (and to a degree that of the prisoners) to vitamin diseases was one of *laissez faire* - what can't be cured must be endured and what one endures long enough, one gets used to living with. Occasional Red Cross medical supplies of thiamine and other vitamin pills checked and reduced these complaints and it has to be said to the credit of the Japanese that although their own people were suffering from the same ailments they did not, except perhaps individually, raid our sometimes superior medical supplies.

As already said, the best way to get a day off work was to have something to show: to a degree a high reading on a thermometer impressed the Japanese but a septic wound could work wonders. In displaying them, however, one might be taking a frightful risk. On one occasion three of the Hong Kong group - Clemo (of whom much more later), Hailstone and Musker - exhibited huge skin ulcers - up to two inches in diameter - which were stubbornly refusing to heal, to a guard who, perhaps, had had some on the spot battlefield surgery experience. He called for a scalpel and forthwith performed on each of them in turn complete excisions without anaesthetic. Even granting that the suppuration or beri beri may have somehow numbed the area the fortitude of these three men who with faces pouring sweat endured these operations without so much as a whimper was truly praiseworthy.

The Second Blessing

Musker Hailstone

Accidents in the dockyard were inescapable and some were serious. Coxhead's diary recounts numerous personal accidents; Squires was knocked off the stocks and falling twenty-five feet was very badly injured; Richards dislocated an ankle which, improperly set, left him a cripple nine months later; Davies dislocated a shoulder. Mancell, who sat at the same table in my room, lost an eye through chipping caustic soda from a barrel (for which he was offered, and refused compensation of 150 Yen!); Kennedy fell into a ship's hold and dislocated a thigh which again was never properly set. Blow and Clemo lost finger joints; one of my legs bears the scar of a plate falling off a truck and ripping open the calf. So it went on - it was all but impossible to work for nearly three years in such a disorganised dockyard as was Habu in those days without regular mishaps.

Accidents in the camp were less common but they occurred. Forrow, larking about on the rusting jetty by the camp, fell through it splitting one foot wide open in the process. It was stitched up there and then - without any form of anaesthetic of

The Second Blessing

course - and with three men holding him down while the operation was performed!

Attacks of colic accompanied by diarrhoea were as common as the English cold and this was hardly surprising considering the astonishing things one ate officially and unofficially. It was remarkable that only one man poisoned himself when one considers the risks which were taken with substances whose nature was doubtful to say the least.

As normal substances became in short supply or vanished entirely from our menu, all manner of extraordinary things for which titles had to be invented such as: "Grass, conge and sea moss," were substituted. On the official side were *inter-alia*: carrot tops, bracken, dried vegetables, sweet potato tops, lily roots, seaweeds, sea slugs, maggot infested rice, sour beans and barley and fish - usually shark - reeking of ammonia.

On one never to be forgotten occasion on returning from work we were supplied with a doubtful mess of uncertain nature (except undoubtedly containing fish) which was as black as the longtitudinal iron trays in which it came. There was quite a generous portion each and it was attacked with gusto. But scarcely had it been eaten than the body was burning hot and hearts were pumping as if they would burst from the body. There was a stampede for the sick bay. All along the corridor the doors were being slid open and men were hastening. The body sensation was such that hardly a man doubted his end was nigh: our skins were aflame and in our chests this tremendous throbbing. The sick bay was soon jam-packed and men were spilling far down the corridor. The Commandant arrived - alarmed that all his charges were about to die and his the responsibility. But no one knew what it was or what to do about it; we were either going to die or time would cure us. Which it did. Our scarlet faces paled, the throbbing eased and, apart from a blinding headache which took the best part of two days to clear, there were no known after effects.

The Second Blessing

On the other hand, away from the tropics, we avoided the real killers: cholera and dysentry while even colds and influenza were uncommon - which is surprising considering that in the winter when one's boots could fairly be described as islands of cardboard holding holes together, one was daily pulling on yesterday's soaked working clothes to issue out into bitter winds, driving rain or snow for the next twelve hours or so. I have never been persuaded since that one catches cold by getting one's feet wet or sitting in a draught! And then again, although our food was meagre and often suspect, it had the merit of being absent of substances on which much ill health is these days blamed: in Innoshima without sugar there was practically no tooth decay, without fat not a single case of heart disorder, and for some quite incomprehensible reason in spite of the fact the some of the Volunteers were well into or even past middle-age, so far as I am aware no such thing as rheumatism.

While most suffered individual bouts of sickness of one kind or another, there were few who were as fortunate to benefit as I was from an illness they didn't have. There had been a serious outbreak of diptheria in Shamshuipo which caused many deaths. It so happened that within a few weeks of the Volunteeers arriving I developed a very sore and discoloured throat which, with diptheria in the forefront of their minds, persuaded the medical orderlies who had arrived with the Hong Kong group I had been stricken and I was immediately whisked off to isolation in one of the single-storied empty huts at the far end of the camp. And there, I was shortly to be joined by one Con 'Buster' Harris.

As can be seen from the photographs which follow there were remarkable differences in the state of health of those who having survived the Dai Nichi voyage, arrived on Innoshima. For my own part all things considered, I looked pretty well whereas Harris was in a dangerous state and was in fact very fortunate to survive.

The Second Blessing

Author (left) and Harris (right) on arrival in Japan.

I stayed for several weeks in isolation. I did not mind in the least; I was quite satisfied I didn't have diptheria and it was bliss lying comfortably on my tatami, covered by my blankets and my futon, listening to the sound of the camp marching off to the cold and miserable dockyard, knowing that the Japanese, who were always terrified of catching things, wouldn't come in and bother me. Con and I were provided with an *hibachi* and a supply of charcoal on which we brewed tea every day. Unforunately our supply of tea leaves was very limited and eventually we simply boiled up the old leaves in a billy can. The colour changed steadily with each succeeding brew, the final few being vivid purple. I count those weeks the most pleasant I had as a prisoner of war: food was still good, our hibachi removed the chill, we were left alone and Harris (who in peacetime had been an on-course bookie) was a warm and interesting companion and in that quiet room a bond was wrought which has stood the test of time. We exchange Christmas cards and send each other postcards from holidays abroad and although more than fifty years have passed still meet occasionally.

The Second Blessing

3

So far as the Commandant, Nimoto, was concerned, the number sent out to work each day was more important than the amount of work they did and this principle was followed to such degree that on occasions men were sent out although they had to be supported to and fro by fellow prisoners. The ruling on rations being halved was generally foiled by sharing and some help from the cookhouse but the policy of no pay or cigarettes was more difficult to circumvent although in Room 6 which had largely been filled with men moved over from the Sick Bay (mostly but not entirely Raffs) and therefore at the time the least fit in the camp, a 'Rules for Room 6 Wages Scheme' was established which required its members to pool all wages and bonuses earned.

It was very unfortunate that through our entire time on the island we lacked a British medical officer whose word would have carried weight in excusing sick men from working. There were occasional visits from a Japanese Army doctor and theoretically we had the Habu Dockyard Hospital medical staff and equipment to call upon. Some injured men were X-rayed while others who needed to be - as for example a man with a fractured femur and another with a broken ankle - were not. At the same time it is fair to say that there was no discrimination shewn against prisoners as such and first aid treatment of an elementary nature of prisoners injured at work was usually rapid while eyeglasses broken at work were replaced free of charge although they had to be paid for otherwise.

There was a dispensary in the camp which was technically under a civilian dockyard employee who had no English and scant medical knowledge and whose main function was to render the necessary medical returns and keep the percentage of men at work as high as possible; but fortunately in the contingent which came from Hong Kong there was a corporal of the Royal Army Medical Corps, E.M. Mogford, who came to run the medical side of things, organized the camp hospital, when it was functioning, and more or less took over the dispensary.

To appraise Mogford properly one has to appreciate the

The Second Blessing

position in which he found himself. A prison camp doctor is not like other men. To begin with he has considerable power. If, as was the case in Japan, his captors decide on the number of men who shall be allowed off sick each day, it is he who arbitrarily decides which they shall be amongst men whose numbers include some who genuinely believe that to be sent out to work may be a death sentence. Some may be hugely overdramatizing but nevertheless all manner of emotions arise which result in wild accusations of favouritism or bribery, embarrassing entreaties from bended knees, cunning stratagems and charges of incompetence. All these have to be resisted with humanity because to achieve what Mogford was to achieve, the camp's understanding and respect had to be won.

His very separateness weakened Mogford's position amongst complainants, setting him apart from the general members of the camp. *Force majeure* he had to become a confidant of the Japanese for he needed their co-operation to do the best he could for those under his care. To obtain their co-operation he had to co-operate with them, treat their wounds and sicknesses and prescribe them drugs which should have been solely for the prisoners. Moreover as he did not have to go off to work at dawn and return at nightfall, ragged and oil-smeared, degraded, he was soon seen by the Japanese in a different light and respected as other prisoners were not.

The pressures and temptations which follow from such situations can seduce all but the strongest-minded. And Mogford was, after all, a man with, at the outset, only the most rudimentary knowledge of the average young serviceman's complaints who overnight was faced with problems which would have taxed the skill of the most experienced practitioner. He was called on to be doctor, surgeon, therapeutist, pathologist, dermatologist, chiropodist, osteopath, masseur, opthamologist and, and by no means least, psychologist, politician and judge. And there was no escape for him. Once surgery was over he was just another prisoner. He could not lock up and go off home.

We did not have the full benefit of Mogford's qualities at the outset for he was not the only R.A.M.C. orderly who came up with the draft. At the beginning it was Furnell who was in

The Second Blessing

charge largely, it seems, because the Japs took to him because he had such a splendid singing voice. This was unfortunate. At the time the dispensary was stocked with adequate supplies of sulphanilimide compounds which the Volunteers had brought up with them from Hong Kong;. *Doctor John*, as he came to be called, used to dish these out like sweets: "Take four now, four before you go to bed and four when you wake up in the morning and here's a dozen aspirin to take the headache away." I had a bout of kidney trouble while on Innoshima which was to result in the loss of a kidney shortly after the war and when my urine was tested prior to the operation it was not perhaps surprising that my doctor having considered the results was to suspect me of trying to cure myself of venereal disease because of the quantity of sulphanilamide discovered in it!

Corporal E.M. ('Dai') Mogford

We were extraordinarily fortunate in having Mogford with us for he was a man of outstanding quality. An entire chapter could be given over to recounting his character and achievements. I will limit myself to a single example to illustrate his virtues.

One of the Hong Kong men, Tom Kennedy, fell off a ship and

The Second Blessing

fractured his femur. It was theoretically reset by the Japanese in Habu Hospital and the man was returned to camp - with one leg two inches shorter than its fellow. It seemed that if nothing was done Kennedy would be crippled for life. Using his imagination, Mogford designed a weird contraption of clamps and straps and bolts and wingnuts which he fixed each evening to the shortened leg and then wound down to stretch it and stop it setting. Although this was not only very painful for Kennedy at the time but through the night which followed, where a lesser man would have weakened in his resolution, Mogford grimly continued with the treatment.

Several months after the accident, the war ended and a Major Artman, an American Army doctor, came to the camp and, having examined the device. was awed. "Kennedy will always have a limp," he told me, "but if it hadn't been for that contraption he would have been a cripple for life. If ever a man deserves a medal, Mogford does."

I wonder if he got it.

CHAPTER ELEVEN

OUR INCOMPREHENSIBLE HOSTS

1

The quality of life in camp depended very much on the temperament of the monthly guards: some were reasonably disposed towards us, others on the lookout for trouble and quite unfathomable.

With roll call at 5.20, there were those who liked to get up earlier than 5.15. On one memorable occasion there were one or two up and about in my billet when one of these monthly guards, a short, tough, stocky fellow appeared in the passage, stood for a moment or two staring in through the glazed doors his face suffused with rage then, abruptly sweeping the doors open, stormed in and proceeded to set about them. When he came to the end of victims he turned his attention to the rest of us. It was a nice decision whether or not it was safer to stay in bed as it was now approaching the official reveille time. Three or four more elected to get up to be promptly set upon and, one after the other, beaten up. The rest, having stayed put, were now aware they were in breach of the rules as it was well past reveille and the guard, as if aware of this, proceeded to start pulling out those still abed as if it was his intention to beat up each and every one of us.

Fortunately for the rest, one of his latter victims ill-advisedly objected with *"wakaran"*(which is a short way of saying *"wakarimasen"*which means "I don't understand.") This, so far as the guard was concerned was apparently the final straw and, as if he had never been so insulted in his life he screamed *"wakaranka?"*and, seizing the objector, picked him up, literally hurled him bodily at the window, smashing it, glared at the rest of us, wheeled round and departed, presumably to

Our Incomprehensible Hosts

look for trouble in the adjacent billet.

There was an American woman who wrote a post war book titled 'How the Japanese tick,' and, if memory serves me correctly, admitted she had had little to do with the Japanese personally but had based her writing on what she had been told about them by others. I cannot believe she interviewed any from Innoshima where the view was generally held that not only was it beyond us, Europeans, to understand the workings of the Japanese mind but as often as not they didn't understand each others'. Certain it is that a remark made one day might so amuse a guard that he would reward the man who had made it with a cigarette and yet the same remark repeated a few days later would send him into a paroxysm of rage. One simply did not know where one was and could never rely on consistency. One of our permanent staff, Sergeant Nagano, behaved so well for the first twelvemonths that he earned the nickname 'Smiler', only overnight for no apparent reason to change and become the most unpleasant of them all.

Then there was Minahero who was quite unfathomable. He had started with us as a cook but as cooking was taken over by prisoners and some permanent N.C.Os left, presumably for the war, he gradually rose in the camp hierachy. Of all the permanent staff, he was regarded as the most dangerous and was the one who usually carried out punishments; he was the only one of ours so far as I know who was arraigned and sentenced for his misdeeds by the War Crimes Tribunal. He had a withered arm for which he made the suspect boast that he had been wounded as a pilot and, discovering I had been one, he used to refer to me sneeringly as: "you pilotto." I sensed that he was only awaiting his opportunity to revenge himself on me and stupidly gave it to him.

Still twenty-one when taken prisoner, I had towards the Japanese a narrow pride and one of the ways I used to express this was by refusing to bellow my number out at roll call. If the rest of the room were happy to shout, that was their business; I, who being room leader was the last to call a number, was going to show my independence. For two years I had no trouble, the various guards taking *Tenko* being apparently prepared to accept winding up with a quiet *sang ju ni* after a bellowed *sang*

171

ju ichi. Then one day, exceptionally, Minnie (as we called him) took Tenko. We went through the performance, Minnie turned to leave, then of a sudden wheeled, glaring at me. *"Nani?"* (What?) he yelled from the doorway. *"Sang ju ni,"* I responded at the same level as before. Now the Japanese had an unpleasant system of eyeball to eyeball confrontation when dealing with wrongdoers. They would advance on their hapless victim, prisoner or fellow Japanese, so close that noses all but touched and glare at him while volleying a stream of abuse and questions which he would answer at his peril. This volley could last a full two minutes - sometimes even longer. Then, abruptly it would cease - but not the nose touching nor the glaring. Sometimes the intervals of silence were punctuated by kicks and blows; sometimes the assault came at the end; either way it was guaranteed. I have seen this staccato performance accompanied by beating last for a full ten minutes.

On this occasion, Minnie, having bellowed *"sang ju ni"* at me from the doorway, and having failed to secure the desired response, applied the system. With my eyesight in its prime and capable of keeping in focus at three or four inches range a pair of glaring eyes, it was an experience to be remembered. The jabbering was of course incomprehensible apart from the frequently repeated *sang ju nis!* whose stressed final syllable turned them into exhortations for me to shout the number back. Stubbornly I would not do so, only repeating it at the same level as before; my pride in front of thirty-one men was at stake and there was something more - the instinct that giving in would doom me to an immediate beating up followed by a week or two in the Little House.

At length, Minnie, realising he was losing face and with the balance of roll call still to take, drew away, rejoined the rifle-toting soldfiers in the doorway, turned to give me a final, malevolent look and the menacing instruction:

"You, after Tenko, office come!"

I went, prepared, like a boy at school heading for the headmaster's study, as best I could be for what lay ahead by wearing my work trousers under my breeches against what in the billet had been voted my most likely minimum punishment: a beating up followed by having to kneel for several hours on a

Our Incomprehensible Hosts

thin bamboo cane - something which I can assure those who have not tried it, is exquisite torture.

The office was astringent with the aroma of the charcoal sticks burning in the hibachi and the night was black outside the uncurtained windows. Minnie was waiting for me. *Sang ju ni!* And we were off again. It was a weird yet oddly intimate exercise - the two of us, a Japanese and an Englishman, nose to nose, alone on a winter's night, the one bellowing *sang ju ni*, the other repeating it at the same muted level. How long we went on, I cannot estimate - it seemed an endless and utterly absurd labour through which my mind gradually numbed and, I suppose because of this, my qualms diminished. Then suddenly it was over. Minnie withdrew. I saw to my astonishment that he was smiling. Pulling a packet from his pocket he offered me a cigarette. We smoked together, even exchanged some sort of conversation. And then he told me to go to bed. And never a word was said about it afterwards.

Then there was the case of my athelete's foot which I collected on my way out to the Far East and have never entirely got rid of to this day for it lies dormant awaiting the right conditions when it breaks out and is an infernal nuisance; at times in Japan it would get so bad that it not only attacked the skin between all my toes but spread over my feet and I would be allowed off sick with it. On one of these occasions as was his wont, the Commandant, Nimoto, took it into his head to find out who were sick and what was the matter with them. A purge usually followed such investigations and punishment was meted out on suspected malingerers, with the fact that you had been excused work no protection. So, even though I had something to show - which was more acceptable - it was with some trepidation that I stood to attention awaiting Nimoto's arrival. However, far from being angry he was intensely interested and insistent he could cure me and to achieve this took me for a walk.

We headed towards Mitsunosho. There were just the two of us: Nimoto's English wasn't bad and by now I could fill in with a fair amount of Japanese. It was spring and everywhere was peach, plum or cherry blossom; the sea was sparkling, and the houses with their heavy tiled roofs as distinct from how they

Our Incomprehensible Hosts

had appeared to us at Moji, looked picturesque. It was the first time (and in fact so far as I can remember was to be the only time) I went out of the camp for a purpose other than taking part in a funeral, that one brief stay in the hospital or going to work and I felt the touch of an affection long since forgotten, freedom.

Presently the hills on our left yielded to a valley, a Shangri-la of sweeping paddy fields, cool, fresh, green, inviting. Between the paddy fields were areas of lush grass. Nimoto ordered me to remove my boots and walk barefoot through these sweet pastures assuring me I would be cured of my affliction. He was gentle and solicitous. I have often wondered the effect on sales of a book based on the horrors of prisoner of war life under the Japanese if for the savage with a two-handed sword about to lop off a head you were to substitute a Commandant all but hand in hand with one of his charges meandering through a paddy field.

It would be nice to report that a cure was effected - sadly it was not.

Another example out of the many that are available may demonstrate how impossible it was for us to measure or forecast the moods and attitudes of our captors. In the summer it was very hot and after a long day in the dockyard there were those, admittedly a minority, who fancied a swim in the sea after we got back. A request would be made, sometimes to be granted, more often refused. One evening while those wanting to swim were in their billets awaiting the decision the corridor was of a sudden aswarm with guards, vibrating with heavy boots and resounding to the shout of

"ALL MEN SWIM! ALL MEN SWIM!"

Except for those sick in bed, none were excused and when all were in the sea the guards lining the beach with their bayonets pointing menacingly forwards, forbade us to come out. Only when it was all but dark and we were shivering with cold were we allowed to do so.

There were occasions when we were able to take advantage of failings in the make up of our captors and score a victory which, if not overdone, could be repeated. One of these games was particularly satisfying. Apart from the evening roll call covering the whole camp, there was also a count of those who had returned from work. The guard taking it had a record of the number who had left camp that morning and we were required to form up in rows so that he could check against it. This was slowly done with the guard laboriously scratching numbers with the butt of his rifle in the dirt of the mustering area and sometimes while his attention was thus engaged, a couple of men would slip from, say, the front row which had been counted to the back row which hadn't been with the result that he ended up with having apparently two more men returned than had gone out. This invariably threw him into a state of considerable confusion especially if after he'd started again at the beginning the ploy was repeated. As likely as not, aware that something was amiss, a higher ranking guard, a corporal (*gaucho*) or a sergeant (*gunso*) perhaps, would come out from the guardroom and demand from the hapless fellow what was going on, and this in no mealy-mouthed way - for while a Japanese didn't like losing face, it didn't seem to worry him if he caused loss of it in others lesser than himself. Most probably the new arrival would now take over and, having found the result to be a correct one, castigate his companion in no uncertain manner even to the extent of slapping and kicking him, or even knocking him to the ground in front of us.

Alfred Lynch, who worked through the whole of our stay in Japan in the same party as I did, reported an even more astonishing example of both the total indifference to the feelings of those of lesser rank or importance which could be shown and the unquestioning acceptance of such conduct by those who had to put up with it. Just after the bombing and machine-gunning of Habu Dockyard (which is recounted in later pages), Lynch and another prisoner were making their way through the yard in the company of a Japanese soldier when they passed a Japanese officer. Both, as they were required to, saluted the officer but, somewhat surprisingly, their guard passed him without doing so whereupon the officer shouted for him to come back and when he had done so ordered Lynch and his companion to punch the fellow. They had no option but to comply.

Our Incomprehensible Hosts

Yet after the officer had gone on his way, the guard presented the two of them with a packet of cigarettes.

Was it to show he nursed no ill feelings? Or was it because they hadn't punched as hard as a compatriot under orders would have done?

2

The Japanese attitude to sickness was diametrically opposed to that held in the Western world. To the European, a sick man merits care and sympathy; to the Japanese he was a burden. The sick man in Europe is given a special diet; the sick man in Japan had his ration cut in half. The function of the soldier was to win or die; that of the civilian to work. It is probably impossible to project to a European mind how total and final was this ethic but if accepted goes a long way to explaining the lack of interest of the Japanese in our deaths on the *Dai Nichi Maru* and of those who toiled for them in the Phillipines, Siam, Burma, Sumatra and the other Indonesian islands.

The Japanese accepted authority unquestioningly and were hooked on statistics. Both Nimoto and the dockyard bosses had to send to Headquarters monthly records of the workdays put in by their charges and were, presumably, rapped on the knuckles if the percentage workforce was less than that of, say, Osaka or Nagasaki. To this end every month each of us was issued with the card illustrated earlier which was stamped on the days on which we worked. These stampings were regarded like good conduct stars at school: when a man succeeded in completing a full card he got a bonus ration of cigarettes and if he avoided having any blanks the Commandant would call a parade, read out his name, deliver a eulogy on the splendid effort he was putting in helping his father and mother *(sic)*, Dai Nippon, bid him step forward from the ranks and reward him with two eggs. Thereafter he was known as an 'egg man' through the camp.

So far as the forced labour workers were concerned a similar, but I imagine more stringent attitude applied - I doubt for example if any of the Koreans got two eggs for regular work; far more likely it was a beating for anything less.

Our Incomprehensible Hosts

On Innoshima there was a large amount of imported labour and not only of Koreans but also of very young Japanese and others who having done their two year military stint had been returned to so-called civilian life. They were housed in hutted camps where a quasi-military discipline obtained and the timetable, rules and routine were much the same as ours.

It is certain that in these camps a man could only get himself excused work if he was very definately ill - and as to a considerable extent the choice of which men in our camp could be excused lay with our own medical orderlies it is probable that it was more difficult for the Koreans and Japanese to be excused in theirs. It can be safely assumed that amongst them malingerers were few and far between. Nevertheless the authorities clearly assumed they existed for every now and then there was a purge and we would be treated to the astonishing sight of a raggle, taggle mob of Koreans, Japanese or what have you, being rushed through the dockyard, still in their bed attire, belaboured by a gang of black-clad kempies beating them with sticks, kicking them with heavy boots and howling imprecations. They swept through the dockyard like a gale - you could see and hear the performance from afar, watch it approach, pass you and disappear into the distance. It was remarkable.

3

Both in the camp and at the dockyard we had far greater opportunities for studying the Japanese than did our less fortunate compatriots building railways through jungles and creating airfields on remote tropical islands; and, certainly, greater opportunities than do the businessmen of today meeting them in boardrooms or in the cosmetic atmosphere of hotel lounge and restaurant. It may be suggested that the level of Japanese workmen we found ourselves talking to in an earth-floored hut was lower than the representatives of Hitachi, Mitsui and Mitsubishi we would be likely to meet in post-war encounters and of course there is a good deal in this. But it must be remembered that with Japan totally geared for war so that few at any level were excused military service and operating a system whereby a man having finished his military service was drafted to work in such places as dockyards, we were involved with many young Japanese who could well have become, or indeed were to become, such representatives.

There were certain aspects of the Japanese character which have remained impressed on my mind through all these years: an insensitivity to suffering in others, fascination with barbarity, blind obedience to orders given by those of higher standing and an apparent inability, sometimes amounting to crass stupidity, to see things other than from their own blinkered standpoint.

A dockyard *Yasumi* was often prolonged by a soldier turned guard or a worker displaying the small stock of photographs he often carried with him. Some of these were truly horrendous: for example of Chinese just decapitated or about to be. And these exhibits were handled lovingly and shown with pride. A worker falling off a ship and lying badly injured invariably attracted a crowd of fellow workmen who would stand around, jabbering and giggling, clearly throughly enjoying the diversion. An amusing pastime was to burn out the eyes of frogs with lighted cigarettes; another to throw a dog into the sea then form a line and pelt it with stones offering it an alternative choice of death: that by drowning. Yet for all this unconcern in the suffering of others the average Japanese was loath to be hurt himself as, for example, one saw in the nervous queues for one or other of the frequent group inoculations for which the authorities appeared to have a passion and which were carried out *en masse* in the yard.

I have already touched on the fact that an Army private could assault civilians with impunity. To a degree this of course happens in any country where the military are in control but in the case of Japan it had roots in the pre-war economy. This was built on a limited number of major business houses who employed their massive staffs from the cradle to the grave. This still obtains today and the vast majority of Japanese workers expect a single employer to pay them, house them, arrange their medical attention, organise their holidays, pension them off and bury them.

Our Incomprehensible Hosts

This goes a long way to explaining the trouble-free labour relationship which has enabled Japan to compete so successfully in the post-war world. How long this will continue is an interesting question. The very success it has brought Japan in the post-war days may very well sow the seeds of its decline. Sooner or later the work force may become aware that it is not getting its fair share of its company's prosperity and make demands difficult to resist. Countries which are not self-supporting in essential raw materials have to export or die - it was after all because it lacked such resources that Japan went to war in the first place intending to meet its problems through the management to its own advantage of what it trumpeted as the *Greater East Asia Co-Prosperity Sphere* - which was of course a euphemism for a new Japanese Empire. It is to be hoped that if the rot sets in those in power do not seek a solution in the re-establishment of a military regime. It will be tempting to them to do so.

4

It was really a nonsense our being in Japan at all. It is doubtful whether taking into account those who had died, those who were sick, those who became cooks or medical orderlies, and two or three who worked in the camp as cobblers and tailors, there were on average more than one hundred and fifty of us working on the same day and towards the end as food and health deteriorated, even less. To provide this pitiful work force the Japanese, (desperately pressed to house, clothe and feed its own population), had to transport us and those who were to die, from Java and Hong Kong, build a camp and staff it with a Commandant, about eight permanent and at least ten transient guards, two interpreters, and in the dockyard a dozen non-working gangers - certainly more than thirty to be housed, clothed and fed - to supervise house, clothe and feed one hundred and fifty unwilling and difficult workers whose opportunities for offsetting such value as they did have were enormous.

There is no limit to examples of our sabotage which could be given these ranging from simple actions such as barely screwing more than a thread or two of bolts on to large plates so that when lifted up into position they clattered to the ground at great risk of life and limb to dropping a handful of nuts and bolts into a pump so that when it was called into service, it ground itself to a standstill.

I have already written of how my own party set about spoiling refrigerated holds when we were stupidly given the task of insulating them but perhaps one of the most effective instances of sabotage was that recounted to me by Henderson of the Genki Boys.

"A great big tanker came into Hachi Dock and they bored a hole in the bottom and we went down with these four gallon tins. They sort of opened up this thing and of course the oil ran out and we were catching it and sending these four gallon tins backwards and forwards along the line and tipping them into this iron bucket. And the crane, the jib, wouldn't stretch over Hachi Dock so they lashed a telegraph pole sort of thing to the end of it. And they put the block and tackle on the end. And we were down below. The idea was to fill this thing, this iron tank, lift it up, run it down to the end of Hachi Dock and tip the oil in this lighter that was there to take it. This was in summer when the oil was soft. In the winter, by when we'd got to the bottom, it had solidified.

When you think about it! - we lit a fire in the hold of this oil tanker to heat the shovels to chop the oil into chunks to put into baskets and lift 'em up on the block and tackle, sitting astride these girders! And this went on, months of it. You must have seen us, we were filthy! Anyway this lighter was getting filled until it got lower and lower in the water. Mori Shigay was our foreman and when we'd filled this lighter up he said he wanted it shifted from there to there. So, the old Volga boatmen, we hauled it along and got it shifted and we had to tie it up, you see. So I did the tying up and I tied one end very tight and the other end very loose and when the tide went out the whole thing tipped over and all the oil went out into the sea. There was hell about that. There was nine months work there. Well, it broke my heart to see all that oil go but nevertheless that was my big war effort!"

Our Incomprehensible Hosts

In ways other than direct sabotage the prisoners were able to make a confounded nuisance of themselves by goading the Japanese. In one case the Genki Boys were engaged in removing rocks from the cliff face of the hill (which has subsequently been removed so that the new dry dock could be constructed), and they were required to shift them away from the area in one of the high-sided two-wheeled carts which provided most of the dockyard mobility in those days. Coming upon a particularly large rock someone suggested to their foreman Mori, (who was the island's wrestling champion and fancied himself as a strong man) that it was even beyond his powers to shift. Mori rising to the challenge like a trout to a mayfly, with much grunting and groaning actually managed to lift the rock and drop it into the cart where it jammed! Not only did the sides of the cart have to be broken away from the chassis before it could be moved but, more importantly, Mori ruptured himself and was absent from the dockyard for quite some time!

On another occasion a party in the woodyard were required to shift the narrow gauge railway which was used for carrying cut timber from the sawmill to the main railway track, a matter of two feet sideways for its entire length. It had been decided that rather than digging up and relaying the track, the prisoners, using stout staves, would lever the rails into the required position. At first all went well for the track lay mostly on top of the soil but after a time they came to a place where the track was well and truly buried and the prisoners half-hearted efforts failed to move it. The foreman, whose name was Mitsui, decided to lend a hand. Placing one end of a stave against the rail and the other end on his shoulder, he indicated that the prisoners should do the same and at the count of *"ichi, ni, sang"* heave with all their strength. Bellowing his *"ichi, ni, sang!"* Mitsui heaved mightily while the prisoners heaved gently and to universal satisfaction heard the crack as Mitsui's collar-bone snapped. He was out of action even longer than Mori Shigay!

5

From time to time searches of the billets took place. These were usually because an edict had gone out through Japan that some material, such as copper or aluminium, was desperately needed and no stone must be left unturned in making good the shortage. It was difficult to understand exactly why such a futile operation which caused everybody including the camp staff considerable inconvenience and yielded at best very little was ordered or why, if it was going to be carried out, we were given advance notice.

A Coxhead diary entry makes the point well:

'Jan 23rd. Yasumi. Inspection. All metal personal possessions had to be declared but only aluminium was taken. By Room 4 word had got around and mess tins moved rapidly.'

The form was that a blanket should be laid out on the tatami and all possessions spread upon it. One stood at attention while these were inspected by the Commandant and his posse. It never seemed to occur to our captors that forbidden items might be concealed elsewhere; that lifting a tatami, or even the blanket might have yielded treasure.

While so far as I know all other pilots who were taken prisoner had destroyed their Log Books because of the incriminating evidence within them of our fearful slaughter of the Japanese on the River Moesi in Sumatra and to a lesser degree in the Cheribon landings in Java, I had stubbornly kept mine intact and when searches took place I simply laid it on the tatami, spread the blanket over it and then my possessions including if possible an item such as a copper spoon prominently displayed. My Log Book, which I have to this day, was no more discovered in half a dozen so-called searches than was any of the Genki Boys' loot.

6

From 1943 we were from time to time provided with batches of *'The Mainichi'* and *'The Nippon Times'* which was a four page broadsheet in English published in Tokyo by Shoichi Kawamura. These papers were of excellent quality and published to meet the needs of neutral nationals who could not read the Japanese script. Whilst obviously heavily slanted to show the progress of the war in the most favourable light for the Axis Powers, nevertheless what was reported was accurate enough for one to have a clear idea of how the war was going.

The Japanese might claim the destruction of absurd numbers of enemy ships, planes and men but they did not make the error of printing rubbish when it came to geographical movements - the Swiss and the Swedes after all had access to their own newspapers. Thus when it was gleefully reported that Tacloban airport had been utterly destroyed by Japanese bombers, once one had discovered where Tacloban was, one had learnt that the Americans had retaken Leyte Island in the Phillipines.

It is a matter of great regret to me that I did not keep more of those old papers or copy out more excerpts than I did. There was a delicious piece of which I took a partial copy about a rear gunner in a Japanese bomber who, having run out of ammunition, threw his lunch (a rice ball) at the attacking American fighter and brought it down and another one about a Japanese pilot in a 'lone Hyabusa' who captured a Mosquito aircraft in mid-air over Burma and brought it back safely to his own airfield. According to the account the intrepid Nippon pilot so terrified his British counterpart by his brilliant flying that the wretched fellow threw in the sponge and, correctly interpreting sign language from his conqueror, accompanied him back to the Japanese base. The story ended with a most touching and lyrical passage describing the two aircraft flying side by side in the rays of the setting sun.

If any reader is able to lay his hands on a copy of that newspaper (Nippon Times, 15th December, 1943) and would care to send me a photostat of the article, I would be most grateful.

Amongst the copies I did keep in full was the article below which was included in The Nippon Times of February 2nd, 1943 and headed :

5th Bougainville Clash.

'The American Navy has carried out one counter attack after

Our Incomprehensible Hosts

another in vain efforts to wrest the sea supremacy from the Japanese Navy but in each attempt they have met with miserable defeat. From the first to the fourth Air Battles of Bougainville in the same area, they suffered the tremendous loss of 60 warships among which were 2 carriers and 4 warships (sic). Under the prevailing excitement of xx airfield, Commander I's voice was cool and steady. A wireless report was received from one scouting plane. "Just sighted a large enemy convoy: an aircraft carrier, x cruisers, x destroyers, position xx." It was x p.m. The convoy was headed for xx island. The young pilots grouped around their commander were equally quiet. Their faces did not betray their excitement. Among them a few even wore a grin on their faces, the peculiar grin of perfect self-confidence. The K attack formation spotted a few lights below them. "At last the enemy convoy!" But the position is slightly different from that expected. Is this the target? The moon is bright but the water below is barely visible. Sub Lieutenant I made several investigating circles. Certainly if he dived low enough the objects below could be identified, but a dive should mean some destruction of the enemy. They dived to attack. Instantly two aircraft carriers were set ablaze and one cruiser together with a huge water column disappeared from the surface. At this moment the H attack formation which had searched the surrounding waters without discovering the enemy heard (sic) the terrific vibrations of the ensuing battle and came to release their share of torpedoes. The oil spilled on the ocean, spread and caught like a prarie fire. Literally this was Hell on earth. With visibility perfect the I formation dove upon the enemy. A cruiser suffering a direct hit split in two and into the gaping side another plane charged in bodily in glorious self-destruction.'

And from The Nippon Times, June 7th, 1944:

'Drinking and excesses of all sorts mark send off parties at American bases, it was disclosed by special Sergeant Major Nakogawa who participated in aerial combats over the New Guinea area and who returned to Fukuoka on June 5th.

"Sometime in July last year I was patrolling the Wewak area in New Guinea when all of a sudden I met a B.26 Martin bomber.

Our Incomprehensible Hosts

Thinking it not worth while to challenge it to combat, I purposely evaded it and the enemy must have mistaken my move for flight for he began to give chase. I lured him to practically the side of a large cliff and then banked so steeply and with such speed that in order to avoid a crash he was forced to land. Among the crew was found a female radio operator. From her we learnt that the Americans at the base were wont to have wild send off parties for their comrades leaving for the front. We were told that on occasions a unit would award medals to those about to leave encouraging them to fly bravely to be worthy of the medals just granted. The wild parties would continue all night, the atmosphere growing more abandoned as night wore on. Fortified by drink, officers often told subordinates that the Japanese were easy rivals, but those who had tasted of this easy rivalry knew better"- so the Radio Operator told.'

And from *Nippon Times* June 4th, 1944 under headline:

'Citation awarded to Major Keijo Ishikawa.'

'The above mentioned sighted an enemy sub while on duty escorting a group of transports sailing in the Indian Ocean. He at once initiated a bomb attack on the enemy. Then as enemy sub discharged torpedoes, he fired on the moving missiles in an attempt to destroy them, but, seeing his efforts unsuccessful, he dived towards the torpedo in defiance of death, carried out the act of hurling himself against the torpedo, thus stopping it. Thus were the transports saved from danger at the glorious sacrifice of his life.'

While most of the columns in these newspapers were filled with such stories or with accounts of the war's progress one did occasionally find lighter entries - as for example poetry which whatever merit it might have possessed when written in Japanese hardly translated impressively.

'And I beheld a single crow
Pecking at - a tomato.'

Or again a complete poem under a note which extolled 'the

author's wonderful communion with nature':

> '*A frog jumped into a pool - splash!*'

Poetry was also used as a vehicle for denigrating the Allies:

> '*The paths we human beings race*
> *Across it they run sideways.*
> *The Anglo-Saxons after all*
> *Are only monkeys.*'

There were of course frequent references to *Kamikazes* in these newspapers and this presented us with a puzzle I have never been able properly to solve.

The theoretical driving force of the Kamikazes (literal translation: 'divine winds') was the spirit of *Bushido* defined in The Nippon Times (October 7th, 1943) as '*the way of the warrior which is represented by death*' Again quoting: '*why death is called the ultimate goal of Bushido is because there is no humanly possible manner by which the infinitely noble honour of the Japanese warrior can be vindicated. Death is his constant partner on the battlefields.*'

The article went on to make the point by an illustration of a certain Major Yokozaki who was reported to have crashed his plane against that of an American bomber: "*for while*", the article went on, "*the Major never forgot to improve his flying technique, he was on the other hand a faithful observer of national traditions and when the technique which he had developed proved insufficient, Major Yokozaki crashed against the foe with all the force of his spiritual stamina.*"

We, on Innoshima, who lived in the closest proximity to the Japanese, found such articles arrant nonsense and scarcely accepted that the *Kamikazes* existed. We considered the constantly re-iterated accounts of their exploits to be no more than confidence tricks to boost a sagging morale and we were

Our Incomprehensible Hosts

inclined to believe that most of the Japanese dockyard workers thought as we did. Yet *Kamikazes* **did** exist and in considerable numbers - just as two thousand Japanese soldiers **did** die to the last man on Attu Island, and just as in other islands retaken bloodily one by one by the Americans the number of Japanese prisoners taken as compared with the number killed was miniscule.

Why was our judgement so at fault? After all we were not a camp whose inmates were limited to young inexperienced servicemen; amongst our number were several score intelligent, well-educated, in some cases exceptionally well-educated, experienced men many of whom had done business with the Japanese for years. I think it was that to believe in *Bushido*, to accept that *Kamikazes* did exist, we would have needed to have sensed a spirit of burning zeal and patriotism in the Japanese around us. And it was not to be found: not in the soldiers in the camp nor in the civilians in the dockyard many of whom were returned soldiers who had done their two year stint.

On my journey back to England after the war had ended I wrote the extensive account of my experiences on which much of this book is based and the following was included:

'During the last few months war production had practically ceased and ships had been lying idle, unpainted since the spring. Construction on ships on slipways even though they had been half-completed was abandoned. The people had lost all interest in the war. The famed spirit of 'Bushido' was entirely lacking. The only interest was in food for which black market prices were soaring. The average Japanese workman was incorrigibly lazy and the average foreman unbelievably obtuse, in many cases his sole interest being to have an easy life without trouble.'

And then again within the *Kamikaze* legend was the idea of courage. Yet where was the evidence of this courage on Innoshima? Surely a race which could produce heroes in such quantity would be free of personal fear? But when the air raid warnings sounded the Japanese looked as fearfully at the sky as did we prisoners and when the strafing and the bombing started were as quick into the caves; and a workman waiting for an injection, or in the camp a soldier waiting for Mogford to use an instrument on him, was a very nervous man.

So the *Kamikaze* business is a puzzling one perhaps best explained by the rigid discipline exercised in the Japanese military and seen for the first time when we were filling up those craters on Kemajoran airfield. When a bomber landed and taxied in, the crew dismounted and stood stiffly to attention awaiting dismissal by their captain. It is hard to imagine the crew of a British Lancaster or an American B.29 doing the same. I still find it difficult to accept that all *Kamikaze* pilots were volunteers in the true sense of the word. Some, the earlier ones, yes; but for the rest it is easier to imagine groups of raw, young pilots, browbeaten into *volunteering* by stirring harangues delivered before assembled officers and ground staff, taking off with insufficient fuel to return from a target area and disgrace certain (and even execution possible) for the cowardice of aborting a flight on a suspect claim of engine misbehaviour.

7

Habu Dockyard was almost unbelievably inefficient. It was managed by a system of watertight compartments co-operation between which was appalling. Wastage was colossal and the packing of perishable commodities in straw bundles prevalent. Workmanship was poor and newly constructed ships would fail their trials and require months of reconstruction. The majority of machine tools had been imported and spares for them were non-existent or at best in short supply. Work such as coaling and emptying oil from bunkers was done by hand thus taking weeks rather than days or even hours to complete even though cranes and pumps which could have been called in to do the job were standing idle. The youngest of children and the oldest of crones were used, presumably on the principle that no scrap of available labour should be left unused, but this was often counter-productive with sketchily trained youngsters doing important tasks such as riveting and making a hopeless bodge of it and the old crones merely an extra clutter in an already over-cluttered dockyard.

Everything was shoddy: clothing, foodstuffs, toilet articles, buildings, transport. As has been said dockyard uniforms were made of wood fibre from which you could pull splinters and it was all but impossible to transfer soap lather to your face; medicines were ineffective or unavailable - a sovereign cure for diarrhoea was to get a bit of burnt wood from the cookhouse fire and chew it. In a week the sole of a brand new boot wore through, metal workers' gloves were of discarded cotton materials stitched in layers which didn't last a day, matches so thin that you had to strike them away from you or they snapped, throwing burning phosper underneath your nails. The list is endless.

Such improvements as were made were in the dockyard with nothing available for such luxuries as roads or sewerage. The provision of new shops and tower cranes certainly increased production but it is an interesting fact that within twenty-one years of the end of the war production in Habu Dockyard had multiplied a staggering twenty-one fold. In fact ships are no longer made in the dockyard which is nowadays titled *'The Innoshima Ship Repair Yard'* and no less than a hundred vessels with an aggregate tonnage approaching four million are these days handled annually in a yard which breathes an efficiency quite unimaginable in our days. It gives one food for thought (and perhaps sounds a warning for the future) to consider how much more difficult it would have been to have defeated the Japanese if today's dynamism had existed then.

Additional to general disorderliness and inefficiency, production was continually blighted by misfortunes and calamities, one of the most amusing of these being the destruction of one of the vital tower cranes as a result of muddle and idiocy.

A party of Koreans had worked with prisoners for months on the construction of bulkheads for the engine room of one of the ships under construction on a slipway. Someone conceived the idea that instead of putting the pieces one by one on to the ship and riveting them *in situ*, they would be riveted together first and then hoisted as a complete article aboard. This, the Koreans told the prisoners working with them, would be done by the *okii kajuki* (the big crane). Well the day was awaited by us with keen interest for it was calculated that the total weight of the agglomeration was in the vicinity of 45 to 50 tons whereas the lifting capacity of the crane was painted in huge letters on the jib arm as being 11 tons at the base, 6 tons midway and 3 tons at the end.

When the day for hoisting arrived, the dockyard was alive with top brass and others drawn from the offices and numerous spectators from the yard to watch the bulkhead lifted into place. Satisfied all was ready the crane driver was signalled to lower the lifting hook; aware of the danger he signalled frantically against this stupidity but, overborne, did so, the hook was engaged and full lifting power applied. According to a witness: "*The crane arm came down at least three feet towards the load and then lifted it about fifteen feet into the air.*" The driver was then signalled to take it round to the slipway and began doing so but when it had made barely a third of its traverse the crane arm broke off at its pivot base and brought the whole thing crashing down with the driver with it. What had been a fine looking tower crane was reduced in seconds into a twisted mess of scrap metal. The driver, who had fallen between fifty and sixty feet, was miraculously unhurt and was pulled out of the wreckage not by any of the Japanese workmen (who saw the whole incident as a screaming joke and were splitting their sides with laughter) but by one of the prisoners, a Welshman, 'Taffy' Thomas who for his pains was handsomely rewarded with cigarettes.

While this typical example of ineptitude occurred in Habu Dockyard, another of a different nature but in its way as bizarre occurred in the smaller, sister dockyard of Mitsunosho. One of the prisoners, a man named Bellamy who worked in the camp as a cobbler, put out an urgent request for leather which he needed desperately for boot repairs. On the day in question it was raining heavily and the ganger in charge of Moulstone's party (which happened to be working at Mitsunosho) only too pleased at being able to find an excuse for sloping off with his friends, led the prisoners into the top storey of a large, neglected building and told them to be quiet and stay there. Naturally they had a good look round to see if there was anything worthwhile looting (and incidentally found numerous old dockets in English going back to the days when it was a

Our Incomprehensible Hosts

British yard) and came upon a large crate and having prised off the lid discovered a leather belt in layers studded together which was about twelve inches wide and forty to fifty feet long and was recognized as being the spare belt for the main pump plant for the dockyard! Having removed the main coupling pin they cut off about twelve feet of the belt, divided it into suitable lengths, tied it around their waists and took it back to the camp.

Bellamy was delighted and it became a normal procedure when he wanted more leather for someone to slip up whenever an opportunity arose and cut off more. In due course when there was none left to take, so as to destroy the evidence there had been a spare belt at all, the crate was dismantled, broken up and dumped into the sea. One morning, while Bellamy was mending boots the Commandant came into the cobbler's shop and very impressed with the quality of the leather Bellamy was using, enquired where it came from. "*Oh, Hong Kong and Java,*" Bellamy told him vaguely. "*Ah, so!*" said Nimoto ("*Ah, so!*" was a favourite expression of our hosts)."*Very good. You make me shoes for my little gir*l." Bellamy did so. One imagines long after we had left Japan all work being brought to an abrupt halt by the pump belt snapping and the mayhem there must have been with everyone rushing around hysterically searching high and low for a vital spare belt which records must have shown to have been delivered!

Nevertheless, in spite of accidents, inefficiency, shoddy workmanship, prisoners' sabotage and, towards the end of the war, Allied air attacks, altogether nineteen ships were launched during our stay of which the majority were very small, the three largest (whose numbers were 1778, 1779 and 2684) were of about ten thousand tons while a similar ship was redesigned to become an aircraft carrier. Each of these four ships had been planned for invasion purposes - which was curious considering that at the time the Japanese had their hands full trying to repel American invasions to recapture islands lost in the first few months of the war. Apart from these larger ships there was a dredger, three or four submarine chasers and the rest were cargo ships varying in size from one to three thousand tons.

Habu's repair facilities were probably of greater value and amongst the many vessels brought in after being damaged by attack of one form or another were quite a number of well-known ships. These included: *President Harrison, Hoyo Maru, Asama Maru, Scharnhorst* (not the German battleship), *Hawaii Maru, Eastern* (the first ship to sight the Russian Fleet in the Russo/Japanese war and a strange old-fashioned four funnelled battleship she was), *Lecompte de Lisle, Seattle Maru, Siberia Maru*, several destroyers and small aircraft carriers and one or two more antiquated battleships. By the time the war came to an end (by which time work at Habu had for all practical purposes ceased) a long line of ships (including the brand new 2684) lay idle, unused, indefensible targets.

8

It will have been seen that compared with the vast majority of Japanese prisoners of war we on Innoshima knew a remarkable degree of freedom. Escape was impossible - on one occasion Minahero, seeing me gazing longingly over the sea wall, suggested I waded in and swam to England and promised to tell no one I had gone. The camp was unwired, there were no such things as sentry boxes or lookout towers and in the dockyard we were able to wander from one end to the other without let or hindrance. As our command of Japanese improved we could, and did (although this was against regulations) strike up conversations not merely with our fellow dockyard workers but with seamen off ships who were a useful source of information on how the war was going. And as well, gleefully able to seize on every reverse, on every damaged ship, on every air raid, we were able to spread doubts in the minds of our captors as to their hopes of victory. If we had in the first instance been brought for propaganda purposes, in the end our presence must have proved a two-edged sword.

News plays an important part in the morale of a prisoner of war camp and it is important that the news is accurate. In Boei Glodok there were two types of news going the rounds: the first based on rumour told of fantastic Allied victories and promised

Our Incomprehensible Hosts

release almost daily; those who put it about insisted they had a source which was unimpeachable but could not be disclosed and waved aside arguments against it based on logic. They were astoundingly believed - one was almost waiting to hear the guns! But a penalty must be paid for living in a fool's paradise and it was paid in deeper gloom and despair when time proved the emptiness of these false and absurd reports.

The other source of news in Java came from a radio which the Army had smuggled in which was well hidden and in spite of a few close shaves never discovered by the Japanese. An official bulletin of accurate news was given out daily but, with the war going badly and being anything but encouraging, was discredited by the majority with the reporters accused of 'holding back the gen.' The radio, dismantled (and the pieces hidden inside bamboo poles) departed with the first draft to Japan leaving Boei Glodok bereft of news until new arrangements could be made.

In Innoshima we were far more fortunate. Apart from the *Mainichi* and the *Nippon Times* and such information as we picked up from visiting seamen, we were to have another source which was to continue to supply us with regular, accurate news right up to Japan's capitulation. As has been mentioned the *Denki* party of four men had a pro-Western foreman and he used to pass on to them news he had heard on the radio and would often bring a newspaper to the docks. Japanese papers are written in two scripts: *Kanji* (the Chinese ideographs which express meanings thus by-passing language) and *Hiro Gana* and *Kata Kana* - forms of syllabic writing. Japanese newspapers use both sets of symbols and so cannot be read except by those who know enough *Kanji*. Fortunately there were men in the camp who did.

After D Day, supplies of *The Mainichi* and *The Nippon Times* abruptly ceased. But by then it hardly mattered. The Commandant had a paper delivered daily which he used to leave on his desk while he had his evening meal and when he was unable to obtain a newspaper in the dockyard, the man one came to regard as leader of the Denki party, Freddie Clemo, used to steal in, borrow it and, before returning it, have the important passages read. I had always believed that this was done by another member of his party, Joe Reid, (who was to die of tuberculosis in Hong Kong in the sixties) but after the war another Volunteer, Patrick Fallon (who had had two years of Chinese schooling) mentioned in a letter that he had been the translator.

Pat Fallon · Joe Reid

In any event after translation Clemo having returned the paper would make his way down the passage calling in on every room to pass on what had been learnt. The door opening and Freddie's: "Gen tonight, chaps"was an important moment. The news was as scrupulously accurate as the source allowed, never highly coloured and always delivered in this rather dramatic way. You could never prise advance information out of Freddie - you waited in your billet and he came to you.

There were only two exceptions to this evening dissemination and both occurred at the dockyard at lunchtime. The first on June 7th, 1944 telling us of the fall from power of Mussolini in words delivered in front of our interpreters: "The modern Napoleon has withdrawn from Caesar's capital!" - and the second the most important news ahead of the Japanese surrender we would hear in our long years of captivity:

It is midday June 8th, 1944, in Habu dockyard. Perhaps one hundred and forty men returned from their morning's work are seated at three long tables. It is high summer and there is the reek of sweat. The men are unshaven, their clothes ripped, stained, patched and frayed, their hair cropped close. Faces are gaunt. The table is bare but for china bowls and plates and cups without handles regularly spaced along both sides and teapots filled with hot water. The cooks have delivered the food, barrowing it from the camp in barrels and are already gone, passing through the dockyard into Habu town to collect fresh supplies. The food has been transferred from the barrels into wooden buckets which steam at the table ends; it consists of daizo and dried vegetables and a thin, soya-flavoured soup. In summer the vegetables are always dried or if there are no vegetables there is bracken. In front of each man, disturbing the tables' regularity are his implements: chopsticks, forks, spoons either factory made or roughly fashioned out of odd bits of metal, bumpy to the tongue. All eyes are on the steaming soup and daizo.

Of a sudden Freddie rises to his feet. It is remembered he has done this once before - when advising us of Mussolini's demise - and the action brings sudden, expectant silence. The low hum of conversation dies away, the occasional chink of crockery abruptly ceases. The interpreters look up, puzzled: Fujita, small, dangerously lean, bespectacled, mean and O'Kana the number two interpreter.

"Just a minute, chaps!"

We know this is a vital moment - and one charged with danger for the man we're listening to.

"We've crossed the moat and breached the Western wall!"

And Freddie sits down again and so silent is the room that the creak of the bench as he does so is clearly audible. Fujita is looking about him, frowning, seeking and failing to find an explanation. And then the chatter breaks out into a vast explosion - for once, even lunch is of secondary importance.

But Freddie's greatest triumph was yet to come.

Our Incomprehensible Hosts

A very brave man - Freddie Clemo.

Mention has been made of two of our interpreters, Fujita and O'Kano; early on we had a third, the Army interpreter who we called *Neckerst*.

They were three distinct types. Fujita, always dressed in riding breeches, bespectacled, very small and rat-like in appearance, cunning, cowardly and untrustworthy, was the official Number One interpreter employed by the dockyard. His English left a good deal to be desired for all that he claimed to have lived for many years in America. There was no doubt he nursed a positive hatred of Westerners; it was believed that he intentionally mis-translated in order to bring about punishments and he delighted in seizing opportunities for punishing men himself. He had a curious weakness. The bow in Japan was in wartime being overtaken by the salute but one did not have to salute civilians; Fujita would offer bribes of clothing or cigarettes in return for being saluted. Rattled by the bombing we saw little of him in the docks through the last few months.

I had one personal brush with him. Shortly after the docks took over from the Army, he called me to the guard room, and started asking me questions about my flying experiences in the Far East war zone. Although I don't suppose it would have mattered much by then if I'd agreed to talk about them, I gave him the standard reply that all I was supposed to tell was my name, rank and number. Although he pressed me, I didn't budge and he then told me that this request for information had come from Zentsuji and I would be well-advised to answer his questions because if I didn't Zentsuji would know the way to make me. I again refused and he told me to go away and think it over. Two weeks later he had me in again and when I again refused to co-operate, repeated the threat making it seem as if almost the very next day I would be dispatched. But I stuck to my guns and I never heard anything more about it - I have always supposed that it was a sudden bright idea of his own to ingratiate himself with higher authority.

O'Kano was a better character. He had the merit of thoroughly disliking both Nimoto and Fujita and was generally speaking held in high regard and there is no doubt he saved many prisoners from serious punishments. His nickname was *Tubby* and his favourite expression: "*I don't want no trouble.*" He had spent many years in Vancouver and returned to Japan as a kempei and early in 1945 was to return to being one but, exceptionally for the tribe, always had a smile and a word for most of us when we ran across him in the dockyard. When the war was over he came back to the camp on the scrounge for clothing and cigarettes and a letter of recommendation which was given.

Neckerst earned the soubriquet because that was the nearest he could get to "next" He was forever drunk and would reel into Tenko reeking of sake and make crass remarks. On one occasion he told us some more prisoners were coming, reeled from the room, staggered back and with finger to his llps said: "*but don't tell, it's a secret.*" His favourite expressions were: "*Commander, he say, very sorry for you; in the case of going to the docks*" and "*if I were Commander, I would do so and so but I am only interpreter."*

He was the subject of any number of amusing incidents. On one occasion, in a drunken stupor, he was put to bed in the hospital during Tenko to save his condition being discovered. He was forever entering the billets and drinking tea through the spout of a kettle and would offer 400 cigarettes he had stolen from somewhere for a tin of bully beef. Something of a musician he was a veritable tonic at a time when one was badly needed - we were sorry when the docks took over running the camp and he departed.

CHAPTER TWELVE

INNOSHIMA ATTACKED

1.

Having been bombed and strafed by Germans, Italians and Japanese, we were now to be bombed and strafed by British and Americans.

Japan was divided into what were known as *Kens* which were similar to our counties and although the name of the camp was changed three times, our Ken was always Hiroshima. If enemy aircraft were sighted heading for Japan a preliminary warning known as a *keikaikeiho* was given, this being in the nature of a general alert advised by the sounding of a continuous siren blast and the displaying of blue and white flags on hillsides and other prominent positions. If aircraft were actually in a Ken and seemingly heading for one's area, a warble was sounded and a red and white flag substituted. Should danger of actual attack appear to be imminent a further continuous blast was sounded and the blue and white flag re-substituted. The all clear was given over the radio and while an air raid was in progress a running commentary given of the number and type of enemy aircaft involved and the towns attacked were named. How accurate this information was, we could not of course have known. None of the warnings given above constituted an instruction to take cover - this was not to be done until a watcher on a hill actually reported seeing approaching aircraft when what was called a *taiho*, or take cover, was broadcast.

Serious bombing of Japan commenced at the beginning of 1945 following the recapture of Saipan Island some fifteen hundred miles distant when daylight attacks were made with B.29s on

Innoshima Attacked

Tokyo and Nagoya. The B.29, or B Ni Ju Ku, soon became a household word in Japan and the population had the greatest respect for its capabilities but as in spite of frequent air raid warnings over the next few months no aircraft had been sighted, initial apprehension amongst the dockers in Habu soon subsided. It was not until March 19th, 1945 we were to see any action.

The warbles were sounded early and the red and white flags put out, anti-aircraft fire was heard and bursts of it seen and then, a little later, a formation of about fifty aircraft passed by at some distance. There followed a period of inactivity until eight fighters appeared, cruising slowly over the dockyard. Assuming these must be Japanese the shipping held its fire. The aircraft then began to circle in pairs and quite suddenly peeled off into a dive at the same time opening fire on the *Lecompte de Lisle* which lay anchored in the bay. Two attacks were made and a few bombs dropped but with only a modicum of success achieved with one bomb striking the bridge, modest strafing damage occurring and some casualties inflicted. (5 fatalities according to Coxhead's diary). The aircraft were believed to have been either Grummans or Vought Sikorskies. They suffered no losses.

The all clear was given but then at 11.00 a.m although no further warnings had been sounded a formation of twenty-seven fighter bombers suddenly appeared over the dockyard. The absurdity of the warning system was dramatically demonstrated for in such a hilly country as Japan, low flying aircraft would be seen just as early by those they were about to attack as those watching out for them. Yet, curiously, in spite of the earlier incident, it was again assumed that these were Japanese machines, a view which we of *Umpanko* pushing a trolley load of wood beside the prime target of Hachi Dock, shared. We stopped work to look up and start counting how many machines there were when the first of the formation, which could hardly have been at more than a thousand feet, peeled off to attack from directly overhead. Miraculously unhit, we scattered wildly for cover and I ran full tilt into an iron pipe projecting from a stack of them and yet was hardly aware of what I'd done for all that by nightfall my chest would

Innoshima Attacked

be bruised black as night and my left arm which had been forced against it, all but immoveable.

The next few minutes were heart-pounding with aircraft low enough to read their markings, numbers and so on, screaming around Habu Dockyard strafing and dropping bombs, but the damage they actually inflicted was only minor: a few bomb-damaged crane tracks, a slipway rather knocked about, a newly constructed aircraft carrier holed with bullets and cannon shells and some more casualties inflicted.

From a morale boosting point of view, however, it was tremendous stuff. The Japanese had been terrified and for the next few days practically no work was done with almost every workman heading for shelter at the first hint of approaching aircraft. As for us, the prisoners of whom none (unless I was to be counted) had been hurt for all that various parties were actually working on the aircraft carrier or in the general vicinity of attacks, it was of course a splendid tonic. For the next few days conversation was about little else, the whole attitude to life was changed and the sense, so long known, of being detached from the outside world abruptly dissipated. We had, after all, been within measurable distance of English or American pilots now safely back on board their aircraft carriers. This was a very positive feeling; it was as if you had held out your hand to freedom and all but touched it.

Meanwhile my bruising started to manifest itself becoming a remarkable sight with almost the whole of my chest turning jet black while my arm seized solid. I had to wait until the end of the day before going back to camp but was to be excused any further work for the next three weeks.

Following this raid many solitary B.29s and other aircraft flew over or in the neighbourhood of the dockyard, maintaining a steady course and a fair altitude, all unmolested either by Japanese fighters or ground defence. It is a really remarkable fact that only on one occasion did we see both an American and a Japanese aircraft in the sky at the same time, and the latter a seaplane which promptly fled. It was clear that the Japanese air force had been for all practical purposes annihilated.

The solitary aircraft were obviously on reconnaissance missions and the photograph below of Habu Dockyard (this one

Innoshima Attacked

was actually taken on July 28th, 1945 - in other words just two weeks before Japan capitulated) is a treasure.

VIC. E.23. 28JULY45. INNO SHIMA. INLAND SEA.

Hachi Dock can be seen directly behind what appear to be two ships lying side by side at anchor (in fact there are three) and the clutch of buildings to the left of it include the Canteen where we ate our lunch; the town of Habu is on the right and our camp a mile and a half or so to the left i.e northwards. Across from Innoshima is one of the many delightful small islands with which the Inland Sea is scattered from which can be seen the rugged nature of the terrain, the way in which every square foot of usable soil is cultivated and the closeness of the houses.

The Japanese soon took to regarding these single B.29s

Innoshima Attacked

flying over them with only a mild curiosity; it is an instructive thought that if the B.29 flown by Colonel Tibbets which dropped the atom bomb on Hiroshima on August 6th took off from Saipan it would have been seen on its passage overhead at thirty thousand feet by the dock workers and prisoners of Habu, for Hiroshima lay about thirty miles distant on a sufficiently direct line for an aircraft travelling at that height to be visible.

After the March 19th attack on Habu, the next six weeks were quiet apart from these individual flights in respect of which the sounding of a warble was soon abandoned but on May 5th things took a more portentous turn. It was a glorious day with winter just turning into spring and the sky about a fifth (or as pilots would say two-tenths) covered by cumulus cloud. At 10.00 a.m. an alert was sounded followed by the displaying of red and white flags and very soon the drone of approaching aircraft engines could be heard. We posted ourselves close to the mouth of a cave in the hillside which had been prepared as a shelter. The drone grew steadily but still no aircraft came in sight and it was not until the sky was alarmingly vibrant with the roar of approaching bombers that the first of a formation of nine four-engined B.24s or B.29s in perfect V-formation emerged at about fifteen thousand feet from a towering bank of cumulus just a little to the south of us. As this nine cleared cloud, on either side appeared the first of two similar V formations each of nine aircraft, making twenty-seven in all. But this treble V proved to be no more than the first of three such groups for two more Vs each of twenty-seven emerged from the cloud on either side making a total of eighty-one of these huge bombers. And if this was not a sufficiently terrifying sight, it was immediately followed by a similar number in an identical V-formation. They came like wraiths against the blue: luminous white, deadly and remorseless, formation succeeding formation. We began to count. Nine, twenty-seven, eighty-one . . . .and still they poured out of the cloud in an unending stream, unstoppable, terrifying yet superbly beautiful. Being a trifle to the side of us we were in no real fear while the Japanese stood spellbound and incredulous, with wonder written on ther faces as they watched

Innoshima Attacked

this deathly, deadly procession while in the near distance, from the mainland, could be heard the awful thud of exploding bombs.

Altogether one hundred and sixty-two passed overhead close by and the sole defence against their progress was a few feeble bursts of anti-aircraft fire which made a Japanese standing close by me make a gesture with his hands and a comment: *"You might as well strike a match underneath them for all the good that that will do."*

On June 23rd we had a similar but rather more nerve wracking experience. On this occasion while numerous B.24s or B.29s were seen in the vicinity instead of being in one huge formation maintaining a steady course, they were operating in batches of ten to thirty with a few single aircraft flying at comparitively low altitudes. The warning system was soon all at sixes and sevens as each time the all clear from *taiho* was given, the drone of a new batch approaching from a different direction could be heard while the Japanese, blindly following the instructions given, were popping in and out of the shelters like startled rabbits while the prisoners loath to miss what was going on, but cautious, mostly stayed out in the open near cave mouths and the like.

Finally a formation of twenty-four having flown southwards across the dockyard turned and came back over it again on a reciprocal course. It looked like a bombing run and with beating hearts we waited peering upwards from the mouth of the cave itself, ready to hurl ourselves inside at the first whistle of falling bombs. But there was only the drone of engines and the formation flew on, to some other pre-determined target.

We were very fortunate. In one of those strange coincidences with which life is studded, I was, when in Sydney on my way back home after the war had ended, to run across the First Lieutenant of the *Indomitable* off which we'd flown to Java and he told me not only that it was aircraft off *Indomitable* which had taken the reconnaissance photographs referred to earlier and shared in the attack which took place that day but also that a major attack by B.29s on Habu Dockyard had been pencilled in and but for Japan capitulating when she did, would

Innoshima Attacked

certainly have been carried out. This, although I did not know it at the time, was confirmed by American Intelligence to Moulstone and others at Yokohama when we were being repatriated when a precise date, August 18th (i.e. just three days after the Japanese capitulated!), was given for a B.29 carpet destruction of the Hachi Dock area. Had it occurred far fewer, if any of us, would have left Japan.

The final, and most dramatic episode was on July 28th.

As has been already mentioned, apart from Habu dockyard there was a small dockyard at Mitsunosho almost abutting the camp, and on the seaward side of the road to the main dockyard and perhaps half a mile distant from it was the foundry of Karoto. Small parties worked now and then in Mitsunosho dockyard and men on light work were sent to Koroto to fettle castings. At the time I was having to put up with a particularly bad outbreak of athelete's foot which had spread across both insteps and soles of my feet so that I could hardly walk and was included with this latter party.

At about 6.00 a.m. on this particular morning the warbles sounded and the radio gave out the information that *kansaki* (carrier borne aircraft) were in the vicinity. For the first time ever we were ordered to remain in camp and a few minutes later when I was in the woodyard area where we sometimes hung out clothes to dry, a number of either Grumman or Avenger aircraft appeared, circled ostentatiously very low, then broke up to attack Mitsunosho dockyard. I enjoyed a ringside seat of an attack on a target not half a mile away. It was a brief but very exciting foray. There was tremendous noise immediately at hand - cannon and machine gun fire from the attacking aircraft and a barrage from ships and gun emplacements which was heavier than it might otherwise have been because of the accidental presence of a couple of invasion barge ships anchored off Mitsunosho which put up a respectable, if ineffective performance. The attacking aircraft all flew off unscathed but inflicted little damage.

When the all clear sounded we were mustered and sent off

Innoshima Attacked

to work, the light duty party peeling off at the gates to Karoto Foundry and before long we were sitting comfortably on the dirt floor carefully fettling castings and then smashing as large a proportion of them as seemed reasonable. Later in the morning, the warbles again sounded but the Karoto bosses gave us no instructions to take shelter and all, prisoners and Japanese, with a sense of apprehension, continued working.

This time there was no warning - one moment there was just the sound of chipping hammers for the casting shop was a quiet place, and the next there was bedlam: the shriek of aircraft engines, the rattle of machine guns, the thudding of cannons, the whistle and crump of bombs. From where we were seated inside our building (which was very like an aircraft hangar) we could see nothing and a minor panic ensued with prisoners and Japanese alike running to get outside. What happened to the others I was working with, I do not know. We were all of one mind, to get outside and find some sort of shelter.

The sides of the foundry consisted of low brick or stone walls to about five or six feet, above which they were glazed right up to roof height. Finding (when I had got myself outside) the sky to be filled with strafing and bombing aircraft and seeing no obvious place to take cover nearby, I threw myself beside this wall; there were better places to be in a sustained air raid than by a sheer wall of glass but to be in the open would have been even worse. And at least I had a ringside seat.

Some forty or fifty Avengers were being used. These were fighter bombers which carried small bombs which were released from open bomb doors underneath the fuselage. The aircraft came in low from the sea, perhaps at twenty or thirty feet, then climbed away after strafing or dropping their bomb loads. It was at once a desperately unpleasant and yet exhilarating business for from where I crouched with the coastline curving, I could actually see bombs falling and striking targets on Mitsunosho although because of the intervening hill the actual results of the main attack on Habu dockyard were hidden from view. Not that this lessened the excitement for many of the Avengers on their run in roared directly overhead and low.

Then, suddenly, as swiftly as it had begun, the raid was

Innoshima Attacked

over and the Avengers gone. An amazing silence reigned. We gathered together and with no one attempting to prevent us made our way out of the Foundry yard and up the hillside against the possibility of a further attack. And here we stayed until below we saw the Habu working party returning, being sent back to camp, and we came down and joined them.

I have been extraordinarily fortunate in possessing photographs not only of the dockyard just prior to it being attacked but also of some of the damage inflicted and for the latter I am indebted to Moulstone - who, very much liking the look of Sydney when we were repatriated through it, decided to get demobilised in Australia and make his life there. Apparently after the war was over one of the Raffs seeing a Japanese walking past the gates of the camp, camera in hand, took possession of it - whether by payment or expropriation, I do not know. The camera was already loaded with a film and the man who had obtained it, apparently interested only in the camera itself, offered Moulstone the film which he accepted and had developed on H.M.S. Ruler, the aircraft carrier on which we were to be taken from Japan to Sydney. I imagine that possession of photographs by an ex-prisoner of war of an enemy target taken immediately before attack from reconnaissance aircraft and close-ups of damage inflicted taken afterwards by an enemy national must be unique!

To return to the attack itself, unlike its predecessors this one had been hugely successful.

The photographs which follow should be read in conjunction with the photograph on page 202 and the dockyard plan on page 73. As will be seen by studying the photograph on page 202 (which has as its reference Vic E.23. 25 July 45, Innoshima. Inland Sea. F714) looking along the quayside from left to right (north to south) there is a pair of sizeable ships moored alongside each other and a smaller ship, moored against them on the seaward side. Southwards of these is another major craft with two small vessels moored again on the seaward side to it and then another large ship with two small craft lying between

Innoshima Attacked

her and the quayside, one of which may be the invasion barge packed with troops which is mentioned later. Further south are two more fairly large ships and between them what appears to be one small ship but was it seems two small anti-aircraft frigates for the protection of the dockyard, moored side by side. There is a large tanker in Hachi Dock (Number 8 Dock) and at the Habu end is another dry dock (part of the new Number 1 Dock) but then known as No 4 Dock which was occupied but open at the time. The long buildings are the shops (pipe, plate, machine shop, foundry and so on) and a half completed ship can be seen on one of the slipways and also tower cranes and ancillary buildings.

The photograph below (which has as its reference Vic G/O. Innoshima Island Sea 100U K/20 Restd) does not extend so far but shows the ships it does cover more clearly.

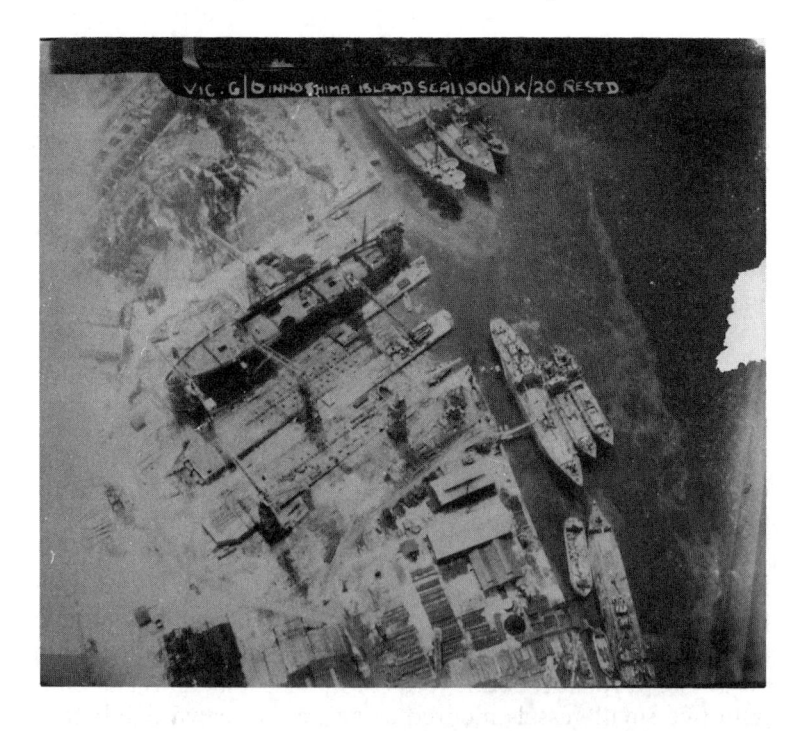

Innoshima Attacked

One of the moored ships (most probably one of the two largest ones moored alongside each other) was the *Hiterus Maru* of between eight and ten thousand tons. This ship was hit amidships and broke in two.

The ship in the small dry dock received a direct hit down an open hatch and as can be seen in the photograph above was hugely twisted by the explosion.

Another lying alongside the quay was sunk and the invasion barge next to it turned turtle drowning the majority of its occupants.

The only set of shear legs in the dockyard collapsed on top of the ship they were serving which was the recently launched No 3311 which was being refitted and after the bombing had to be refloated.

The two frigates were both hit and sunk

As for the buildings themselves the final photograph

which follows gives some indication of the damage caused. Summarising the pipe shop was no more; the machine shop received several direct hits and was badly mauled with most of the machinery ruined; the plate shop was damaged. The electricity depot was hit and electricity could not be supplied for several days.

There were numerous other hits both here and on other installations and in fact almost everything except, strangely, Hachi Dock and the slipways, was put out of commission. So far as casualties were concerned, these were put at four hundred (including one hundred and sixty killed) not one of which was a prisoner - which was remarkable considering we made up about five per cent of the work force.

Equally remarkable was the fact that although our camp (obviously mistaken as an appendage of Mitsunosho dockyard) was attacked, no casualties resulted. The photograph on page 58 shows not only damage to the camp but also the almost complete destruction of a house across the road.

There is some disagreement as to whether or not this house

Innoshima Attacked

was damaged in the air raid or rather later by parachuted supplies in 50 gallon drums dropped on us after the war was over missing their target. My own view (with which Coxhead's diary agrees) is that it was caused by bombing; on the other hand a diary kept by Flight Sergeant Price is categoric that it was caused by the supply drop and several others I have questioned go along with him. If it was by the supply drop, the fact that a house could be so easily wrecked gives the clearest indication of the flimsiness of Japanese construction and explains why the devastation caused by fires and bombing was so horrendous. A woman and two children in the house were killed and a collection was raised in the camp to assist in the refurnishing and reconstruction.

Coming back to the raid itself, one stick of bombs straddled the camp exploding in the sea and badly damaging the single-storied hut we had occupied prior to the Volunteers arrival and others landed in the woodyard and on the Mitsunosho dockyard machine shop hard by it. The photograph shows the roof of what was the Japanese administration quarters marked PW - which was done after the war as an aid to the aircraft dropping supplies.

As may be imagined the camp was in a terrible mess with rubble and debris everywhere. Large boulders had been hurled on to the thin roofs and had crashed through on to the floors below and in turn through them leaving gaping holes while a minor tidal wave had swept over from the sea damaging more than poor Smithy's vegetables. It was a chaotic day. The whole island was in a highly nervous state and with the electricity out of action frequent air raid alarms given verbally continually interrupted the task of clearing up the shambles. To make things worse with both the well and the pumping station put out of action, our water supply was severely interrupted. There was however one consolation - food had by now reached a catastrophically low level and our evening meal was to have consisted of a few small potatoes and a meagre soup; but the bombs had stunned numerous fish, some weighing several pounds and the Japanese were far too distracted by their own problems to bother to stop us wading out and helping ourselves to the gasping creatures.

Innoshima Attacked

One might have expected that our captors incensed by these happenings would have revenged themselves on us. I have no recollection that they did so. Perhaps this was because even to the most jingoistic Japanese on Innoshima the raid of July 28th finally made it clear that the war was lost to them.

When the tide of war turned and it became obvious to us that however long it might take, we would win the war, there were Japanese who would say to us that we had no reason for looking cheerful in that only two alternatives faced us. The first that they would win, in which case we would go on working in Habu Dockyard for the rest of our lives; the second that they would lose in which case we would be put up against a wall and shot before the Americans could get to us.

This was said seriously and would not, I think, have been far out. Many stories have been put about that careful plans had been laid for the extermination of prisoners when the first Americans landed on Japan. I cannot vouch for them - but whether pre-planned or not, I have not the least doubt that this is what would have happened. Had their homeland been invaded, the Japanese would have fought like tigers to defend it and they would certainly not have wasted food, time and fighting men to look after inconvenient prisoners. We were aware of this and found it difficult to reconcile good news with the inevitability which followed from it. As a topic of conversation it was largely avoided; no comforting answer was imaginable. But then no one imagined the atom bomb. And so our delight at the events of July 28th was tempered by the realisation that the crunch time would not be too long delayed.

There were no more raids on Innoshima. - and, in fact, to have attacked it would have been wasted effort and material. Output, which at no time had been startling and had over the past twelvemonths slowed to a crawl, as good as ceased. An air raid warning sent every worker into shelter and even the distant sound of an aircraft engine had all on their feet and those on ships hastening down the gangplank. It occurred to no one that defence was possible - we were simply a practice range. And this of course was exactly what the whole of Japan had

Innoshima Attacked

become by now.

In the two weeks before the end the crumps and reverberations of nearby raids became commonplace. Bombing by night and day was constant with huge quantities of bombs dropped and the power behind some of the explosions gigantic for although the actual sound was faint, our buildings shook. Our sleep was constantly interrupted by large formations of aircraft rumbling alarmingly low overhead and attacking nearby targets and the sky was often reddened by distant flames. I made a diary note that on August 8th the sky was aglow with fire and that we understood there had been a large incendiary raid on Hiroshima which at that time was no more to us than a nearby Japanese town after which our camp was named. On August 9th the sound of bombing reached its climax with continuous huge explosions - indeed hearing so many of them, we were tempted to believe a naval bombardment was in progress and the invasion was at hand.

As for the atom bomb, did we hear it? Many times I have been asked that question. And the answer is that I do not know; a blockbuster dropped nearby would probably sound at least as loud as an atom bomb dropped thirty miles away. But this I do know - the atom bombs on Hiroshima and Nagasaki killed many, many thousands. But by providing the Japanese with an excuse to capitulate they saved incomparably many more. Had it been necessary to invade Japan the carnage on both sides would have been astronomical - and amongst the first to die would have been the prisoners.

CHAPTER THIRTEEN

FREEDOM REGAINED

1

Coming events cast their shadows before and we might have guessed that so far as at least as some of the Japanese hierarchy were concerned the writing of their defeat was on the wall when on July 19th, 1945 at 6.15 a.m before we left for work, Nimoto, through Fujita, addressed us:

"Today I am under orders to leave for another camp. During my time here, since the beginning of this camp, most of you have kept in good health and have worked well. I hope that you will continue to do so until your are able to return to your homes.

Although I am leaving the camp, I must remind you that there will be another commandant in charge of you and he may have different ideas from mine. Nevertheless you must obey his orders and those of Sergeant Kimura and Mr Minnchara as well as the dock officers.

Take good care of your health during the rest of your stay here."

A few days later, in fact on Friday July 24th, when those who had been in the dockyard returned, all in the camp were mustered for an address by 2nd Lt Mori, the new Camp Commandant:

"I am Lieutenant Mori. I am posted to be Commandant of this camp in place of Captain Nimoto. I have not as much experience as Captain Nimoto, but I will do my best in this position. For the present I shall follow the routine of Captain Nimoto; later on if changes are required they will be made.

Freedom Regained

If you are expecting your country to win the war soon and on that account take advantage, you will incur heavy punishment. I must warn you to obey all the rules of the camp. I have heard that the English are gentlemen, and therefore I expect you to behave well.

You may feel dissatisfied with your food rations but throughout Japan the food situation is difficult at present. You are receiving almost as much food as the Japanese soldiers. You have been prisoners for more than two years. I know that the life of a prisoner-of-war is disagreeable, but if you bear it with fortitude, you will be rewarded by returning to your homes."

2

August 15th, 1945 was the strangest day. It began like all the others: Tenko, an apology for breakfast, fall in for work, march to work - the same tatterdemalion column of listless men with bellies empty and minds filled with the drear thought of another endless day ahead. At Karoto a handful of sick men peeling off to spend the day chipping and smashing castings; the rest of us continuing past the Kempeitai's hut into the dockyard. The falling into parties, the taiso; the foremen standing by to direct their charges to the barrowing, sledgehammering, bunkering, pushing, pulling, lifting, heaving; and the new thing: the listening for the sound of aircraft engines. The one new thing - but otherwise just another of about one thousand days spent in Habu Dockyard.

Until mid-morning.

There was an announcement over the dockyard system that there would be a radio broadcast at some stated time and in due course the entire Japanese labour force trooped off to gather in various places while the prisoners were shepherded together out of earshot. After the broadcast the Japanese came back and resumed working. But the rumour spread that it had been Hirohito himself who had addressed them - an unimaginable happening from a man who until then had been to his people divine. So the morning went on with rumour countering rumour. A Korean sidling up told us that the war was over, Japan had been defeated. Others heard this also. In the Canteen at lunchtime, I challenged Freddie who denied it. We went back to work and then, rather early were ordered back to the camp - to find the guards had temporarily deserted it. Through the evening meal there was a babel of discussion but finally doubt was put at rest. Freddie was at the door, grinning at me : *"Gen tonight, chaps. Today Japan capitulated unconditionally. The war is over!"* Freddie wasn't going to be scooped - not at the very end.

I did something I had always resolved to do - sat down and wrote my immediate reactions. Sadly, what I wrote I have long since mislaid but the gist of it was a crushing sense of anti-climax, an emotion shared widely through the camp. There was no tank smashing through a wall; there were no paratroops. It was an evening exactly like a thousand others: the same thin faces around one at a table, the same miserable apology for a meal, the same hunger when it had been eaten, the same legs swollen by beri beri, the same dearth of tobacco - yet all the props of life of a sudden knocked away and nothing to replace them. Just that one first whoop of joy and then, throughout the camp, a universal feeling of emptiness and depression.

Just as I finished writing an odd thing happened. Our new Commandant came into the room, a man who struck us as a fairly harmless individual. Seeing me writing, he came across. *"What are you writing?"* he asked. *"What I feel,"* I told him. He held out his hand - it was Hobson's choice; we had still to be officially informed. I handed him the piece of paper and he went away with it. A few minutes later the air raid warning warbled. I reflected on what I'd written - and wondered. But the tension lasted for only a little while. The all clear sounded and there was no summons to the office. And later my writing was returned to me.

It took us several hours to adjust and for once there was little sleep in that camp beside the Inland Sea known now as Hiroshima 5. We looked across the moonlit water and dared to start making plans; we stretched out on our tatamis, restless without the boon of automatic sleep which normally protected

Freedom Regained

us from the hosts of fleas and mosquitos which were our constant companions through the summer months. We looked at our lice-ridden dockyard uniforms, finding it difficult to believe they would never be worn again.

3

A few days later we were all assembled and Mori read a speech to us:

"I am pleased to inform you that we received military orders for stoppage of warfare on August 18th.

Since you were interned in this camp you have doubtless had to go through much trouble and ageing due to the extension of your stay here as prisoners of war. But you have overcome them and the news that the day for which you longed day and night, the day on which you could return to your dear homeland, where your beloved wives and children, parents and brothers and sisters are eagerly awaiting you has become a fact, is probably your supreme joy.

I would like to extend to you very most sincere congratulations but at the same time I sympathise most deeply with those who have been unable, due to illness or some other unfortunate reason, to greet this joyous day.

By order, we, the camp staff, have done all in our power towards your management and protection but, owing to the destitute internal conditions here, we regret that we were unable to do half of what we wanted to do for you. But I trust in your understanding on this point.

Several days ago at one camp, the prisoners presented the camp staff and factory foreman with part of their valuable relief foodstuffs and personal belongings, while at other camps, prisoners have asked for permission to present civilian war sufferers with their personal belongings. This, I know, is an expression of your understanding, open-hearted gentlemenliness, and we, the camp staff, are deeply moved.

Until you are transferred over to allied hands at a point to be designated later, you will have to wait at this camp. Therefore, I sincerely wish that you will wait quietly for the day when you can return to your homeland, behaving according to camp regulations, holding fast your pride and honour as people of a great nation and taking care of your health."

4

We were to remain for almost a full month on Innoshima - one hundred and eighty two unarmed men on a small island on which lived several thousands of Japanese. It was pointed out to us by our new Commandant that a peace treaty had yet to be signed and that many soldiers were already here or would be returning home some of whom would be very bitter; he beseeched us to do nothing rash. It might be, he suggested, that the roles were now reversed, that we who had been the prisoners were now the victors - but habits which had endured for a thousand and more days would die hard and whereas the camp staff might grudgingly accept orders from those they had expected to give orders previously i.e. from the Warrant Officers, orders given to them by those they had come to look upon as mere dockyard labourers could easily incense them. Again prisoners of war who took it into their heads to go out of the camp in search of food and cigarettes, to seek out and goad their former foremen or merely to enjoy the freedom of strolling the island, could easily arouse a hornet's nest.

This is what he conveyed if not in so many words and it made good sense but, as we were to discover his fears were largely unjustified for the vast majority of the men and women on Innoshima were only too pleased to be done with the war in general and with air raids in particular. Those whose behaviour had been reasonable took to coming to the camp on the lookout for cast-off clothing, food and cigarettes; most of the others quietly vanished. And with a few exceptions the anger we had nursed at what at the time we had considered monstrous treatment, soon evaporated. One or two made good dire threats of what they were going to do to their foreman one day but even these only because the men in question were stupid enough to present themselves at the camp. For the great

Freedom Regained

majority it was sufficient to have enough to eat and smoke, to be able to swim, play cards, paint or fish, to be freed of anxiety and apprehension, to be finished with the dockyard and to laze the days away feeling strength returning, watching flesh being recovered at a truly amazing rate, to dream of the loved ones with whom they would soon be re-united and to make plans which could at last be realised.

Service discipline was re-established: the Raffs and the handful of Army men on the whole accepted this automatically and the Volunteers, although no more than civilians who had climbed into uniforms for a few days fighting, were mostly sensible men who accepted that an imperfect solution was better than none. We had no trouble. There was no immediate swarming over the island; there was no great rush to try to quit it.

Apart from Japanese who called at the camp trying to scrounge or buy clothing, food and possessions and a boatload of thirty Geishas offered by a Japanese entrepreneur promptly sent packing, we had a quartet of surprising visitors - these were two Englishmen with Japanese wives who turned up at the camp gate. Having lived on Innoshima since the 1914-1918 war they spoke fluent Japanese while their English still had a Cockney accent. They told us that many times they would have liked to have spoken to us while we were prisoners but the Japanese kept a very strict eye on them and they had never dared to do so.

Another visitor was Bill May, the Hurricane pilot with whom I had played bridge on the way out on *Indomitable* and who had had shared the same hold on the *Dai Nichi Maru*. He came over by boat from Mukaishima camp to see me, bringing with him Walter B. Ross, First Lieutenant Bombardier, one of the crew of a B.29 shot down a few days before the end of the war. Being on the mainland and their self-assurance bolstered by a group of Americans super confident of their country's might, the prisoners in Mukaishima were very much more in control and knew so much more than we did: not merely details of the war but of other things of which we had no knowledge: German concentration camps, penicillin, a man named Frank Sinatra.

Freedom Regained

The party stayed only for an hour on Innoshima and they took me back with them to see things from the other side.

This proved to be a memorable experience. Bill suggested I might like to take some sake back with me. "We can buy as much as you want at 200 yen a crate," he told me. I pointed out I didn't have five yen let alone two hundred. "No trouble,: he said. "All we need is some red armbands and I'll lend you the money and you can pay it back later on." Mystified I accompanied him to a godown. We each put a bit of red ribbon round our arms and entered the official sake store, plonked the two hundred yen Bill had lent me on the counter and ordered a crate of sake. It was supplied without demur. Somewhat bemused I reached out to lift the crate but Bill shook his head and signalled to a nearby Jap to carry it outside, which he did. We were immediately besieged by other Japanese begging to buy bottles off us. Bill said: 'Black market price is two hundred yen a bottle," and taking one out of the crate sold it and pocketed the money. "All yours," he said with a grin indicating the balance of the crate. "If you want you can sell the lot and go in and buy more and be a yen millionaire in no time!"

When I returned it was to find our camp bristling with discontent; the comparison now was not that we were far better off than we had been but that we were far worse off than those at Mukaishima.

Something had to be done. Now accepted by the Japanese as a Warrant Officer and guilty at having accidentally been responsible for raising something of a hornet's nest, I organised a meeting in the dockyard offices with the managing director, the new commandant, the chief kempei, the head of the island commissariat and the local bank manager. Sitting at the Board Room table with one of the Hong Kong Sergeant Majors I explained the position and made demands using the threat that if these were not met the men would be over the camp walls and trouble would ensue. Already our rations had been increased but everything demanded - vegetables, meat, fish, cigarettes, a boat - was agreed to. After three and a half years of being obliged instantly to obey orders however fatuous or

Freedom Regained

unreasonable - often given by transient guards whose sanity one sometimes doubted - it was heady stuff and I was carried away to make a final and quite absurd demand - money as part payment for the years spent slaving in the dockyard again using the threat that if it was not forthcoming, the men would be over the wall ransacking the local shops. It was pointed out that there was nothing in the shops on which to spend money but I was obdurate. How much money then?, I was asked. Two hundred yen a man I said plucking a figure from the air. And where do we get all that money? I indicated the bank manager, he'd have plenty. The bank manager was firm - it wasn't his money to give. We had reached an impasse - but I don't suppose I really imagined anyone was going to trot out something like thirty-six thousand yen! I was a youth who had been cut off from the world since he was twenty-one years of age overwhelmed by the sudden sense of power over my former captors and enjoying myself. But then an extraordinary thing happened. The Commandant, Lieutenant Mori, asked me how, if he was to advance this large sum personally, he would get it refunded. Simple, I said. We both sign a document that you have advanced this money in good faith and it should be repaid by the occupying forces. And he believed me - perhaps I believed it myself. Anyway we wrote something on a piece of paper and we both signed it and then Mori pulled out a chequebook and wrote a cheque and the bank manager went away and after a time he came back with the thirty-six thousand yen in the bottom half of a shoe box. And I took it back to the camp and distributed it and later when we went by train to Yokohama most of it was thrown out of the windows like confetti to children we passed en route.

That demand and its acceptance has always been on my conscience. Mori, who I have since been told, had been before the war, manager of a shipping line, Osaka Shosen Kaisha in Hong Kong, had since his recent arrival behaved entirely decently. I have over the years been rather haunted by the thought of him presenting his promissory note to the first American soldier he ran across and watching it being used as a spill to light the G.I's cigar. And the devil of it is that of the many who were in that camp with me I have since re-met only

Freedom Regained

a handful who even remember receiving the money at all.

Mind you that is understandable because almost immediately afterwards something occurred which made the possession of paper money of little value except as useful souvenirs on which to collect signatures of those with whom one had shared the years. - a B.29 flew over and dropped supplies of such quality as to make anything still available in Japan seem quite irrelevant.

Typical signed banknote (reduced in scale)

On the side of the B.29 painted in huge letters were the words: *The Uninvited*. Never was an uninvited guest more welcome! It made a low run over the camp, turned, came back more slowly at a higher altitude and at once parachutes supporting pairs of oil drums welded together were to be seen falling from it. It was not the most accurate of drops. Some parachutes didn't open and none landed within the camp itself. Never mind - parties went out and scoured the hillsides and great quantities of food and cigarettes were recovered and, I suppose medical supplies, toilet requisites and so on.

Not all was recovered and some of the local Japanese did well gleaning cans of apricots and tins of meat on the hillsides and in the paddy fields. We didn't begrudge them what they found. Japan was all but starving, they were as hungry as we had been and we had ample now.

Apart from the supplies we received from the air drop, we were also showered with leaflets from an earlier B.29 which flew low over the camp about, so far as my memory serves, two days before 'The Uninvited.'

> **TO ALL ALLIED PRISONERS OF WAR**
>
> **THE JAPANESE FORCES HAVE SURRENDERED UNCONDITIONALLY AND THE WAR IS OVER**
>
> WE will get supplies to you as soon as it is humanly possible and we will make arrangements to get you out. Because of the distances involved it may be some time before we can achieve this.
>
> YOU will help us and yourselves if you act as follows:
>
> 1. Stay in your camp until you get further orders from us.
> 2. Start preparing nominal rolls of personnel giving the fullest particulars.
> 3. List your most urgent necessities.
> 4. If you have been starved and underfed for long periods do not eat large quantities of solid food, fruit or vegetables at first. It is dangerous for you to do so. Small quantities at frequent intervals are much safer and will strengthen you far more quickly.
>
>   For those who are really ill or very weak fluids such as broths and soups, making use of the water in which rice and other foods have been boiled, are much the best.
>
>   Gifts of food from the local population should be cooked. We want to get you back home quickly, safe and sound, and we do not want you to risk getting diarrhoea, dysentery and cholera at this last stage.
>
> 5. Local authorities and/or Allied officers will take charge of your affairs in a very short time. Be guided by their advice.

A few days later we received a letter dated August 27th from Fritz W. Bellfringer, representative of the International Red Cross.

Freedom Regained

The hour of your liberation has come. Representatives of protecting parties (Switzerland, America, Britain, Sweden and Netherlands etc and the undersigned) are in touch with the Allied High Command and will assist the Japanese in your evacuation. A speedy and comfortable evacuation can only be assured if you collaborate and maintain order to the last. For this reason, you are requested to follow the instructions of your Camp representative who will be in contact with us and will receive the necessary information.

Therefore please be patient, and do not create any disturbance which may delay your evacuation.

Japan should see you leave with all your honour and dignity,
The Delegate of the International Red Cross,
Fritz W. Bellfringer.

On Tuesday, September 11th, after more than three and a half years of being prisoners and some four weeks after Japan's capitulation, a small pinnace, flying the White Ensign, pulled up at the damaged jetty and with a cry of *"The Navy's here,"* an officer, off I believe the battleship King George V, together with some American officers and enlisted men sprang ashore. Their purpose was to make lists of those they had liberated and give us instructions for leaving for Yokohama and repatriation on the following day.

We must have learnt much that was new to us and yet of that meeting there are only two things which stand out in my memory: the first that doctor's praise of Mogford and the other the hardening of the camp's division from almost the very instant that Naval officer stepped ashore. He knew at once that here were two separate groups of men and he reacted to them accordingly. To the Raffs he was punctiliously considerate; but with the Volunteers he was at ease. He was not concerned that this man had crumbled under pressure or that one had shown integrity and strength; he was not to know. He recognized in the one group a social status he found lacking in the other and it was apparent.

Freedom Regained

It is perhaps unsurprising that whereas on the voyage away from Japan a group photograph of the H.K.V.D.C. ex-prisoners was organised, no similar photograph was taken of the R.A.F.

H.K.V.D.C. ex-prisoners on H.M.S Ruler

However, there were few who took exception to the Naval officers attitude and in a curious way his mien helped to fill a void. For approaching four years our basic way of life had been decided by others; we had been allowed a degree of freedom, perhaps roughly equivalent to that of children who can express themselves as they like in a playground but must obey the classroom rules. And not all had behaved in that playground as they would have wished to behave or as they might have been expected to. Now, all at once, that had to be put behind. The vacuum left by Japan's defeat was filled by the reality of convention. The Genki Boys were no longer Genki Boys but just so many Raffs and Volunteers; already the cooks were barely distinguishable from their fellows; Freddie Clemo was no longer a purveyor of news and Mogford was just another medical orderly. The pledge never to waste a cigarette was already mocked by overflowing ashtrays; the carefully collected menus were forgotten. And a reversal of history restored the certainty which captivity had destroyed: just as the slate had been wiped clean of all a man had done before he became a prisoner, so now it was wiped clean of all he had done while being one. Ahead lay a future based not on the immediate past but on the past of life before captivity.

It had to be so because there was no way we could base our future lives on the way we had led our lives in that camp. Yet, except for the want of women and children, Hiroshima 5 had been a near perfect microcosm. We had had our rich and poor, our known and unknown, our well educated and our poorly educated, our young and old - a society in which within clearly defined limits we were free to live by such standards as we chose. The Japanese apart from 'Tenko' and the occasional search rarely came into our billets; they provided the raw materials of food which we cooked and distributed and whether fairly or unfairly was our business, not theirs. They provided a sick bay and some medicines and stipulated the number allowed off work each day and on the whole left it to the medical orderlies to decide who most needed rest or treatment. They provided a spotless new camp which by their standards was of a very high standard indeed; heat, clothing and bed coverings equal to their own; a bath of near scalding water every night. They allowed concerts to be arranged, sing songs to be sung, lectures to be given, church services to be held. They permitted men when not at work to dress exactly as they pleased and to demonstrate or develop their personalities as they chose.

In an odd sort of way they took away many of those problems which in normal life so beset a man he cannot be himself but, forever concerned about his job, his rates and taxes, the conventions of society, the latest fashions, the never-ending decisions he has to make, is forced into a pattern of behaviour

Freedom Regained

which but for these pressures he would not adopt.

Then again being a prisoner in Japan was a different thing from being one in say Singapore or the Phillipines where one could imagine as island after island was retaken by the Allies the glorious moment when that tank *would* come driving through the gates. With the atom bomb unimaginable the presumed defeat of Japan itself could only have come about through invasion - and no doubt this presumption was correct. Had Japan been invaded the battle would have been bloody and difficult and millions would have died and amongst them most certainly their prisoners.

With the country in such a parlous state with food, fuel, clothing, indeed all necessities of life already in such short supply, the disruption of invasion would have created havoc with distribution of the little that there was, and the effort of protecting Western prisoners against the temper of a hungry, vengeful mob would not have been worth the candle even if the military had felt inclined to do so.

There is not the least doubt that quite soon, if not on the very day of invasion, we would have been taken out and shot.

This probability which was believed if not openly admitted by the majority created an ambivalent state of mind which strangely was not difficult to live with and in general the camp did no more than touch lightly on the likely result of an obviously approaching victory which uplifted spirits. In seeking an answer to an attitude which defied all logic, I am inclined to think the reason lay in this feeling of being cocooned in a sense of timelessness and in a way of life in which decisions of any importance were no longer our concern. Unlike how it had been in Java when presumed victory was at most a year away, we had learnt to live with time. Our third anniversary of captivity had come and gone and we were heading for our fourth. Even with the fall of Okinawa, the nearest allied troops were still three hundred miles from the southernmost tip of Japan. If it could, as it did, take eighty-two days to subdue an island only five miles in length defended by a mere sixty thousand Japanese or, even more to the point, in spite of one of the heaviest bombardments of the war more than a month to take tiny Iwo Jima, the first scrap of Japan proper to be taken into allied hands, how much preparation must first be necessary to invade a country as rugged as Japan itself which would be fought for yard by yard by four or five million soldiers backed by a ninety million population?

No, the prospect was too vague seriously to contemplate; we could enjoy the fruits of more distant victories and push aside finality as do many when faced with the first symptoms of a terminal disease. And because this was so, because we were not bedevilled by concern at how others might judge our behaviour whilst prisoners, we could be ourselves more completely than we would ever dare to be in civilian life.

But now, suddenly, by the dropping of a single bomb, all that was changed. Our future attitudes and behaviour would once again be conditioned by the pressures of a larger world; in - as Tolstoy puts it - 'the elemental swarm-life in which he (man) inevitably obeys laws laid down for him.'

This is not at all to suggest those bitter years left no imprint: there would be those who because of them would have lost what could never be regained be it innocence or self-belief and others who would use what they had seen to good account. There would be none without a reservoir of recollection to call upon when things looked bleak or when they saw men harshly judged for minor faults. Above all there would not be one who wouldn't have a better knowledge of himself.

I have never looked back on those three and a half years I spent as a prisoner of the Japanese as a total waste of life - I have even sometimes wondered if I could go back to that morning when we cut cards on the stoep of the Hotel der Nederlanden in Batavia to decide who should stay behind to fly the last few Hurricanes and I slid off the topmost card, if, knowing what I know now, I *would* after all have cut a little deeper - for by doing so, by cutting perhaps a king of spades instead of my miserable four of clubs I would have missed a most valuable experience.